ON COMING TO LAW

AN INTRODUCTION TO LAW IN LIBERAL SOCIETIES

F.C. DeCoste

Butterworths

A Member of the LexisNexis Group

On Coming to Law: An Introduction to Law in Liberal Societies
© Butterworths Canada Ltd. 2001
September 2001

The Butterworth Group of Companies

Canada:
75 Clegg Road, MARKHAM, Ontario L6G 1A1
and
1721-808 Nelson St., Box 12148, VANCOUVER, B.C. V6Z 2H2
Australia:
Butterworths Pty Ltd., SYDNEY
Ireland:
Butterworth (Ireland) Ltd., DUBLIN
Malaysia:
Malayan Law Journal Sdn Bhd, KUALA LUMPUR
New Zealand:
Butterworths of New Zealand Ltd., WELLINGTON
Singapore:
Butterworths Asia, SINGAPORE
South Africa:
Butterworth Publishers (Pty.) Ltd., DURBAN
United Kingdom:
Butterworth & Co. (Publishers) Ltd., LONDON
United States:
LEXIS Publishing, CHARLOTTESVILLE, Virginia

National Library of Canada Cataloguing in Publication Data

DeCoste, Frederick Charles, 1946-
    On coming to law: an introduction to law in liberal societies

Includes bibliographical references and index.
ISBN 0-433-43831-2

    1. Law. I. Title

K230.D44 2001   340   C2001-901948-3

Printed and bound in Canada.

This book is dedicated to those many students,
in my law school and elsewhere, with whom over the years,
I first charted this path to, and through, law.

We love law, not because reason requires it, but because our commitment to our discipline serves the needs of the public to whom, and for whom, we are responsible.

Paul Carrington

[L]awyers ... are prophets. ... They show their community what its values are, and how much their values cost.

Thomas L. Shaffer

He who seeks justice must believe in justice, who like all divinities, shows her face only to the faithful.

Piero Calamandrei

Preface

Over the past 25 years or so, myriad books have been written with the intention of introducing their readers to the law. Though many of these have receded both in memory and in use, every few years, it seems, a new title is added to this sizeable body of literature. This book is one of these, and it is reasonable to demand of its author a justification for its appearance in this already crowded field.

Though I hope that others will read it with profit, this volume is intended primarily for use by students, those who have just begun, and those who are seriously entertaining, the study of law. More particularly, I wrote this book for students in courses, in law schools and elsewhere, which aim to provide a general introduction to law. Though justification for this work cannot then be found in its intended readership, it can, I hope, be discovered in its more specific purposes and methods.

Most introductions to law exhibit an approach and an attitude very different from that followed in this book. Most, first of all, proceed from the pre-reflective view that law is simply law, in broad brush the same in all societies and at all times. And virtually all take what may be termed an outsider's attitude to law. That is, they view the law in the same clinical fashion as do observers, like sociologists or economists, and their purposes therefore exclude the view of law of those — lawyers, law professors, judges and, yes, law students — who experience the law as participants in its institutions and practices.

Introductions to law which proceed in either of these fashions carry some very real costs for their readers. By adopting an outsider's attitude towards the law, they prevent their readers from encountering the premise on which all else in legal education and legal practice finally depends, namely, that a proper lawyerly view of law and legal practice is somehow uniquely indigenous to the profession. By failing to localize law politically, they obscure from view a host of inquiries which are necessary to any adequate understanding of law. Chief among these is the relationship between law and the terms and conditions of individual and collective life in the society whose law is the object of consideration.

This book aims to provide *a lawyer's view of the institutions and practices of law in societies such as ours*. The lawyer's view which I construct is the perspective of a perhaps ideal lawyer, one who not only takes the law seriously as an institution, practice, and way of life, but is also fully and intelligently informed about law and the understandings and commitments that it requires of its practitioners. When I propose, then, to introduce readers to law through the eyes of members of the legal community — and this will become more apparent as we proceed — I am not making a descriptive or empirical or sociological claim about the attitudes towards law of present members of the bench, bar and legal academy. Though most lawyers experience law, in part at least, along the lines I explore, my claim is instead normative. I am claiming that, from the point of view of a judge or lawyer or law professor in societies such as ours, law can make sense only if it is experienced and explained in the ways I designate as lawyerly.

Societies such as ours are, of course, liberal democratic societies. They qualify as such through their public declaration of, and adherence to, the values of liberty and equality. Coming to terms with our law, in consequence, requires two things. One must first acquire knowledge of the institutions and practices which comprise "the legal system" as the institutions and practices of a society devoted to liberty and equality. Then, one must come to a view on how those institutions and practices serve those values, on how they are justified in terms of liberty and equality. It is the premise of this book that neither of these requirements can be met unless those who would understand law, and especially those new to law, adopt *the legal point of view*, the view of the legal community, of the judges, lawyers and law professors whom the law names and obligates as its practitioners.

Organizationally, this book tracks these requirements of understanding. Part I ("Describing Law") aims to describe what the law looks like from the perspective of the legal community. The first chapter grounds this undertaking by offering a lawyer's answer to the question "what is law?" Subsequent chapters deal with the structure of the legal community (Chapter 2), the sources of law (Chapter 3) and the nature of legal argument (Chapter 4). Chapter 5 is a brief afterword which serves as a conceptual bridge to the remainder of the book.

The purpose of Part II ("Explaining Law") is to justify the legal system described in Part I in terms of liberal democratic political values. The features of our law which were there identified — for instance, the law's dependence on rules, the independence of the legal community, the practice of precedent — set the threshold for the explanation of law offered in Part II. After first making a number of necessary conceptual distinctions (Chapter 6), I then offer, and explore, the Rule of Law as the sole and exclusive justification for law in societies such as ours (Chapter 7). As we shall see, one of the requirements of the Rule of Law is a body of public and private law. The main categories of public and private law are introduced in a separate chapter (Chapter 8).

Part III ("Living the Law") canvasses the implications of this explanation of law for contemporary legal education and practice. Chapter 9 explores the conditions of service on which the authority of legal community depends. The "Conclusion" attempts to make clear just how much societies such as ours depend on lawyers being good lawyers and what, finally, goodness requires of them.

Though this book has as its primary focus Anglo-Canadian law — which is to say, Canadian law excluding the civil law of Quebec — and in the main uses Canadian and English law to illustrate matters, the view of law it offers is general in its intent, and national details aside, applies with equal force to the legal systems of any and all modern liberal states. In part to make this plain, most chapters are followed by a list of further readings deliberately (and eclectically) drawn from a wide variety of national sources. In selecting readings, I was concerned as well with the cultural amnesia which is the unhappy estate of far too many judges, lawyers and law professors. So in a modest attempt at preventing the spread of this disease among those new to law — and with the hope that this book might be an ongoing resource for those who take up a life in the law — the readings include important works relevant to the matters discussed in each chapter. In addition, an appendix lists some of the milestone works produced by lawyers over the history of their community. Unhappily, the readings were not able to relieve the text from the burden of footnotes, which are used throughout whenever clarity or attribution requires them.*

I wrote this book as a law professor and lawyer who loves the law. I hope that readers will leave it with cause to share my affection. I hope, in particular, that they will come to know our law as an accomplishment of singular and universal significance, and to appreciate the goodness it alone offers, not only to those many who benefit from its rule, but to those few who are called to spend their lives as its faithful stewards. Though many of the matters with which this book deals will place demands on the reader, and though progress towards revealing the whole will be incremental, if I have done my job at all well, the reader's efforts in following the course of the book will be amply rewarded, I hope, finally with just that knowledge and recognition.

F.C. DeCoste
Edmonton, Alberta

---

*   Incidentally, lawyers use the Latin words *supra* ("above") and *infra* ("below") to direct their readers to previously and yet-to-be cited works.

Table of Contents

PART II — EXPLAINING LAW

PART I

DESCRIBING LAW

Chapter 1

What is Law?

Law [is] a community of speakers of a certain kind, ... a culture of argument perpetually remade by its participants. ... It is the true nature of law to constitute a 'we' and to establish a conversation by which that 'we' can determine what our 'wants' are and should be. ... The law should take as its most central question what kind of community we should be, with what values, motives, and aims.

James Boyd White

A.   INTRODUCTION

Much has been written about the nature of law. Legal theorists and philosophers have been motivated to define law in order to distinguish law from other systems of rules and from gratuitous commands backed by threats of the sort issued by a bank robber or mugger. Other scholars have had more modest, less philosophical ambitions, and have sought to reveal the nature of law through sociological description and economic analysis. However, for lawyers, the whole of this ongoing investigation and debate has been entirely pointless. None of the descriptions it has offered, and none of the fine distinctions and definitions it has constructed, matters to the judge or to the lawyer, because for them, the nature of law — what law is, and is not — is always clear and beyond dispute. It is the purpose of this chapter to explain both why this is so, and what follows from its being so. We shall begin by exploring the two approaches which inform all discussions about the nature of law. And we shall discover that how one describes law turns on whether one approaches law from the perspective of a member of the legal community or from the perspective of an external observer.

B.   OBSERVERS OR PARTICIPANTS?

In order to describe law, we must begin by deciding what it is we are attempting to describe. We could, for instance, take the view that law is a social fact about the world, and have as our objective the accurate portrayal of the complex of institutions and actors which comprise that fact. On the other hand, we could think that what is important is the very idea of law, and take as our purpose the analysis of its conceptual content. Finally, we could think of law as a kind of practice and aim, first, to describe the practice as it is pursued by its practitioners, and then to explain the point of pursuing a practice of that sort.

Descriptions of law which proceed from the view that law is a fact about the world invariably approach law from the observer's point of view. They do not seek, nor can they seek, to understand law from the first-person point of view of a participant in the institutions which they purport to describe. Their objective, rather, is to provide hopefully accurate reports about those institutions, their structure, their relationship to one another and to other institutions, and so on. But statements about law of that third-person sort do not capture anything about the beliefs of committed legal actors within those institutions. In consequence, descriptions of law as social fact are both misleading (they take what is at best a part of the picture for the whole) and unacceptable (they fail to tell us about matters — the experiences and beliefs of legal actors — about which we might reasonably expect a description to inform us). They are also mistaken in a more fundamental way. Since law is minimally about legal rules, and since legal rules do not describe the world, but instead make prescriptions about conduct, to describe law as a fact is both to misrepresent its nature and to misconceive its relationship to society. For all of these reasons, definitions and descriptions of law which proceed from the view that law is a fact about the world about which, like the weather or population density, accurate reports are possible, are of no interest or utility to lawyers or, more generally, to anyone who is seeking to understand law as lawyers do.

Though they are much more sophisticated in style and substance, conceptual definitions of law too are largely irrelevant to lawyers. Definitions of this sort consist of claims about the idea of law. Their purpose is to identify which of the manifold prescriptive rules operative in any given society are legal in nature. Though they avoid mistaking law for fact, they are no more successful than the law-as-fact definitions in capturing the point of view of legal actors, because, like fact definitions, they take an observer's attitude to law. Conceptual definitions of law consist of statements about when a legal system might be said to exist, and about the validity of rules in such a system; but, without much more, statements of that sort do not account for the point of view of participants in law. Conceptual definitions of law have never offered such a view, and have instead merely observed that, whatever their individual reasons for doing so, lawyers and judges have to believe in law in order for law to exist. This observation does not tell us anything about the lawyer's point of view, and it leads to descriptions of law which are so general and so abstract that the actual substance of law and lawyering very easily becomes lost. Because they, in these ways, fail to disclose either how law is experienced by lawyers, or how lawyers view law, conceptual definitions of law have little to offer lawyers.

From the lawyer's point of view, law is a practice which is performed, rather than a concept to be defined, or a fact to be described. But not all of those who think that law is a practice describe and explain law from the lawyer's point of view. Indeed, many descriptions of law as a practice take the observer's view of matters. This they do by locating the point of legal practice outside of the law. In consequence, law is viewed by them as an instrument, or technique, for the advancement of some extra-legal social end or ends. Some instrumentalists support law, and think that the ends of law — say, conflict resolution, social stability, economic efficiency or even personal liberty — are good ends, and that what law requires is a continued refinement of its techniques and processes. Other instrumentalists are legal dissidents. They think that the present ends of law are repugnant — law, it is most often said, is an instrument, variously, of class, or race, or sex, domination, subordination and exploitation — and they advance either the replacement of these diseased ends with other healthy ends, like economic, gender or race justice, or else the abolition of law altogether. The views of each of these sorts of legal instrumentalists are, however, united in the view that the sense of law is to be found, not in law itself, but beyond the law in some extra-legal philosophy, morality or system of values. Instrumentalists of all sorts, dissidents and supporters alike, thereby situate themselves outside of law; and, in consequence, their views of legal practice do not, and cannot, account for the experiences of judges and lawyers who perform the practices which the instrumentalists purport to describe and explain. That some instrumentalists speak well of law, while others seek to diminish and denigrate law, does change their joint failure to take seriously the views of lawyers and judges who practise law seriously, not as a tool for the achievement of some social end, but as something they have chosen to do for its own sake.

It is possible to describe and explain law, as a practice, from the point of view of lawyers and judges who have chosen law, and who are its good faith practitioners. According to this view, the doing of those activities which constitute legal practice leads judges and lawyers to experience law in ways which are fundamentally different from the ways an observer can possibly experience law. Such a view claims that a *distinctively legal point of view* inheres in the practice of law, and that it is that point of view which alone accounts for the way lawyers and judges, as practitioners, experience law. From this legal point of view — and here our journey really begins — law is, descriptively speaking, an *independent communal practice* with its own intrinsic values which can only adequately be explained by establishing the *point* of our having a community of that sort.

C. LAW AS COMMUNITY

Law is a community in an unadorned sociological sense. Only individuals who are admitted to the legal community — who are called to the bar — can practise law. As a consequence, certain actors who are often associated with law in institutional terms, legislators and the police in particular, are not members of the legal community. However, though law is, indeed, a community in this rough empirical sense, viewing law as a community exclusively in this institutional fashion fails to capture the more profound sense in which law is the legal community.

The legal point of view is the point of view of lawyers and judges who accept and believe in law, as a practice and an institution, which is worthy as an end in its own right. Law is experienced and understood by them as a community of a certain sort. More particularly, from their vantage, *law is a set of activities, exclusively practised by members of the legal community, in certain defined contexts, namely, activities which minimally involve writing and speaking about legal rules.*

This lawyer's description of law raises two different sets of questions which we shall attempt to answer in Part I, before we proceed, in Part II, to determine the point of a community of this sort. It raises, first of all, certain *institutional questions*, which will concern us in Chapters 2 through 5. It also raises a number of *definitional questions*, to which answers will be provided in the remainder of the present chapter. First, we shall have to decide what we mean by "societies such as ours". We shall have then to address the meaning of "rules", "legal" and "contexts", as those terms are used in our lawyer's description of law. But, before we turn to any of this, there is the matter first of the meaning of "community" and of "practice", since together they constitute the core of our lawyer's definition of law.

(i)   The Meaning of Community

From the lawyer's point of view, law is a community which depends upon status, and which binds its members together in terms of the obligations which derive from status. In consequence, it is also a community which requires observance of, and fidelity to, its own tradition. Consider, first, status. Lawyers are lawyers, and judges are judges, by reason alone of their status as members of the legal community. And they are members of the legal community on account alone of their sharing common credentials and methods of membership. Membership status, in turn, signals participation in a tradition of practice, which binds the legal community together, and from which it draws the complex of obligations — to other members, to clients, to third parties, to society — which define lawyerly observance and fidelity. Being a lawyer requires a lawyer to know and to value the practices of lawyering. The lawyer does not invent those practices, but encounters them as a tradition, a standing set of practices which will continue to exist after any individual lawyer departs the legal community.

Lawyers and judges use a common language to communicate and argue which not only unites them in community, but constitutes them as well as participants in a specific culture. Law is, in this sense, a culture of conversation and contestation, a community of discourse, which subsists in, and by virtue of, a particular tradition. Viewing law as a culture in this fashion demands that we ask what kind of meaning this culture serves to create, and what kind of persons it requires its practitioners to be. Law requires its members to be persons who are competent, ethically as well as practically to seek its cultural good. Being a lawyer is a matter of being a certain kind of person, a person who not only has an adequate sense of the tradition, but forms his or her personality as a lawyer with regard to the virtues the tradition communicates.

Some members of the legal community — judges, legal scholars and practitioners alike — have reimagined the legal tradition and community along functionalist lines. Because the view of law as community and tradition nonetheless survives, the result has been conflict and confusion about the nature of law and of legal education and practice especially. However, for committed, good faith lawyers, law remains a tradition and community of practice which demands and deserves their allegiance.

(ii) Defining Practice

To say that lawyers and judges are members of the legal community, and that they, therefore, experience law as participants in legal tradition and culture, is to place the notion of practice at the heart of matters. For community, culture and tradition each relate to practice, and differ only in providing distinct vantages for understanding practice. Community directs our attention to the status of those who perform the practice, tradition to the nature of the practice, and culture to its means. Even before our exploration of the meaning of community along these lines, the term "practice" stood unadorned at the centre of our lawyer's description of law. But, though we have been talking in terms of practice from the very start, we have yet to define the term. It is to just that task which we must now briefly turn.

Our usage of "practice" has been somewhat precise, at least by implication, all along. For we have used the term to denote the activities of groups of individuals, and such social practices, which define and govern the relations of individuals in groups, are very different from the "practices" of individuals, which are really not practices at all, but more properly habits. *Social practices* are understandings of standards of human behaviour shared by members of some community. Whether or not a social practice is governed by explicit rules, a practice consists of a set of activities, recognized by some community, which together constitute, not only that community's way of doing things, but its way of life.

That practices are both ways of proceeding and, more fundamentally, ways of life, means that they have a point, that they are not merely intended, but purposeful. We have also been using the term "point" in this discussion, and it is a crucial one as regards all practices, for it introduces the idea of justification. If a social practice is, by definition, a set of purposeful activities, it makes sense to ask why we engage in those activities. And to answer this question is, of course, to justify the practice, to declare it to be worthy as a way of proceeding and as a way of life.

But how do we determine the point of a social practice? Is the point of any such practice simply some principle, or set of principles, apart from the practice, by reference to which the practice is justified, in an over-the-shoulder, after-the-fact sort of way? Or, is something more at play? Because a practice is, by definition, an understanding about the requirements of conduct which is shared by some community, the point of a practice cannot be some external, abstract principle against which a practice is judged; its point, rather, inheres in that understanding of those requirements. Just because the point of a practice is, in this way, constitutive of the practice, to determine the point of any practice requires that we adopt the point of view of those who pursue the practice, that we see the practice as they do.

Law is a complex social practice. It consists of numerous subpractices, each of which has meaning by virtue of its being part of the practice as a whole. This is to include, under the point of the practice, subpractices which may appear to be autonomous, and to exclude practices which may otherwise appear to be subsumed by the point. Judicial adjudication, for instance, may appear to be a practice in its own right, but judging is very much a part of the practice of law which stands to be justified by the same point which applies to the rest of the legal community. On the other hand, though they may appear to be subpractices of law, law-making and law enforcement are autonomous social practices, subject to justification through their own points.

Law is, by its own declaration, *a professional practice* as well. This claim distinguishes law from any number of other complex practices and places it in the family of those practices which claim the distinction of professionalism. The term "profession" comes from the Latin word *professionem*, which means to make a public declaration. Lawyers and judges are professionals because they are required to make a public declaration of their fidelity to the public morality of which law is the practice and the legal community the custodian. They are professionals, that is, because they profess the point of their practice.

(iii) "In Societies Such as Ours"

Law is a practice pursued, with a particular point or purpose, by the legal community, but only in societies such as ours. Our lawyer's description of law is expressly the view of lawyers in a certain kind of society, since only lawyers and judges in societies of that general sort would, or could, experience law in that way. In other kinds of societies, lawyers would experience law in a manner fundamentally different from lawyers in our society, and their community would have a practice, point and purpose very different from ours.

Describing societies such as ours in a fashion which is both fair and sufficiently informative and general is a precarious proposition at best. To what does one direct attention? Our society's aspirational qualities? If so, one is open to charges of social blindness, since societies such as ours are, in fact, characterized by inequalities which significantly affect the life chances of all sorts of people. If, on the other hand, one were to focus on just those matters, the aspirations and accomplishments of societies such as ours would unfairly be hidden. In order to avoid these difficulties, we shall aim for a description to which a reasonably informed, reasonable person, resident in any liberal democratic society could assent. With this test in mind, we shall, for present purposes, take as a fair and general description of such a society that it is *governed by law*, and is otherwise characterized by *freedom, protection of personal integrity, equality of opportunity, privacy* and *general standards of welfare*. We shall briefly consider each in turn before directing our attention to formulating a preliminary statement of the values which inform these characteristics.

Reasonable people in societies such as ours think that their societies are societies governed by law, rather than by the will or whimsy of the government. They believe that authorities which have a public purpose should comport themselves in accordance with rules which are known to people in advance and to which they can reasonably conform. More particularly, they believe their society to be one in which people can both avoid penalties and depend upon others, precisely because their societies are ruled by law, and not by the individuals who happen, at any point in time, to hold authority.

Reasonable people in societies such as ours also believe that their societies are, and ought to be, characterized by personal freedom. They believe that, provided only that they do not harm others in significant ways, people should be left to their own devices, free from government control and control by others, in making decisions about their own lives. They believe this, despite knowing in advance that many individuals will make bad decisions about their lives and will be worse off on that account.

Reasonable people in societies such as ours believe as well that law, at the very minimum, should afford protection from personal injury caused by force or stealth. They believe this, because they believe that personal freedom would be rendered empty in a society in which individuals are subject to losing their personal security and their property, at the whim either of the government or of any individual who happens to be strong or tricky enough to overcome them. They believe, that is, that law is necessary to avoid barbarity and to permit civilized life to flourish.

But, in societies such as ours, reasonable people believe their society to be dedicated to wider purposes than protection from these sorts of core injuries, however central such protection might be for them. First of all, they believe that theirs is the kind of society in which everyone, regardless of their sex, race, sexual orientation, or political or ethnic affiliation or origin, has, and ought to have, an equal opportunity to reap the rewards of society. They believe that discriminating between people on the basis of individual characteristics of these sorts is unfair and unacceptable, and that only effort, ability, and personal choice should determine the course of an individual's life.

Second, reasonable people believe that privacy is a separate, free-standing good of societies such as theirs. They believe that their having control over the information others — not only the government, but private organizations and persons as well — have about them, is somehow constitutive of the kinds of lives people ought properly be able to lead in their kind of society. And they believe that their society must protect the possibilities for solitude and for intimacy, and the personal affairs of its members more generally, by drawing a sharp line, as regards its political and legal arrangements, between the public and private aspects of people's lives. Otherwise, they believe, important personal relationships and practices will be lost, and important individual interests, such as our interest in protecting our reputations, will be jeopardized.

Finally, in societies such as ours, reasonable people believe that everyone is entitled to a minimal standard of living. They believe that everyone, whatever their abilities and however bad their choices, has a share in the rewards of society, and that personal necessities — such as food, clothing, shelter and physical security — must, therefore, be available to all. They believe this because reasonable people recognize the role that luck plays in human affairs, and because they are in consequence moved by benevolence for others.

It is reasonable for people in societies such as ours to think that a description along these lines is proper to their society, simply because these descriptions resonate in the core values of liberal democracy.[1] First among the values which found societies such as ours is the claim that *only individuals count*. According to this value, what counts in law and politics is the impact which social arrangements and policies have on individuals. In liberal democratic societies, law is about, and only about, the individual, simply because liberal law arises from, and is dedicated to, the interests of real, flesh-and-blood individuals. Consequently, if there exists, at law, a choice between two results, one which would improve the situation of individuals and another which would diminish their life circumstances, say, by favouring some group or a collectivity, the legal decision-maker is bound, as a matter of law, to choose the former.

The second core value of liberal democracy consists in the view that *individuals are equal as persons*, and that, in consequence, *each of us counts as one, and none of us as more than one*. This value expresses the understanding that human persons share equally whatever it is about them that makes them worthy of consideration; and it prohibits societies such as ours from preferring, in matters of law and politics, any of the differences which inevitably obtain between us. Consequently, in liberal democratic societies, political arrangements and legal entitlements cannot be premised upon individual differences such as, say, intelligence or ambition or belief, or upon collective differences such as race or gender. More widely stated, this prohibition renders indefensible in such societies any proposal which would have the legitimacy of public authority rest on any basis other than equality.

---

[1] I depend here on D. Johnston, *The Idea of a Liberal Theory* (Princeton: Princeton University Press, 1994), at pp. 17-27.

The final value resides in the view that *individuals are, as persons, free*. Often, freedom of this constitutive sort is associated with our capacity as agents, namely, our capacity to conceive of values and projects with which to guide and lead our lives and to act on them. But, in liberal democratic societies, one need not have the capacity of agency, either fully (as in the case of children) or, indeed, at all (as in the case of the severely disabled) in order to count as an individual due equal protection by our political and legal arrangements. In such societies, being an individual person is alone sufficient to make one count equally to others, and differences as regards agency speak, instead, to the nature and quality of the protection which is owed.

Societies such as ours, then, are characterized by certain broad political understandings which are founded upon certain core values, values in terms of which alone such perceptions make sense. Societies such as ours are also societies in which lawyers experience law as a practice exclusive to their community. We may conclude at this point that because our society is indeed one which is governed by law, and founded upon a certain core of values, this lawyer's understanding of law has the possibility of justification in terms of those fundamental characteristics.

(iv) The Nature of Rules

Lawyers speak and write about legal rules.[2] But describing their practice in this way tells us nothing about the quality of the rules which are the objects of their practice. Since so much about law, both its description and its point, turns on rules, it is absolutely necessary for anyone who would understand law to understand the nature of rules first.

Legal rules are *prescriptive* rather than descriptive. There is, for instance, a world of difference between the laws of gravity and the laws of property. The laws of gravity consist of statements about the empirical world which purport to predict what will probably happen or to explain what has already happened. The laws of property, on the other hand, are not statements about the world at all; they are interventions into the lives of people, which purport to prescribe conditions for human relationship. While descriptive rules attempt to disclose the nature of the world, prescriptive rules attempt to stipulate conditions for acting in the world. For this very reason, it makes sense to refer to prescriptive rules, as lawyers are wont to do, as "tests". For legal rules, like all prescriptive rules, set conditions which, if met, control interactions among persons.

That prescriptive rules have normative force in this way is what distinguishes them from maxims, or rules of thumb. The maxim, "An apple a day keeps the doctor away", is very different from the rule, "No smoking in the law school", because the maxim, unlike the rule, is merely an optional guide to conduct. It is

---

[2] The understanding of rules which follows is drawn from F. Schauer, *Playing by the Rules* (Oxford: Clarendon Press, 1991).

optional, because its instruction applies only if one wishes to achieve the result
— here, health — it commends, and because, even if one does, only on the condition that one believes that compliance with its direction will produce the de-
sired result. Maxims, then, do not, by themselves, apply normative pressure.
Rules, on the other hand, do. Our no smoking rule, unlike our maxim, is mandatory in just that sense. Where it applies, it provides a reason, simply by virtue
of its existence, for compliance. It has independent normative force just because
it is a rule.

Mandatory rules are of two sorts. Regulative mandatory rules govern activities which exist independent from, and prior to, the rule. Our no smoking rule is
a good example. As the history of our move to regulate smoking indicates, the
capacity to smoke is separate from, and existed prior to, any rule designed to
govern that activity. Constitutive mandatory rules, on the other hand, create the
conduct which they govern. Take, for example, the rule in hockey concerning
icing the puck. That rule not only governs, it creates the activity of icing. So too
the rules of all games. Without the rule governing crowning in checkers, or the
rule governing castling in chess, no activity called crowning or castling would,
or could, exist. Further on, we shall discover that, although law is concerned
with regulative rules, its practice yet depends on certain foundational rules, concerning structure and procedure, which constitute the very possibility of a practice of that sort.

Though descriptive and prescriptive rules differ markedly in these ways, they
are both necessarily *generalizations*. Descriptive rules do not describe singulari-
ties or particulars, but consist instead of statements of predication or reportage
about types of events or occurrences. Prescriptive rules, too, concern classes or
categories; but rather than empirical regularities, their object is human action.
To qualify as a rule of either sort, a putative rule must offer a generalization
which claims to govern either a multiplicity of instances or a multiplicity of actions. In neither case, and indeed in no case, may there be a rule which governs a
non-regularity or a particular.

That prescriptive rules are generalizations means that commands are disquali-
fied as rules of that sort. This is an especially important result as regards law,
since it has been often proposed[3] that law consists of a set of commands, issued
by someone or some body having *de facto* authority, and backed by sanctions.
But, if legal rules, as a variety of prescriptive rules, are generalizations, this cannot be correct. Compare the command, "Clear the road" issued by a police officer, and the rule, "Maximum Speed 100". The command demands simple
obedience from some particular person or persons with respect to some particular event, and if the obedience is forthcoming, the command is then used up. The
rule, on the other hand, creates an obligation which applies to all who are caught
by the rule — in our example, all present and future drivers on the road in ques-

---

[3]   Most famously by John Austin. See: J. Austin, *The Province of Jurisprudence Determined*
(1832) (London: Weidenfeld & Nicholson, 1954).

tion — and survives present, past or future compliance by any of them. Particular prescriptions are commands, and commands cannot be rules, because their particularity prevents them from doing the things that rules uniquely do.

Because they are generalizations, prescriptive rules also have a characteristic form or structure. They consist of a *conditional factual predicate*, or hypothesis, followed by a *consequent*, and are typically expressed as "if *a*, then *r* result follows" statements. Take, for instance, our rule about culpable homicide, which roughly states that "if one causes the death of another human being either intentionally or negligently, then one has committed either murder, or manslaughter, or negligent homicide". The "if" clause, the factual predicate, describes the facts which have to obtain for the rule to apply, and the "then" clause prescribes what is to happen when those facts are made out. In the case of the culpable homicide rule, absent some good excuse or defence, the result would be punishment of the accused person according to the law of murder, manslaughter or negligent homicide.

Sometimes rules are formulated in a way that obscures their form. Take our rule, "Maximum Speed 100", which is formulated so as to hide both the factual predicate and the consequent. Nonetheless, all such fragmentary statements of prescriptive rules may be reformulated in standard form. In this case, the full rule would read, "if you drive in excess of 100 kilometres per hour on this road, then you must pay a fine of 60 dollars". Any rule can be recast to take the form of predicate followed by consequent.

There is more to discover about rules than simple disclosure of the factual predicate and the consequent can possibly tell us. Can we not ask where the generalization, stated in the predicate, comes from? In answering this question, a third element of prescriptive rules becomes available to us. Take again our rule about speeding. By asking on what the factual predicate — "if you drive in excess of 100 kph" — the generalization which governs the application of the consequent, is based, we are asking about the goal which the rule seeks to achieve or the evil which it seeks to prevent. We are asking that the rule be justified. And, in this case, the rule's generalization could be justified on grounds either of achieving public order or of preventing avoidable human harm.

Every prescriptive rule has a *background justification* of this kind. Justifications only work if a rule's factual predicate can be seen to be an instantiation of its background justification, and that turns on our believing that the facts which govern the rule will contribute to the purpose which the justification declares. Justifications themselves exist at different levels. The first order justification of public order, in our example, might in turn be itself justified by a second order justification, say public safety, and that justification, in turn, might be justified by still other ends, and so on. This is especially important to our project of explaining law, which presumes that law as a whole is an instantiation of some discernible background justification or point. It is important as well to legal practice, since this characteristic of legal rules, among others, provides lawyers with a fund of arguments concerning their meaning and application.

Prescriptive rules, such as the rules of law, are a complex human invention. Rules of this sort constitute a complex relationship between some end (the background justification or point), some means (the factual predicate's instantiation of that justification), and a result (the consequent which is compelled in all cases to which the rule applies). This richer picture of rules begs for further analysis to determine the background justification for prescriptive rules themselves as a way of proceeding.

Prescriptive rules not only constrain the activities of those to whom they apply; they also constrain the people — in law, lawyers and judges — who are entrusted with their application. This second sense of constraint is especially important. For it means that in adopting a system of rules, we are disabling certain decision-makers from considering factors which they might otherwise think important, and therefore from making decisions which they might otherwise consider proper. Think again of our rule about speeding, which has both of these effects. Suppose you are a judge in a traffic court, and a case comes before you in which the application of our rule would have, in your view, unduly harsh consequences. Let's imagine that the fine would take from the person charged with speeding the only funds he or she has available to meet an important prior obligation, say, purchasing a much-needed medication for a sick child. Because our rule governs the case, you would as judge be prohibited from considering these extraordinary circumstances, however much you might wish, and however meritorious you might otherwise consider them to be. Proceeding with rules at all is premised on a prior decision that constraining the power of decision-makers in this way is itself a good idea. So viewed, *prescriptive rules are devices for allocating power to decision-makers*. And our choosing a device of that sort has itself to be justified.

(v) The Adjective "Legal"

We have seen that rules are distinguished from both commands and rules of thumb or instructions, because they impose obligations. Prescriptive rules are, by definition and as a practice, *compulsory*. When they apply, they apply independently from either our consent or dissent and, more particularly, independently from our individual appraisal of their substantive value or their moral or political acceptability. They are, rather, mandatory.

Rules, as such, are compulsory, then, because they require us to act in ways which we might not otherwise choose and, in so doing, constrain our liberty and independence. But legal rules are compulsory in an additional sense, just because they are legal. From the external point of view, law is most properly defined as a system of rules, and "a legal system [as] a coercive order of public rules".[4] Now, it is very important that we understand with some precision what,

---

[4] J. Rawls, *A Theory of Justice* (Cambridge, MA: Harvard University Press, 1971), at p. 235.

independent from the compulsiveness which attends their status as rules, makes legal rules *coercive* in this special, additional way.

Viewing legal rules as commands backed by sanctions cannot account for this added measure of compulsiveness. Any notion that associates law's special co-erciveness to the view that laws are commands is simply inaccurate descrip-tively. Unless one stretches the word "sanction" beyond all recognition, most rules of law are not backed by threats of sanction. More importantly, any such view obscures the important way in which those prescriptive rules, which are legal rules, differ from those which are not.

Some legal rules — typically those which create criminal and other offences — are backed by sanctions, but other legal rules — say the rule that a benefici-ary of a will cannot serve as a witness to the will — are not. Yet both are legal rules by virtue of some other, and additional, quality of coerciveness which is not shared by social rules to which the adjective "legal" does not properly apply. A prescriptive rule becomes a legal rule by virtue of its being a *public* rule in the sense that the state acknowledges or backs it.

Legal rules are backed by the state through its own institutions, especially and typically through its court system. This generally happens at the behest of citizens themselves, and only in certain defined and limited circumstances, on the state's own initiative. In either event, the point of state endorsement is the possibility of public vindication. And it is just this possibility of organized, pub-lic confirmation which, minimally, distinguishes legal rules from other social rules, and which discloses the special, added coerciveness which is characteristic of legal rules.

That legal rules may be vindicated through public institutions means that le-gal rules, unlike all other rules, apply comprehensively. Where they apply, they regulate the whole of our conduct, even when such conduct might otherwise be the subject of some other, non-legal prescriptive rule. Law, in this way, "defines the basic structure in which the pursuit of all other activities takes place", be-cause all other rules and associations are subordinate to it.[5] Legal rules, then, add to the compulsiveness which is definitive of rules more generally, not merely because they are rules which the state endorses, but more specifically because public vindication of that sort means that state rules have priority over all the other rules by which men and women attempt to guide the conduct of their lives.

(vi) The Contexts of Lawyerly Labour

The different institutional contexts in which lawyers work define both the structure of the legal community and the primary subpractices of law. The first matter will concern us, at some length, in the next chapter. What we must now do is explore, in finer detail, what precisely it is that lawyers do. We shall start

---

[5]   *Ibid.*, at p. 236.

with describing the practice of law as whole, before then considering how law is practised in each of its institutional settings.

To practise law at all is to speak and write about legal rules. But, this description of practice, though accurate, does not tell us which aspects of legal rules concern legal practitioners. One aspect of legal rules is, for instance, their moral goodness. Another is their utility. But neither of these aspects are a concern of lawyerly practice. Nor, with certain caveats to which we'll eventually come, is their justice. The aspects of legal rules which provide the stuff of practice are of a rather more mundane variety. The whole of lawyerly conversation and practice, concerns three deceptively simple inquiries about rules, namely, *what they are*, *what they mean* and *when they apply*. And though conversation about these matters can be nuanced in a variety of relatively complex ways, when lawyers and judges speak as members of the legal community, it is about one, or more, of these that they are speaking. Understanding legal practice requires, at the very least, that we understand what is finally at issue in each of these lawyerly questions.

We have first to remember that these questions form the basis of the practices of the legal community. To conceive of them as tasks which can be conclusively performed or consciously completed is seriously to miss the point. The practices which these inquiries inform are, instead, the ongoing, never-to-be concluded, constitutive activities of the legal community and, therefore, of law. With that caution in mind, we can now characterize, in general terms, the practice which each inquiry defines. The first question, "what are the rules?", defines as one of the practices of the legal community, the identification of those prescriptive rules which are properly rules of law. Because the identification of rules is an ongoing practise of the legal community, identification cannot consist of looking to some source in which the rules of law are codified or listed. Happily, the practice of law, including this particular practice, is never as mindless or as uninspired as that. On the contrary, though judges and lawyers typically use certain texts as sources for rule identification, what they do with those texts, and why, cannot at all be construed as a practice of simply discovering or unearthing rules which happen to be contained in those texts. Law has no rule book in that sense.

The second question, "what do the rules mean?", defines another practice. Suppose that, by examining those texts to which lawyers refer, we have identified the rule, "No vehicles in the park", to be a rule of law. Suppose, too, that we are then presented, as lawyers, with questions concerning whether our rule prohibits a baby carriage, or a military tank erected on a war memorial, or a motor bike which someone proposes to push through the park. Our having identified the rule as a legal rule will not help us to answer. Questions such as these, rather, are an occasion for a entirely different and distinct kind of practice. For answering questions of this kind requires us to determine what the rule means, and doing that requires us to interpret the rule.

Suppose we know exactly what the relevant rule is, and what precisely it means. Suppose we are then asked, "does it now apply?". That question signals a third practice, namely, the practice of proving the conditions contained in the rule's factual predicate. The practice of proving the facts proceeds on the legal community's understanding of what has to be proved and how.

We have dealt with *identification, interpretation* and *proof* as distinct moments of legal practice. And, though surely they are, the three often overlap and merge in practice. For instance, we will discover that identification is sometimes synonymous with interpretation, and that applying a rule is, in certain circumstances, indistinguishable from identifying it as a rule at all, or knowing what it means. Yet, these practices are conceptually distinct, and observing that distinction will best serve our ongoing purpose of describing law.

Members of the legal community identify, interpret and apply legal rules, but they do not perform these practices in the same way at all times. How they approach any of these practices depends, rather, on the institutional context in which the practice is being performed. And it is to those contexts to which we must now turn, since they alone disclose both critical differences in the practices of the legal community and, in a curious and important way, what nonetheless unites them as legal practices.

Members of the legal community practice in five different contexts, each of which defines a separate and distinct subpractice. From *the point of view of the practising lawyer*, two contexts are important. Lawyers meet with clients in their firms, and they represent their clients in court and before other kinds of tribunals and in meetings with lawyers representing other clients. These two contexts are central to the practising lawyer's life, because they constitute the two, different and distinct patterns of practice available to the lawyer. When a lawyer meets with a client in the firm's offices, the lawyer's practice as regards the identification, meaning, and application of rules is characterized by *advice and counsel*. When, on the other hand, a lawyer represents the client to others — to other lawyers or before courts and other tribunals — the lawyer's practice is characterized by *advocacy*. These practices are very different. When a lawyer is practising as an adviser or counsellor, the lawyer consults with the client as regards the client's best course of conduct in light of the rules of law and the client's particular circumstances. When, however, the lawyer is representing the client to others, deliberation of this sort is replaced by advancement of the client's interests and cause. Consequently, depending upon institutional context, lawyers may practice either as advisers or advocates.

From *the point of view of judges*, the practice of identifying, interpreting and applying rules informs a subpractice of a fundamentally different character. Unlike practising lawyers who may, depending on context, be advisers or advocates, judges have only one course open to them, just because they hold judicial office. To be a judge is, exclusively, to deliberate upon, and to reach a conclusion about, the rule (or rules) of law pertaining to some actual occurrence, some real case. Unlike lawyers, it is not for judges either to advise or to advocate. Their particular practice, rather, is *authoritatively to determine the identity, meaning and application of the law governing some lived experience of life.*

Legal practice has, finally, still another meaning for academic lawyers. From *the point of view of those who teach law* to those who would someday join the legal community, the practices of identification, interpretation and application define two distinct subpractices, namely, *professional preparation* and *communal criticism*. The practice of professional preparation has two aims. The first is to educate students in lawyerly competencies. This includes not only imparting to them the specialized vocabularies out of which the rules of law are built, but also inculcating in them the crafts on which lawyers so much depend. The academic lawyer aims secondly to transmit to students the ethics and morality of the legal tradition and community, in the hope that the lives which they will later live in law might make the law a yet better practice.

Scholars are legal scholars — and not, say, philosophers or historians or sociologists or economists — by virtue of their membership in the legal community. Their membership directs their scholarship to a special audience and causes it to have a peculiar aim and form. The primary audience for legal scholarship is the legal community itself — judges, practising lawyers, other legal scholars and sometimes law students. Scholarship directed to that audience necessarily takes the form of criticism. Legal scholars explore, refine and defend the values and point of law. Legal scholarship is the practice of holding the legal community to account, demanding that it make good the promise of its traditions and values, that it honour the point of its existence.

There are, then, five subpractices to the lawyerly practices of identifying, interpreting and applying legal rules, each of which devolves from the different institutional contexts in which lawyers work. These subpractices — *advising, advocating, adjudicating* and *professional preparation and criticism* — are, however, united by more than their being about legal rules, as important as that is. They are united as well by a characteristic which, just as much as rules, defines them as legal practices. Each of these practices depends upon the needs of specific groups of persons who are not themselves members of the legal community. Counselling and advocacy exist by virtue of the needs of clients; adjudication exists because of the needs of the parties to a case; and legal education exists primarily because of the needs of those who would join the legal community. *The practices of the legal community are by definition practices which depend upon others.*

This dependency has a number of implications for our description of law. First of all, it means, as regards advocacy and adjudication, that those practices are both particular and — in a special sense — adversarial. Advocacy and adjudication are client dependent. Advocacy does not arise without there being a client, and adjudication cannot arise unless that client is presented to a court as a party. That this is so makes advocacy and adjudication client and party centred in a special added way. *Lawyers and judges care, and only can care, about individual cases, individual clients and individual parties.* If they conceive of the general at all, they perceive it through the lens of the needs of the particular client or the particular parties before them.

It is often claimed that ours is an adversarial system of law. But we have to be careful with claims of this sort. For ours is an adversary system only as regards certain of our practices, *i.e.*, advocacy and adjudication. Claims about the adversarial nature of our law cannot describe either the substance of judging or those other subpractices of law which we have identified as equally definitive of law in societies such as ours. The claim is even limited sociologically. The fact is that most lawyers are counsellors first, and only rarely engage in advocacy. That said, if understood correctly, the claim does impart some important truths about advocacy and adjudication.

Our system is indeed adversarial, because the interests of the clients are necessarily both paramount and adverse. Because advocacy and adjudication only happen when a lawyer represents a client against others who are also represented by lawyers, both practices can only concern the interests of the clients who are parties to the matter, and those interests must be pursued in a partisan way by the lawyers involved. The first truth in the claim that our system of law is adversarial is that the clients themselves control the nature of their claims, and that it falls to each, through their lawyers, to put forward the strongest case possible.

Another important truth follows from this, as regards adjudication. Because adjudication proceeds from the understanding that the parties will pursue their partisan interests, to claim that adjudication takes place in an adversarial context is to make a claim about both the role of the judge and the nature of judicial process. It is to claim that judges are neutral and passive decision-makers, and this in turn is to claim that, though they are part of an adversarial process, judges are not themselves advocates, and are properly held to standards of fairness and not to the standards of partisanship which quite properly apply to lawyers. So far as judicial process more generally is concerned, it is also to claim that out of the partisan presentation of proofs by the parties is most likely to come the information necessary for fair and neutral determination by a judge.

So advocacy is adversarial because lawyers, when acting as advocates, pursue the interests of their clients against the interests of other parties, typically against the clients of other lawyers; and, though it presumes that the judge might yet be fair, adjudication has as its substance the partisan presentation of evidence by the parties. But none of this makes our system as a whole adversarial. Indeed, as we have seen, the other practices of our law are anything but adversarial in the required sense. Moreover, even when lawyers do act as advocates, the outcome is more often than not a negotiated settlement which avoids costly and time-consuming litigation; and even where the parties fail in that regard, and go on to court, the judge will often advise and counsel, and act as a mediator between, the parties in order to attempt to salvage a settlement. The claim that our system is adversarial is, then, a very limited truth.

FURTHER READINGS TO CHAPTER 1

1.   The Internal Point of View

Hart, H.L.A. *The Concept of Law*. 2nd ed. Oxford: Clarendon Press, 1994. At
pp. 56-57 and 88-90.
Litowitz, D.E. "Internal versus External Perspectives on Law". (1998), 26 Flor-
ida State University L. Rev. 127.
Postema, G.J. "The Normativity of Law". In Gavison, R., ed. *Issues in Contem-
porary Legal Philosophy*. Oxford: Oxford University Press, 1987. At p. 81.
Raz, J. "The Problem About the Nature of Law". In Raz, J. *Ethics in the Public
Domain*. Oxford: Clarendon Press, 1994. At p. 179.
Tamanaha, B.Z. "The Internal/External Distinction and the Notion of a 'Prac-
tice' in Legal Theory and Sociolegal Studies". (1996), 30 Law & Society
Rev. 163.

2.   The Notion of Practice

MacIntyre, A. *After Virtue*. Notre Dame: University of Notre Dame Press, 1984.
Chapter 15.
Shapiro I., and J. Wagner DeCrew, eds. *Theory and Practice: Nomos XXXVII*.
New York: New York University Press, 1995.
Tunick, M. *Practices and Principles: Approaches to Ethical and Legal Judg-
ment*. Princeton: Princeton University Press, 1998.

3.   Law as Tradition, Community and Culture

Ball, M.S. *Lying Down Together*. Madison: University of Wisconsin Press,
1985.
———. *The Word and the Law*. Chicago: University of Chicago Press, 1993.
Berman, H.J. "The Western Legal Tradition in a Millennial Perspective: Past
and Future". (2000), 60 Louisiana L. Rev. 739.
Gibson, J.L. "The Legal Cultures of Europe". (1996), 30 Law & Society Rev.
55.
Goodman, E. *The Origins of the Western Legal Tradition*. New South Wales:
Federation Press, 1984.
White, E.J. *Legal Traditions and Other Essays*. St. Louis: Thomas Law Book
Co., 1927.
White, J.B. *The Legal Imagination*. Chicago: University of Chicago Press, 1973.
———. *Heracles' Bow*. Madison: University of Wisconsin Press, 1985.
———. "Reading Texts, Reading Traditions: African Masks and American
Law". (2000), 12 Yale J. of Law & Humanities 117.

4. Legal Rules

Ganz, J.S. *Rules: A Systematic Study*. The Hague: Mouton, 1971.

Fletcher, G.P. "Rules and Discretion". In Fletcher, G.P., ed. *Basic Concepts of Legal Thought*. New York: Oxford University Press, 1996. At p. 43.

Meyer, L., ed. *Rules and Reasoning*. Oxford: Hart Publishing, 1999.

Rawls, J. "Two Conceptions of Rules". (1955), 64 Philosophical Review 3.

Schauer, F. *Playing By the Rules*. Oxford: Clarendon Press, 1991.

———. "Rules and the Rule of Law". (1991), 14 Harvard J. of Law & Public Policy 645.

Chapter 2

The Structure of the Legal Community

*Let us examine, then, the nature of this freedom which belongs to the bar-
risters, and which has been so glorified and so criticized. We will see that it
is but a portion of the liberty that is natural to all men, which other men
have been deprived of, and which only barristers have conserved.*

Malesherbes, Mémoire sur les avocets (1774)

A. INTRODUCTION

It is an easy matter to identify the branches of the legal community. The legal
community consists of: a *judicial branch* composed of lawyers appointed to
adjudicate the claims of parties to cases and, in so doing, authoritatively to declare the law; a *practising branch* composed of lawyers who advise and advocate on behalf of their clients; and an *academic branch* composed of lawyers
who prepare others to be lawyers and who produce scholarship intended to hold
the other branches to account. These practising lawyers, judges and law professors alone are members of the legal community. Excluded, therefore, is everyone else: federal, provincial, and municipal legislators, governmental officials,[1]
the police and citizens at large. It is a bit more difficult to determine why this is
so and what it means, and more difficult still to defend the exclusionary character of the legal community. This chapter is devoted to the task of explaining the
why and the what.

The legal community exists and has the configuration it has because there
exist rules which constitute and confer powers to each of its branches. Absent
those rules, the practices of the legal community would not exist. We shall explore the constitutive and jurisdictional rules which relate to the judicial, practising and academic branches in turn before proceeding to the issue of the
character of the community so constituted. Though we shall use Canadian rules
to illustrate the ways in which the legal community is constituted, similar rules
exist in all modern liberal states. And the character portrait to which these

---

[1] There is a caveat to this. Some government officials are practising lawyers. Though these lawyers are involved in a range of matters, especially important are those who serve the state as
prosecutors in criminal trials or as appellate counsel.

particular rules will lead us is applicable, without qualification, to legal communities in all such states.

B.   THE JUDICIAL BRANCH

The judicial branch of the legal community owes its structure to a variety of constitutive and jurisdictional rules which we will canvass in some detail. These rules implicate two other matters — namely, judicial hierarchy and the appointment and discipline of judges — on which we must also dwell.

(i)   Structure

The Canadian judicial branch is complex. Our courts are constituted by different rules, have different jurisdictions and names, and relate to one another in terms of a specific hierarchy. Happily, this maze is made manageable through classification. Every court in Canada belongs to one of four categories of courts. Together these categories constitute and establish the structure of the judicial branch. The categories are: provincial superior courts, provincial inferior courts, the Federal Court and the Supreme Court of Canada. We shall consider each in turn.

PROVINCIAL SUPERIOR COURTS

Consistent with the overall complexity of the system, there are two kinds of superior provincial courts — the provincial superior trial courts and the provincial superior appeal courts — which are constituted by one means and staffed by another. Both courts are constituted by virtue of the provincial power over "the administration of justice in the province" which resides in s. 92(14) of the *Constitution Act, 1867*.[2] In Alberta, for example, the provincial superior trial court is constituted by the *Court of Queen's Bench Act*[3] and the superior appeal court by the *Court of Appeal Act*.[4] However, the power to appoint judges to these courts — and the obligation to pay them — resides with the federal government under s. 96 of the *Constitution Act, 1867* and, for this reason, lawyers commonly refer to these courts as "section 96 courts".

Both "section 96 courts" are courts of *general jurisdiction*, which means that they have unlimited legal right to hear any matter of law except where a statute expressly confers jurisdiction over a particular class of cases to some other tribunal. Tribunals of this latter sort are, therefore, constituted with limited — as opposed to general — jurisdiction which is typically confined to some area of

---

[2]   (U.K.), 30 & 31 Vict., c. 3.
[3]   R.S.A. 1980, c. C-29.
[4]   R.S.A. 1980, c. C-28.

expertise. For instance, the jurisdiction of the labour relations tribunals which are constituted by various provincial statutes is limited to matters relating to trade unions and the relations between organized labour and management; and the jurisdiction of the Canadian Radio-television and Telecommunications Commission, a creature of federal statute, is limited to matters having to do with regulation of broadcasting.

The name of the provincial superior trial courts varies by province. In Alberta, Saskatchewan, Manitoba and New Brunswick, the court is called the Court of Queen's Bench. In Ontario, it is known as the Superior Court of Justice. In all other provinces, save Quebec, it is called the Superior Court (Trial Division). In Quebec, the court is known as the *Cour Supérieure*. But whatever they are called, the provincial superior trial courts are the cornerstone of the court structure in Canada. This is so because of their relationship to the courts below and above, because of their history, and because they try all serious cases, civil and criminal.

In each province, the decisions of the provincial superior trial court may be appealed to the provincial court of appeal.[5] Though for this very reason, "section 96 appeal courts" are superior to "section 96 trial courts", the trial courts remain at the very heart of the structure because their jurisdiction, unlike the jurisdiction of the appeal courts, is *original*. This means that the superior trial courts have jurisdiction at the inception of matters — lawyers call this jurisdiction *in first instance* — and having taken cognizance of a matter, they may try it and deliver a judgment on the facts and law at issue. The jurisdiction of appeal courts, on the other hand, is not original[6] simply because it is parasitic upon the jurisdiction of the trial courts. Only if a matter has first been decided by a trial court and only if one or both of the parties asks the appeal court to review the outcome, does the appeal court become seized of jurisdiction. Lawyers call this jurisdiction *appellate*.[7]

The centrality of the provincial superior courts of original jurisdiction is also a result of legal history. For these courts are the successors to the original 18th century courts of common law and equity. All other courts — appeal courts at all levels and inferior courts — are the invention of later legal history and were consciously additions to the core structure provided by the superior courts of original jurisdiction. This history is critically important. Though these courts are

---

[5] The names of the provincial appeal courts also vary according to provincial legislation. In New Brunswick, Quebec, Ontario, Manitoba, Saskatchewan, Alberta and British Columbia, the court is called the Court of Appeal. In other provinces, it is known as the Appeal or Appellate Division of the Supreme Court.

[6] There is a caveat. Provincial superior appeal courts have a limited original jurisdiction which resides in their authority to receive, hear and deliver judgments on matters of law directed to them by provincial attorneys general. However, since reference cases of this sort are relatively rare, so too is the original jurisdiction of the courts of appeal.

[7] Though appellate jurisdiction captures the whole of the determinations made by trial courts, appeal courts typically defer to the trial courts' determinations of questions of fact.

constituted by legislation, they are not contingent on that legislation and they do not depend upon political or governmental sufferance. Their existence and status is derived, rather, from the reception of legal history and from the recognition that societies such as ours require courts of this sort, courts with the inherent jurisdiction to hear citizens on all matter of fact and law. So, if the these courts are dependent upon anything, they are dependent not upon political will, but upon our society continuing as a liberal democratic one.

PROVINCIAL INFERIOR COURTS

The provincial inferior courts are constituted by provincial legislation — the authority for which resides in s. 92(14) of the *Constitution Act, 1867* — and their judges are both appointed and paid by the provincial governments. The structure of the inferior courts varies from province to province. In every province, the provincial court has a civil and a criminal division. At a minimum, the civil division includes a small claims court. The criminal division may also have a specialized traffic court. Some provinces also have specialized youth and family divisions of provincial court.

Provincial courts have absolute jurisdiction over all offences created by provincial statute, for instance, highway traffic offences and offences arising out of land use and environmental regulation. In addition, the provincial courts have overlapping jurisdiction with the provincial superior trial courts on civil and criminal matters. The jurisdiction of the inferior court in civil matters — which are everywhere tried in small claims courts — varies by province according to the amount of money involved in any claim. Whatever the details of these provisions, the jurisdiction of the provincial inferior courts in civil matters is confined to minor cases.

Jurisdiction in criminal matters is somewhat more complicated. The *Criminal Code*[8] of Canada defines three types of offences — summary conviction offences, indictable offences and hybrid offences — the first two of which impact and, in certain cases, determine the question of jurisdiction as between the provincial inferior courts and provincial superior trial courts. Indictable offences are more serious offences, summary conviction offences less serious ones.[9] For instance, murder, robbery and break and entry are indictable offences, and indecent exposure, communication for the purposes of prostitution and causing a disturbance in a public place are summary conviction offences. A person who stands accused of a indictable offence — which, prior to recent amendments to the *Criminal Code*, was easily defined as one having a maximum penalty greater than six months imprisonment and/or a fine of $2,000 — may, with certain exceptions, elect to be tried by provincial inferior court or by provincial

---

[8]   R.S.C. 1985, c. C-46.
[9]   English and American law use the traditional designations "misdemeanours" and "felonies" in place of the Canadian neologisms "summary"and "indictable".

superior trial judge or by provincial superior trial judge and jury. Excepted are those offences — for example, murder and treason — listed in the *Criminal Code* as within the absolute jurisdiction of the superior court. Excepted as well are those indictable offenses which recent amendments to the *Criminal Code* place in the absolute jurisdiction of the inferior courts. So, these exceptions aside, as regards indictable offences, jurisdiction turns on election by the accused and is, in consequence, overlapping as between the superior and inferior courts. Jurisdiction over summary conviction offenses, on the other hand, resides absolutely with the inferior court.

To summarize then: a) the inferior provincial courts have absolute jurisdiction over all provincially created offences, over all federally created summary conviction criminal offences, and over those federally created indictable offences which the *Criminal Code* identifies as falling to their jurisdiction; and b) the inferior provincial courts have contingent jurisdiction on other federally created indictable offences and limited jurisdiction on civil matters.

Civil and criminal judgments of the provincial inferior courts are, of course, appealable to the provincial superior courts on grounds and by procedures which vary by province.

THE FEDERAL COURT

Section 101 of the *Constitution Act, 1867* authorizes the federal government to constitute "a general court of appeal for Canada". Passed pursuant to this power in 1875, the *Supreme Court Act*[10] constituted the Supreme Court of Canada, the role and importance of which we shall consider shortly. Section 101 also empowers the federal government to establish "additional courts for the better administration of the laws of Canada". In 1970, the Federal Court of Canada was created under this residual s. 101 power.

The Federal Court has a Trial Division and a Court of Appeal, and its judges are appointed and paid by the federal government.[11] Either division of the Court may sit in any place in Canada. The Court's jurisdiction is limited to purely federal law, though, of course, not all federal law, most notably the *Criminal Code*, comes under its purview.[12] The Federal Court, rather, as a court of *exceptional jurisdiction*, hears cases arising from specialized areas of federal law such as patents, immigration and customs and income tax law. In addition, the Court hears matters arising out of the conduct and decisions of federally created administrative tribunals and agencies as well as actions against the federal government.

---

[10] S.C. 1875, c. 11.
[11] The Court is comprised of a Chief Justice, an Associate Chief Justice and not more than 23 other judges. The Chief Justice and ten other judges sit as the federal Court of Appeal. These ten may be drawn from any of the 23 federal justices since members of the Federal Court appointed in one division are also *ex officio* members of the other division.
[12] This is the case because, unlike the provincial superior courts, the Federal Court is a court of exceptional and not general jurisdiction.

THE SUPREME COURT OF CANADA

Though the Supreme Court of Canada has existed since 1875, it did not really become "supreme" until 1949. Prior to the amendments to the *Supreme Court Act*[13] of that year, decisions of the Supreme Court were subject to further appeal to the Judicial Committee of the Privy Council in Britain. Moreover, appeals from the decisions of the provincial appeal courts could proceed directly to the Privy Council without any involvement by the Supreme Court. The 1949 amendments abolished the right of appeal to Britain and thereafter the Supreme Court of Canada became "supreme" in fact as well as in name — its exercise of its general jurisdiction on matters of law became final and binding on all other courts. From that point indeed, the Supreme Court of Canada became more "supreme" than similar courts in many other states because of the nature of its jurisdiction. First, because s. 101 of the *Constitution Act, 1867* defines the Supreme Court as a general court of appeal, the Canadian Court — unlike, say, its American counterpart — has jurisdiction over all matters of law, federal, provincial and municipal, and including all administrative agencies or tribunals created under any of those bodies of law. Second, the Supreme Court's jurisdiction includes both the law of the common law provinces and the civil law of Quebec.

The Supreme Court hears appeals from the provincial superior courts and from the Federal Court of Appeal. Since 1974, leave is required for most appeals.[14] Leave may be granted by the Supreme Court itself or, notionally at least, by a provincial court of appeal. In either case, whether leave is granted turns most often upon whether a case involves matters of national significance. In addition to appeals from these sources, the Supreme Court also hears references cases directed to it by the federal government. References cases generally involve the constitutional validity of some federal statute.

The Supreme Court consists of nine judges who are appointed and paid by the federal government. The *Supreme Court Act* requires that three of the judges be from Quebec. Over time, a convention has become established with respect to the provincial location, at the time of appointment, of the remaining six justices: three of the justices are appointed from Ontario, two from the four Western provinces, and one from Atlantic Canada. The Chief Justice of the Supreme Court is selected from among the nine justices by the federal government and is the Chief Justice of Canada.

(ii)   Hierarchy

We have already touched on the judicial hierarchy which is created by this structure. But since how courts relate to one another is very much a defining

---

[13]   R.S.C. 1927, c. 35 (am. 1949, 2 Sess.), c. 37.

[14]   Though a small category of appeal as of right remains, most of the Court's cases arise from its discretionary jurisdiction.

characteristic of the judicial branch, it is important to be precise. The following chart offers a simplified view of the hierarchal structure of the entire judicial branch in Canada.

Figure 2.1

STRUCTURE OF CANADIAN COURTS

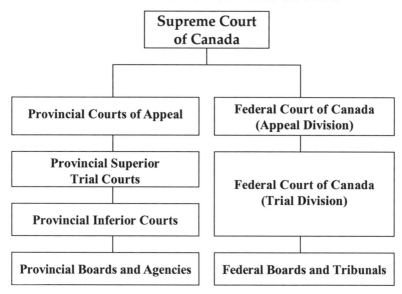

As we have seen, courts exist to render authoritative determinations of the identity, meaning and application of legal rules. It is important to recognize, however, that the reach of their authority depends upon their place in this hierarchy. The Supreme Court of Canada's authority is *final* as regards the parties to the case, and it is *binding* on all lower courts as regards all future determinations by those courts. The authority of all other courts is confined in both of these respects. Because the decisions of provincial courts — superior as well as inferior — are subject to appeal, their authority to bind the parties is much less significant. The force of their decisions in this respect does, of course, increase with the place of the court in this hierarchy. Decisions of the provincial superior appeal courts are much more binding than the decisions of superior trial courts and the provincial inferior courts simply because they may be appealed only with leave. But that aside, the authority of these courts to bind citizens is by definition circumscribed.

The authority of all courts other than the Supreme Court to bind other courts is also limited. Even where they are not appealed to the Supreme Court, the determinations of a provincial appeal court, for instance, bind only courts subordinate to it within its province. As regards courts in other jurisdictions, an appeal court's decisions may merely persuade, and this turns on many factors, not the least of which is the status and reputation of the court within the legal community. The reputations of courts waft and wane according to their membership at any point in time. The same holds for the decisions of superior trial courts. Though they bind only inferior courts in the same jurisdiction, they might yet have persuasive force in other jurisdictions depending upon the reputation of the judge. There have been judges, in Canada and elsewhere, whose reputations for judicial competence and honour were so well established that their influence on the law far exceeded their subordinate station and that of their contemporaries in the courts above them.

Judicial titles and forms of address replicate in a very public way this structural hierarchy. Until quite recently, judges of the superior provincial courts, the Federal Courts, and the Supreme Court of Canada were addressed in court as "My Lord" or "My Lady". Though this continues to be proper practice as regards the first two, in October, 2000, the Supreme Court renounced those titles in favour of "Justice". Use of "My Lord" and "My Lady" arises from the British practice, despite the fact that Canada, unlike Britain, neither has a system of peerage nor designates its superior court judges as peers. This curious anachronism is not, however, carried over into the titles of these judges who are known not as "Lord" or "Lady", but simply instead as "Mr. Justice" or "Madame Justice" and who, outside of court, are addressed as "The Honourable Mr. Justice" or "The Honourable Madame Justice." In law reports and scholarly writing, they are referred to differently still. In those contexts, these judges — except for chief justices — are identified with a simple "J." behind their surname or, in the case of appeal court judges, with a "J." followed by the letter "A" for "appeal". Thus, in Alberta, a Queen's Bench judge is identified as, say, Moreau J. and a judge of the Court of Appeal as, for example, Foisey J.A. The Chief Justice of Canada is identified as C.J.C. and the provincial chief justices as C.J. followed by the first letter of their province. Judges of the provincial inferior courts, especially those in the criminal division, are generally addressed simply as "Your Honour."

(iii) Appointment and Discipline

APPOINTMENT

The authority to appoint judges resides, as we have seen, in ss. 92(14), 96 and 101 of the *Constitution Act, 1867*. Those provisions, however, do not prescribe a process of appointment. In consequence, the matter has fallen entirely within the discretion of the federal and provincial governments. The system of appointment which has developed over time exists then by convention only, and is very much contingent on political will either to maintain or change it. We will briefly canvass the present processes of appointment to each of the courts of the judicial system in Canada before proceeding to the question of discipline, including removal. Canadian appointment practices are increasingly controversial, particularly as regards the degree of discretion which they vest in the executive branch of government and their overall lack of transparency.[15]

Judges hold office on good behaviour until they retire.[16] Perhaps surprisingly, to be eligible for appointment, a candidate must only have been a member of a provincial law society for a certain minimum period of time, most often ten years. Other than that there are no criteria, none at least which are public. With the exception of appointments to our highest court, however, there now exists an abundant process. Supreme Court appointments are made and the Chief Justice selected at the will of the Prime Minister at the time of openings.

Until the 1970s, appointments to "section 96 courts" — and, after its constitution, to the Federal Court — were as freewheeling as appointments to the Supreme Court continue to be, except only that it was the federal Minister of Justice, and not the Prime Minister, who wielded the discretion. Since then, there has been progress towards widening and formalizing the consultation necessary prior to appointment. These developments culminated in the process installed by the Mulroney government in 1988, which with minor adjustments remains intact. Under this regime, a committee of seven members in each province and territory sits to review applications for appointment which are required initially to be submitted to the Office of the Commissioner of Federal Judicial Affairs which is situated in the federal Department of Justice. The members of these Advisory Committees are appointed by the federal Minister of Justice under the following scheme: one member is nominated by the provincial law society and another by the provincial branch of the Canadian Bar Association; a superior court judge is nominated by the provincial or territorial Chief Justice; a person (generally a non-lawyer) is nominated by the provincial Attorney General or by the territorial Minister of Justice; two non-lawyers and a lawyer are nominated by the federal Minister of Justice. Members hold office for three year terms.

Whether the constitution of these committees is an improvement to the federal appointment process is a matter of much debate. Several things at least are clear. There are no guidelines to which the committees are bound. They cannot solicit applications and are confined instead to the applications directed to them by the Federal Commissioner. They are mandated to reach but the very baldest of conclusions with respect to applications, namely, that an applicant is "recommended" or "highly recommended" or that the committee is "unable to recommend". And though their recommendations are forwarded to the federal Minister of Justice, the Minister is not bound by law to select from the list of recommended applicants. Finally, elevation within the federal judiciary and the selection of chief justices are beyond the committees' competence as in practice are elevations to the federal judiciary of sitting provincial inferior judges.

---

[15] See for example the essays collected in F.C. DeCoste (guest editor), "Special Issue on Judicial Appointments" (2000), 38(3) Alberta L. Rev. 603-940.

[16] Depending on their appointment, the age of compulsory retirement for judges is either 70 or 75.

Provincial inferior court judges are appointed by the provincial cabinets using a variety of appointment procedures. Most provinces have some sort of judicial council, appointed by the Minister of Justice, which is mandated variously to vet lists of candidates submitted to it by the Minister or independently to recommend candidates to the Minister. Alberta and Ontario have recently instituted procedures allegedly designed to make appointments more accountable, transparent, and merit-based.

DISCIPLINE

Section 99(1) of the *Constitution Act, 1867* declares that superior court judges "hold office during good behaviour, but shall be removable by the Governor General on Address of the Senate and House of Commons".[17] No superior court judge has ever been removed by joint address and, in consequence, how it would be undertaken and on what grounds remain something of a mystery. The tenure of judges is more typically qualified, if at all, by procedures which fall short of removal.

The Canadian Judicial Council was established in 1971 pursuant to what is now s. 59(1) of the federal *Judges Act*.[18] The Council is comprised of the Chief Justices and Associate Chief Justices of all the federal and provincial superior courts and is chaired by the Chief Justice of Canada. Among other matters — most notably judicial education — the Council is charged with the discipline of judges[19] and, more particularly, with hearing complaints against judges. Pursuant to its own by-laws, the Council has established a Judicial Conduct Committee to handle these complaints. In 1998, the Council adopted a rather anodyne code of ethics for federally appointed judges which was published as *Ethical Principles for Judges*.

With the exception of Prince Edward Island, provincially appointed judges are disciplined by variously mandated provincial judicial councils which are constituted under the provisions of the various statutes governing the provincial court systems. Ontario and Manitoba have recently adopted procedures intended to sophisticate the disciplinary process in those provinces.

---

[17] The *Supreme Court Act*, R.S.C. 1985, c. S-26 and the *Federal Court Act*, R.S.C. 1985, c. F-7, reproduce the "good behaviour" condition for justices of the Supreme Court and the Federal Court. The federal *Judges Act*, R.S.C. 1985, c. J-1 establishes the condition for other federally appointed judges.

[18] R.S.C. 1985, c. J-1, as am.

[19] Though the Council's disciplinary mandate includes the authority to recommend to the federal Minister of Justice that a judge be removed from office, s. 99(1) continues to govern and superior court judges can only finally be removed through a joint address.

C. THE PRACTISING BRANCH

The practising branch is the core of the legal community. The judicial branch and the academic branch exist only because the practising branch of client advisers and advocates exists. Before we can understand why this is so and what it means, it is necessary first to come to terms with the organization and constitution of the practising profession.

(i) Organization

The practising branch is organized exclusively on a provincial basis.[20] In each province, there exists a body — in most provinces, called the law society[21] — which is charged with governing practising lawyers. These bodies are constituted by provincial legislation — generally a Legal Profession Act[22] — under the authority of ss. 92(11) and 92(14) of the *Constitution Act, 1867*. Each of the provincial societies is governed by a small group of lawyers elected from the membership for set terms. These governing members are called "benchers", a term borrowed from the English system of governance.

This structure is the only structure relevant to the practising branch, and the distinction between benchers and members is the only distinction which that structure defines and acknowledges. More particularly, there is in Canada no distinction between barristers and solicitors, no distinction which arises from honorifics such as Queen's Counsel designation, no distinction which depends upon the economic organization of lawyers, and no distinction which resides on specialization.

In England, the practising branch is divided between barristers and solicitors. Barristers are lawyers who are called to the bar which means that their practice consists of courtroom advocacy. Solicitors, on the other hand, may not appear in court, at least not in the superior courts in which barristers appear, and their practice by and large consists of advising clients and, as the need arises, directing them to barristers. In Canada, outside of Quebec, the practising branch is fused. Everyone admitted to a law society becomes at once a barrister and solicitor.

Most provincial governments[23] and the federal government make annual awards of the designation Queen's Counsel or Q.C. Though they do so by virtue of legislation enacted for that purpose — for example, the Alberta *Queen's*

---

[20] In consequence, other forms of organization of lawyers — for instance, the Canadian Bar Association — do not share the constitutive character and importance of the law societies and may appropriately be classed as either fraternal or self-protection organizations.

[21] Hence: the Law Society of Alberta; the Law Society of British Columbia; in Ontario, the Law Society of Upper Canada, and so on. The exceptions are the Nova Scotia and New Brunswick Barrister's Society and the *Barreau du Québec*.

[22] But not always; see, for example, the *Solicitors Act*, R.S.O. 1990, c. S.15, in Ontario.

[23] Ontario is the exception.

Counsel Act[24] — the practice is English in origin. There the award was originally given to barristers thought worthy of appearing in court on behalf of the Crown. And though that meaning has since been lost, it remains in England an honour awarded only to barristers of senior rank and reputation. In Canada, it may be awarded to any lawyer, rank, reputation and nature of practice notwithstanding. For just these reasons, the Canadian practice has been much criticized as political patronage which confuses the public. In any event, the designation does not legitimately segregate between practising lawyers.[25]

Economically and in terms of the delivery of legal services, the practising branch is organized around law firms and sole practitioners. Law firms consist of a partnership and typically include lawyers, known as associates, who are not partners. Unlike partners, who have security of tenure and who draw on the profits of the firm, the tenure and compensation of associates are matters determined by their employment contracts. Subject to whatever rules have been adopted by their society, individual lawyers may seek permission to carry on practice as a professional corporation. This designation permits lawyers to register under and to take advantage of the provisions of legislation governing corporations. Increasingly, sole practitioners seek permission and share office space and expenses with other incorporated sole practitioners. Associates and partners also may avail themselves of the designation. Though all of these economic arrangements are governed by the law societies and though they may produce real socio-economic stratification among members, neither the arrangements nor their economic consequences constitute differences which may be counted as regards the status of being a lawyer. However they practice and to whatever degree of benefit to themselves, lawyers are *equal as members* of the society to which they have been admitted and their society knows and governs them on that basis alone. The society of lawyers, that is, is a *society of equals*.

Law societies are seized of an abundance of authority. Typically, they are charged with: a) administering the affairs of the society including the creation of offices and the selection of officers, the constitution of committees and more generally the enactment of by-laws and rules; b) the operation of legal aid; c) setting and collecting annual fees; d) arranging for a practice insurance plan; e) establishing standards for admission to the society and f) disciplining lawyers including the suspension and termination of membership. Their *raison d'être* resides, however, in the final two. *Law societies exist to declare who may become a lawyer and who may continue to be a lawyer.* This exhaustive jurisdiction over membership in the profession carries a number of meanings which are critical not only as regards the nature of practising branch itself but to the judicial and academic branches as well.

---

[24]   R.S.A. 1980, c. Q-2.

[25]   For those Queen's Counsellors whose practice is courtroom advocacy, there remain two privileges: they may wear silk robes and they may plead from within the bar, which places them nearer to the judge.

(ii)   Self-governance

Law societies alone may award the status barrister and solicitor. Because this jurisdiction over admission and continuance is exclusive, the practising branch is self-governing absolutely. It does not matter that the societies in their modern, Canadian form are constituted under provincial legislation. Like the legislation constituting the judicial superior branch, the legislation which establishes the societies is an acknowledgement and reception of the ancient practices of the legal community which remains dependent upon those practices and not upon their contemporary codification in statute. No government, then, could diminish the self-governance of the legal community without altering in a fundamental way the nature and quality of our politics, law, and communal life.

A second meaning follows from this absolute jurisdiction over lawyerly status. If the society of lawyers alone may determine who may be a lawyer, then being a lawyer is a *privilege* and not a right. But not only that: the award of that privilege must therefore depend upon conditions which the law society alone may identify. Articulating and then applying the conditions for membership comprise the central task and obligation of lawyers through their law societies. And it is their accomplishments in collectively making good those requirements that makes the practising branch the bedrock of the legal community.

(iii)   Admission and Membership

Though the conditions for award and maintenance of lawyerly status are variously stated, they everywhere concern one matter only. To gain and maintain the privilege, the applicant must be *fit* to be a lawyer. Fitness itself always involves two categories of conditions, namely, *competence* and *character*. In Canada, law societies have determined competence for admission minimally to require: a pre-law university education (most often baccalaureate graduation from a recognized university, though sometimes — as in Alberta — successful completion of just two years); successful completion of a degree in law — an LL.B., B.C.L. or now, in the case of the law school at the University of Toronto, a J.D. — at a recognized university law school; successful completion of a one-year period of articles of clerkship with a member in good standing of the society;[26] and attendance at and successful completion of the society's bar admission course. That these requirements are minimal — both as regards admission and continuance — follows directly from the deliberate limitation on the nature of the claims which can be made by lawyers with respect to specialization. When persons are admitted to the bar, they are admitted as generalists — as barristers and solicitors *simpliciter* — and not as specialists in some specific variety of practice or of

---

[26]   The member is called "the principal" and the clerk "the student-at-law" and the agreement between the two — which has to be filed with and approved by the society — the "Articles of Clerkship". Lawyers can only enter Articles of Clerkship if they have been members for at least five years.

law. And though this is now often fudged in practice and sometimes in principle, the point remains: though their interests and practices may in fact be different, other things being equal, those differences provide no basis for segregating between lawyers. All lawyers, rather, are equal as members of the society to which they have been admitted.

The matter of competence does not end on admission. The conduct of lawyers remains open to review on grounds of competence though law societies do not require — as they would need to if specialization were permitted — periodic competency tests. Competence is governed under the provisions of the codes of conduct adopted by the societies. And matters of competence which come to a society's attention will be investigated pursuant to those provisions and where appropriate, they will lead to disciplinary proceedings.

Character as well applies to fitness both on admission and on continuance. In order to be eligible for the status of lawyer, an otherwise competent applicant typically must provide proof of good character and reputation.[27] Law societies generally require written testimonials regarding both matters. The applicant's past conduct or past or present beliefs may also be relevant to character. Suppose, for instance, it comes to a society's attention that an applicant for admission has a criminal record or that the applicant is a member of, say, the Ku Klux Klan or the Aryan Nations. In cases such as these, an inquiry may be undertaken and, if matters warrant, a hearing held on the applicant's fitness.

Once admitted, a lawyer remains held to a standard of conduct which in the society's view is conduct becoming a lawyer. Like the standards of competence, these standards of character are found in a society's code of conduct and are grounds for investigation and discipline. Such codes call for the lawyer to honour five different sets of obligations: their obligations to their clients, to the court understood as the forum of justice, to their profession, to other lawyers, and to society at large. For instance, among many other obligations, lawyers owe to clients confidentiality and zealous representation; to the courts, maintenance of due process and of the practices of justice; to their profession, maintenance and advancement of its standards and reputation; to other lawyers, candour and honourable treatment; to society more generally, maintenance of the institutions of justice and provision of legal service. The status of lawyer, then, is suffused with obligations of competence and character and the award of the privilege of that status properly depends upon their being honoured.

(iv) The Primacy of the Profession

The practising branch is the core of the legal community because the other branches are secondary to it. This is so for two reasons. First, the judicial and academic branches are contingent upon the practising branch in a very real and obvious sense. The judicial branch depends on the profession because the courts

---

[27]   And proof as well of Canadian citizenship or lawful admission to permanent residence in Canada.

must be staffed by persons whom the practising branch alone can certify and supply. Likewise the law schools: had not the practising branch specified a university degree in law as the threshold for competence, the academic branch of the profession simply would not exist. Were this specification to change, law schools would necessarily cease to be professional schools and would become instead departments in the university whose scholars happen, along with colleagues in other departments, to teach and write about law. And though these deprofessionalised schools might continue to employ lawyers as professors, their professional status would be personal to them as barristers and solicitors and could no longer depend on their institutional status as law professors since that designation would no longer exist.

There is a less obvious sense in which the judicial and academic branches owe their existence to the practising branch. In Chapter 1, we saw that the legal community is itself a dependent community. There is no lawyering unless and until a client appears; there is no judicial process or outcome unless and until parties appear; and there is no professional preparation in the law schools unless and until law students appear. But matters are more complex than that. Everything finally depends upon the appearance of clients before members of the practising branch. This is fairly clear in the case of the judicial branch. There can be no judicial action without parties and, by and large, there can be no parties without lawyers having first received the parties into law. Moreover, the courts depend upon the lawyers before them to provide the arguments and the evidence out of which authoritative determinations are forged. The academic branch also depends upon the practising branch having first received persons into the processes and practices of the legal community. Professional preparation in the law schools is dependent in this sense because otherwise there is nothing for which students may be prepared, no language, skill and craft for them to learn. Communal criticism is dependent because, absent the practising bar's receiving clients, there is nothing to criticize.

Despite the hierarchy which obtains between the branches, the *practising branch alone initiates the practices of the legal community.*

D. THE ACADEMIC BRANCH

Unlike the situation in the United States — where some law schools are part of state universities and others (indeed the most renowned)[28] are faculties of private universities — Canadian law schools are without exception located in state-sponsored universities. In consequence, the 21 schools[29] which comprise the

---

[28] For instance, the law schools at Harvard, Duke, Yale, Stanford and Cornell.

[29] They are located at the universities of Alberta, British Columbia, Calgary, Dalhousie, Laval, Manitoba, McGill, Moncton, Montreal, New Brunswick, Ottawa (common law and civil), Québec à Montréal, Queens, Saskatchewan, Sherbrooke, Toronto, Victoria, Western Ontario, Windsor and

academic branch in Canada find themselves constituted under provincial legislation, a university statute, enacted pursuant to the education power found in s.
93 of the *Constitution Act, 1867*. This common origin could be viewed as com-
promising the independence of the law schools from governmental policy. However, the situation of the law schools is in this respect no different from that of
the judicial or practising branches. Though the academic branch is constituted
through provincial legislation, it is not thereby made vulnerable to political
whimsy. The legislation governing universities, like the legislation constituting
the judiciary and the practising branch, is an acknowledgement and reception of
traditions having to do with how societies such as ours are constituted and conduct themselves. That the law schools are located in state universities is much
less important so far as independence is concerned than their owing their place
in the legal community to the always reviewable policy of the law societies to
require that their members hold a university degree in law. There are however
other influences that affect the quality of both professional legal education and
the academic branch's membership in the legal community to which we shall
now turn.

(i)   Law Schools: Professional or Academic?

As we have seen, it falls to the academic branch to prepare law students for their
professional futures and to serve as a source of professional criticism of the legal
community as a whole. Honouring these obligations requires that law schools
take seriously their place in the legal community. To do that, they must view
themselves first and foremost as professional schools, as institutions whose obligations arise not from their location in the university, but from their membership in the legal community. Otherwise, these defining obligations tend to lose
out to those less precise ones which attach to and flow from the location of the
law schools in the university. When that happens, law professors tend to think of
themselves as professors who happen to teach law and not as lawyers attached to
the academic branch of the legal community.

Anyone who is entertaining taking up legal studies, not as an academic discipline, but with a view to professional practice, should be aware that the mandate
and obligations of the contemporary legal academy are the subject of much controversy. Some professors view the law school institutionally as a specialized
faculty of the university, law as (just another) specialized discipline, and scholarly obligation as residing in honouring the scholarly life. Others take the opposite view: for them, the legal academy is a co-equal branch of the legal
community which is seized of special and distinct, though peculiarly legal, obligations. The contest between these views has led to a widespread confusion
about role and standards. Professors outside of the law schools question the

---

York. Carleton University and Laurentian University have departments of law, but neither grants
an LL.B. and neither is a professional law school.

scholarship of law professors and indeed the whole of their way of leading the scholarly life. Law students, on the other hand, think that their professors are too much a part of the university way of life and accuse them of being too "theoretical" and of paying too little attention to their professional preparation. The practising bar accuses the academy of having lost sight of professional standards and of delivering students to articles who have neither lawyerly skill nor spirit. For its part, the judicial branch increasingly decries scholarly criticism of judicial conduct and judgment. And, among themselves, law professors criticize one another for being either too much or too little a lawyer or too little or too much a professor.

With this situation in mind, we can now describe the context and substance of contemporary legal education. As regards context, two matters are critical — the structure of the legal academy and the process of student admissions. As regards substance, we will want to focus on curriculum and on the methods of law school teaching and study.

(ii) The Structure of Law Faculties

Law schools are structured on the same model as other, much larger faculties such as arts or science. The faculty is lead by a dean appointed, in consultation with law school's tenured members of faculty, by the university's board of governors, generally for a five-year term which is renewable only once. The dean is assisted by one or more associate deans who are generally appointed by the dean on the advice of members of faculty for a period of two or three years.

Though a dean has authority over a number of important matters — chief among them, teaching assignments and initial assessments of merit in tenure and promotion — the dean does not have authority to govern the faculty. Rather, as is the case in other faculties of the modern university, governance resides in the faculty as a collectivity. Generally, this takes the form of a council whose membership consists of all tenured or tenurable members of faculty. The dean is a member of this council as a member of faculty and not as dean and, in most law schools, is prohibited from chairing the council which responsibility falls instead to a person elected from the membership or to an associate dean. In addition, law faculty councils generally have elected student members and representatives from the university board of governors and, notably, from the law society of the province in which the school is located. Law faculty councils govern the affairs of law schools through a system of standing committees — minimally, a separate committee for admissions, curriculum, tenure and promotion, and staff selection — whose members are elected annually from faculty and, in case of certain committees, from the student population. The committees report and are responsible to the councils and have no independent authority.

Only tenured and tenurable professors are members of faculty. Members are selected by the faculty itself through a standing committee of the governing council which, when a position becomes available, shortlists and interviews candidates and selects from among them. In Canada, candidates for professorial appointments in law schools generally must hold an undergraduate degree and two degrees in law, an LL.B. and a LL.M. (a master of laws). It is not necessary that they be members in good standing of a law society, though whether this should be required remains a matter of some contention. Law faculties have in the recent past become more integrated into the university and significantly more of their appointments have been at the doctoral level.

Members of faculty are initially appointed on probationary status and at the rank of assistant professor. Generally, the probationary period is six years, after which the professor either becomes a tenured member of faculty or is released. Tenure is a lifetime status which immunizes the professor who holds it from summary dismissal. It does not, however, immunize the holder from review or from dismissal for cause. In most universities, the performance of professors is reviewed annually and persistent poor performance may lay the foundation for dismissal with cause. Everywhere in the modern university performance review is peer review conducted by a standing committee of the governing council on grounds of annual reports which members of faculty — including those members who happen to sit on the review committee — are required to submit to it, generally through the dean. These reports are reviewed and judgments made according to whatever criteria — generally teaching quality, scholarship and community service — are specified by the governing council. In most universities, the review committee judgments take the form of merit awards to which are attached dollars which increment faculty salaries. Since these awards themselves attach permanently to professorial salaries, they are the object of competition among professors.

Faculty members may hold tenure at the rank of assistant professor, associate professor or (full) professor. This ranking system is independent from tenure and relies instead on an independent merit system of promotion. Promotion from one rank to another is a matter which falls to a standing committee of the governing council on application initiated by individual professors. This peer review involves the committee in assessing the applicant's contribution — to scholarship, teaching, and community service — over the long term and, in the case of appointment to full professor, over the whole of the applicant's appointment. Generally, assistant professors apply for promotion to associate at or about the time they are awarded tenure. Associate professors will not normally apply for professorship before they have completed at least ten years of service. There is, of course, no right to promotion and no obligation to apply. In consequence, some professors may end their service at the associate or even the assistant rank. Because rank impacts on salary, professors very much desire promotion and, like merit awards, promotion is a matter of competition among them.

Some faculties employ persons in addition to their tenured and tenurable members as teachers. Known variously as sessionals or adjunct professors, these teachers are not members of faculty as their service is neither tenurable nor eligible for promotion and they are not selected according to the criteria and processes which apply to tenurable positions. Law schools in particular tend to employ a healthy number of sessional instructors drawn from the practising branch. When these lawyers are senior members of the bar, this practice is most beneficial both to students and to the law academy. Acting as classroom instructors, senior members of the bar expose students to the standards and processes of law practice. So far as the legal academy is concerned, the presence of senior members of the bar among the professoriate not only keeps the academy close to the profession, but serves as a reminder that the legal academy is a professional school whose true home is the legal community. Junior members of the bar are also sometimes contracted as sessionals.

(iii) Admission to Law School

Members of the law faculty, through a standing committee drawn from their number, select students for admission. Putting special admissions aside for the moment, admission to law school minimally requires university education, most often an undergraduate degree and rarely a mere two years of university study. Law schools do not require any particular course of studies of their applicants.

Most Canadian law schools[30] also require applicants to take the Law School Admissions Test, the (in)famous and much criticized LSAT. Administered by the Law School Admission Council, the LSAT is designed to test skills which are thought to be essential for success in law school. According to the Council, these essentials consist in the abilities to read and comprehend complex texts with accuracy and insight, to organize and manage information and to draw reasonable inferences from it, to reason critically, and to analyze and evaluate the reasoning and argument of others. Consistent with this understanding, four of the test's five 35-minute sections of multiple-choice questions address reading comprehension (one section), analytical reasoning (one section) and logical reasoning (two sections). The fifth section, which does not contribute to the test taker's score, is used to test new questions. In addition, in the last 30 minutes of the exam, test takers are required to write a short argument on a specific fact situation. The Law School Admissions Council sends this writing sample to all of the law schools to which the test taker is applying, but it does not score or otherwise evaluate it.

Law schools rely on a composite of LSAT score and grade point average to rank applicants, but they do not do so in any uniform way. Some weigh GPA more than do others, and some claim to rely on the LSAT score only in exceptional cases. Whatever the details of the formulae used by different law schools, students who have performed best in undergraduate studies and on the LSAT are everywhere ranked highest and thought the most desirable candidates for law school admission.

---

[30] The exceptions are the French-language common law schools at Ottawa and Moncton and all of the French-language civil schools in Quebec.

There is, however, a caveat to this story. All Canadian law schools have recently implemented policies which establish two categories of alternative admissions.[31] A mature applicant category is meant to open legal studies to persons who have not had any university education or whose university grades fall below the minimum, provided in both cases, they are of a certain age (minimally mid-20s) and have otherwise demonstrated (generally as evidenced by a biographical statement) merit in their work or social experience. The special applicant category is designed to attract and admit candidates from social groups historically disadvantaged by reason of race and ethnicity. Though only a certain number of students may be admitted under either of these categories in any given year, law schools do not reserve places for mature and special applicants and the number in fact admitted turns on the number and merit of the applications received. Both mature and special applicants are required to take the LSAT.

(iv) Curriculum

In Canada, law schools generally provide a three-year course of studies towards either a Bachelor of Laws (LL.B.) or a Doctorate of Jurisprudence (J.D.). Though the details of the three years vary by school — for example, some have more required courses than others, and some stress clinical experience and offer internships while others do not — the curriculum is everywhere united in terms of its origin and by the requirements and nature of the first year of law school.

The contemporary model of legal education is, historically, the Harvard or Langdellian model. Christopher Columbus Langdell was appointed the first Dean of Harvard Law School in 1870, and it was Langdell who created the three-year, first-year centred model of university legal education. It was Langdell as well who first took the view that law is foremost a university discipline and that law professors are primarily university professors rather than academic lawyers.

The first-year programme was meant by Langdell to provide students with a foundation for legal studies and practice by exposing one and all to the fundamental areas of public and private law. In consequence, the first-year programme is mandatory; there are no optional courses. The fundaments of private law are provided in separate, year-long courses on contracts (the law of promises), torts (the law of private harms) and property (the law of ownership). Students are introduced to public law in courses on criminal law and constitutional law. These courses too are generally taught through the whole of first year. Some law schools round out the first-year programme with a course on civil procedure, others with a general introduction to law and legal research. In addition, virtually all law schools require first-year students to prepare and present a moot appellate case. The case is *moot* because the issues and the parties are

---

[31] In addition, some schools consider the regional origin of candidates.

hypothetical. Students are required to research the law governing the case, pre-pare and submit a written *factum* (which is a statement of the facts and law) and argue the case on behalf of either the *appellant* (the party appealing a lower court decision) or the *respondent* (the party who contends against the appeal) before a three-member panel of moot judges (drawn variously from the judici-ary, the bar and the law school).

The second and third years are intended to build on the foundation of public and private law provided by the first-year curriculum. Schools vary in the num-ber of mandatory courses they require in second- and third-year law. Some re-quire none. Others require certain courses in public law (administrative law particularly and in some instances conflict of laws as well)[32] and private law (company law especially).[33] Some also require that during either their second or third years, law students take a course on jurisprudence.[34] Some schools have the additional requirement that students prepare and submit a major paper re-searched in association with a course of their choosing. Whatever the details in these regards, the second- and third-year curriculum is everywhere the same structurally. Essentially, four categories of courses are offered. First, there are the statute-based courses which, as a group, comprise the majority of courses in the upper years curriculum. These courses may concern private law (for in-stance, the law of wills and estates and family law) or public law (for instance, tax law and environmental law). Second, there is a category of specialist courses which provide views on law from a variety of perspectives (for instance, law and literature, legal history, and law and poverty). Third, there is a group of courses which are not statute based and offer advanced study of judge-made law (for instance, advanced torts, equity and remedies). Finally, there is a group of courses which concern legal procedure rather than substantive law (for instance, civil and criminal procedure and evidence). These courses may or may not in-volve statutes and may involve either public or private law.

The upper-year curriculum is also everywhere characterized by the nature of the choices made by students. Despite the wider range of courses now on offer, students tend to be very traditional in their course selections. Without any insti-tutional urging, the typical student may select Administrative Law, Company Law, Income Tax, Evidence, Wills and Estates, Land Titles, Real Estate Trans-actions, Family Law and Credit Transactions. And this selection, of course, leaves out a host of specialized and substantive law courses.

---

[32] Administrative law governs the relations between state agents, tribunals and boards and citizens. Conflict of laws concerns those cases to which the law of more than one jurisdiction applies and determines which law will govern.

[33] Company law governs the relations between persons formally associated to carry on a commer-cial enterprize.

[34] Jurisprudence — or as it is sometimes called, legal theory — concerns the history of ideas about the nature of law.

(v) Teaching and Studying

Harvard's Langdell is also responsible for the methodologies of law school teaching and study. It was Langdell's lifework to make law a respected university discipline and to turn law teachers into respected university scholars. The key to both of these rewards, he thought, was to transform law into a science. In the Preface to his *A Selection of Cases on the Law of Contract*, Langdell describes legal science in the following terms:

> Law, considered as a science, consists of certain principles or doctrines. To have such a mastery of these as to be able to apply them with constant facility and certainty to the ever-tangled skein of human affairs, is what constitutes a true lawyer. ... If these doctrines could be so classified and arranged that each should be found in its proper place, and nowhere else, they would cease to be formidable from their number.[35]

But if law is the science of discovering and classifying legal doctrines, then there had to be some matter — akin to nature for the physical sciences — which would serve as the legal scientist's subject of inquiry and as the new science's raw material. Langdell found law's datum in appellate decisions and in so doing, he committed legal education to what has come to be called *the case method*.

According to Langdell, "all of the available materials of [legal] science are contained in printed books",[36] and the law library is the "proper workshop" for lawyers, since it is for them precisely what "the laboratories of the university are to the chemists and physicists, the museum of natural history to the zoologists, the botanical garden to the botanists".[37] Under this understanding, "the case is both a laboratory and a library", and "the facts of the case" are properly comparable "to the specimen" and "the opinion of the court, announcing the principles of law to be applied to the facts ... to the memoir of the discoverer of a great scientific truth".[38] But if reported cases thus became the stuff of legal science, they became as well the stuff of legal education. For if "the true lawyer" has "mastery" over legal principles and doctrines and if these principles and doctrines are found only in reported cases, then it falls to those who teach those who would become true lawyers to locate the cases in which those principles and doctrines are expressed and to use those cases as the foundation of their teaching.

So we have the case method. Law teachers teach the law as it is found in reported cases, predominantly cases which report the decisions of appellate courts.

---

[35] C. Langdell, *A Selection of Cases on the Law of Contracts*, 1st ed. (Boston: Little, Brown, 1871), at pp. vi-vii.

[36] Quoted in A.F. Sutherland, *The Law at Harvard: A History of Ideas and Men, 1817-1967* (Cambridge, MA: Harvard University Press, 1967), at p. 175.

[37] C. Langdell, "1886 Speech Delivered on the Occasion of the 250th Anniversary of Harvard University" (1887), 21 American L. Rev. 123 at 124.

[38] W.A. Keener, "The Inductive Method in Legal Education" (1894), 28 American L. Rev. 709 at 713.

This defining feature in turn determines how law teachers teach and how law students study.

Law is typically taught from what are called *casebooks*, which contain the cases establishing the doctrines and principles which govern the area of law which is the subject matter of the course. At one time, it fell to individual law teachers to compile and continually to update casebooks. Though some teachers continue this practice,[39] most take advantage of the plethora of commercially produced casebooks now available.

Everything else which may be used by either law teachers or law students is secondary to the casebook. This priority is especially important because it has structured the entire field of resources for legal education. Cases alone are the primary resource. And though there are other resources — what lawyers call "textbooks" which are book-length treatises on a particular area of law — they are secondary not only in the obvious sense that law teachers as a rule do not teach from them, but also because they are considered within the legal community to be of inferior authority. At one time, they were thought to be of inferior quality as well. For until quite recently, most textbooks took the form of "black-letter law" books so-called because rules appeared in them in bold type followed by case authorities and sometimes brief commentary.[40]

---

[39] Either because they find all of the commercial casebooks for their area somehow wanting or because no established national casebook is yet available. The latter occurs especially when new areas of law — say, native law or environmental law — are added to the curriculum. Often, in such cases, one of the casebooks developed by an individual will later be published by a commercial law publisher and join the ranks of national casebooks.

[40] Over time, as lawyers and judges come to rely on them, some textbooks become elevated in authority. At different points in legal history, the following classics, most of which remain most rewarding reading, were so elevated: Sir Edward Coke, *Institutes of the Laws of England*, Four Parts (London: M. Flesher, 1628); Sir William Blackstone, *Commentaries on the Laws of England*, 4 Vol. (Oxford: Clarendon Press, 1765); J. Chitty, *A Treatise on the Law of Contracts* (London: Sweet & Maxwell, 1826); J.H. Wigmore, *A Treatise on the System of Evidence at Common Law Trials*, 5 Vols., Canadian ed. (Toronto: Canada Law Book, 1905); G.C. Cheshire & C.H.S. Fifoot, *Law of Contract* (London: Butterworths, 1945); R.E. Megarry, *A Manual of the Law of Real Property* (London: Butterworths, 1954); and C. Vaines, *Personal Property* (London: Butterworths, 1954). But such elevation is rare and it seems always temporary. In any event, most textbooks have a much more modest fate. They are used as a convenience by lawyers and students but only so long as their treatment of the law remains current. This fact of life has moved some publishers to impose upon textbook writers periodically to update their books, a practice which, so far as students are concerned, has proved more expensive than productive. Some of the leading contemporary Canadian textbooks to which first year law students often refer are: L. Klar, *Tort Law*, 2nd ed. (Scarborough, ON: Carswell, 1996); D. Stuart, *Canadian Criminal Law: A Treatise*, 3rd ed. (Scarborough, ON: Carswell, 1995); S.M. Waddams, *The Law of Contract*, 4th ed. (Toronto: Canada Law Book, 1999); B.H. Ziff, *Principles of Property Law*, 2nd ed. (Scarborough, ON: Carswell, 1996); and P.W. Hogg, *The Constitutional Law of Canada*, student ed. (Scarborough, ON: Carswell, 1999). A final note. Legal treatises — such as theoretical investigations of law more generally or legal histories — which are not textbooks are not at all vulnerable to the fickleness of changing legal doctrine and have, therefore, a much better chance of making a lasting impact on the thinking of the legal community. J. Austin's *The*

Law teachers do not all teach in the same way. Some professors follow what is known as the *Socratic method*. Until quite recently the dominant approach, this method requires law teachers to interrogate law students about cases with the intention of involving them directly in the discovery of the legal rules and doctrines resident in case law. In its purest form, the Socratic method prohibits professors from ever identifying the law for students and even from offering their own view of the law. Though some professors simply lecture their students on the law, most now adopt an approach which mixes a kinder and gentler Socratic method with lecturing. Under this format, law teachers will typically solicit — but not demand — student views on the cases under consideration and then, whether discussion ensues or not, summarize the law for students.

Studying law largely tracks teaching methodology. Law students are expected to have read assigned cases before class and during class they are expected, but no longer generally required, to participate in the formulation of legal principles and doctrines from the case materials. Typically, this expectation involves students in the lawyerly practice of *briefing cases*. In addition, many students often rely on textbooks, especially on those which professors either recommend or require for their courses. Finally, law students may chose to rely as well on one another, especially in first year. There is a long standing law school tradition of students combining, on a entirely voluntary and undirected basis, into what lawyers know as *study groups*, each consisting of between five and ten members. These groups devote themselves not only to the study of case law and to exam preparation, but also to making less insular and less competitive the law school experience.

With the exception of term paper courses, and these are generally specialist or perspectival courses, courses in law school culminate with an examination. Law school exams are different from other university exams as regards both their timing and their method. Traditionally, courses, even year-long courses, were examined only once. Though this tradition has been somewhat eroded in recent times — in first-year courses, for instance, it is not now uncommon for students to sit two exams, one at midterm and the final — law students still remain largely free from ongoing evaluation and much, in consequence, continues to ride on their capacity to perform on exams. Since law school exams are rather

Province of Jurisprudence Determined (1832) (Cambridge: Cambridge University Press, 1995), A.V. Dicey's *Introduction to the Study of the Law of the Constitution* (1885), 8th ed. (London: MacMillan, 1924) and, more recently, H.L.A. Hart's *The Concept of Law* (1961), 2nd ed. (Oxford: Clarendon Press, 1994) are works of such quality and influence. Contemporary works which just might stand the test of time include R. Dworkin's *Law's Empire* (1986) (Cambridge, MA: Harvard University Press, 1995) and *Taking Rights Seriously* (1977) (Cambridge, MA: Harvard University Press, 1977), J. Raz's *The Authority of Law* (1979) (Oxford: Oxford University Press, 1979) and *The Concept of a Legal System* (1970), 2nd ed. (Oxford: Clarendon Press, 1980) and E. Weinrib's *The Idea of Private Law* (1995) (Cambridge, MA: Harvard University Press, 1995). A bibliography of leading contemporary works appears in the appendix to this book.

gruelling affairs — exams for full-year courses are set for three hours and for half-year courses for two hours — law students are wise to think about and to adopt a strategy for preparing and writing them.

Law school exams are different from other university exams in terms of what it is that they intend to examine. Their method belies this special intention. Traditionally, law school exams contain one or more of what lawyers know as *hypotheticals*. A hypothetical is a statement of assumed facts and circumstances. For example, a final exam in first-year torts might contain the following hypothetical:

> It was a stormy Boxing Day in Alberta. Despite widely publicized police road advisories warning citizens of the dangers of road travel, John Grey undertook to drive himself and his seven-months pregnant wife, Elsa, from Edmonton to Red Deer to visit his aged and ailing mother, Martha. Neither John nor Elsa wore a seatbelt during their aborted journey; and John had drunk two beers with lunch prior to leaving.
>
> Under the Alberta *Municipalities Act*, the City of Edmonton has statutory power to maintain roadways within city boundaries. On the day in question, the City dispatched snow plows to various locations throughout the City, including to Calgary Trail South, the main route from Edmonton to Red Deer. It is City policy that employees who operate its vehicles, including snow plows, are required to conduct a vehicle safety check prior to leaving the City's Central Vehicle Depot from which all its vehicles are dispatched. Peter Workman was operating the snow plow on Calgary Trail South into which John Grey's car was ultimately to crash. Prior to leaving the Depot on Boxing Day, Peter conducted the nine-point examination which City policy prescribed for snow plows including a check of the emergency warning lighting system which controlled the flashing red lights on the top and back of the plow and which was designed and installed to make the City's snow plows easily visible in poor weather conditions. This he did by flicking the system's switch, located on the dash, on and off. On observing that the dash's red indicator light was flashing, Peter assumed the system was operational and forwent a visual inspection of the lights on the outside of the vehicle. Peter was wrong. The switch had somehow become disconnected from the system. In consequence, Peter was operating his plow on Calgary Trail without the warning system. As a result of this, John saw the plow through the heavy snow too late, and crashed into the back of it. His vehicle then careened off the snow plow and into a City of Edmonton electrical transformer, destroying it and taking out electrical service to the whole of southwest Edmonton.
>
> John was not seriously injured in the collision; but he was seriously dazed, confused and disoriented by it. Elsa, however, was seriously hurt. Because Elsa is a hemophiliac, and because pregnancy can aggravate that condition, the otherwise fairly minor facial cuts and abrasions she sustained in hitting the windshield bled profusely. Later that day, Elsa's baby was delivered prematurely and with permanent brain damage.
>
> Quite by chance, a crew of CFRB-TV, a regional TV station, was at the location of the accident, televising a live-to-air edition of CFRB's very popular *Road Report Show*. When the accident occurred, the reporter, Barbara Newsflash, instructed her TV crew to videotape the aftermath, which was thereupon broadcast live and included graphic close-ups of the bleeding Elsa. By the time the telecast concluded, Barbara realized that Elsa was in

need of immediate medical attention, and considered using CFRB's broadcast van to transport Elsa to Blue Nuns Hospital which was located some six kilometres from the site of the accident. Since, however, CFRB policy prohibited the use of company vehicles for private use of any sort, she promptly rejected this idea, and she and her crew left immediately. Medical evidence will show that in the case of pregnant hemophiliacs, the greater the blood loss, the greater the danger to the fetus.

An ambulance was called by Peter Workman through his dispatcher; and it finally arrived some 15 minutes after the CFRB crew left the scene. The two-man crew of the Northern Alta Ambulance Service, a privately held corporation, immediately attempted to stabilize Elsa, and promptly transferred her to the ambulance for the short trip to Blue Nuns. Thinking Elsa's condition critical, Roger Worry, the attendant driving the ambulance, resolved to make the trip as quickly as possible. The evidence will show that in doing so, he excessively exceeded the speed limit and with disastrous results. The ambulance went out of control on the icy streets, and slid into a ditch approximately two kilometres from the hospital. Roger and his fellow attendant were able to get the vehicle out of the ditch, but their and Elsa's arrival at the hospital was delayed another 15 minutes.

A City of Edmonton police cruiser, manned by Constable Tim Control, arrived on the scene at about the same time as did the ambulance. Constable Control began immediately to interview John Grey about the accident. On noticing that Grey was generally disoriented, and on detecting the scent of alcohol on his breath, the Constable concluded that Grey was drunk, and decided to take Grey into custody. When, however, he ordered Grey to sit in the back seat of the cruiser — where he intended to administer a breathalyzer — John refused, and began yelling at the officer and accusing him of uncaring incompetence. The Constable very quickly had had enough, and proceeded to force Grey into the cruiser. This he finally succeeded in doing, but only after a scuffle in which Grey slipped on the ice and fractured his left arm. The breathalyzer subsequently revealed that Grey was well under the blood/alcohol level of drunkenness.

Besides the harms suffered by Elsa, John, and their child, the accident had a number of other consequences:

    a)   On seeing the live telecast of Elsa's injuries, John's mother, Martha, suffered and continues to suffer morbid depression.

    b)   John — who always had an unsettled personality — became increasingly agitated after the accident, and began to drink heavily. In one drinking bout, some six months after the accident, he fell down stairs and broke his neck, and is now permanently paralyzed from the waist down.

    c)   Elsa has been informed that due to complications caused by the premature delivery, she will not be able to bear any more children.

    d)   Peter Workman suffers from chronic back pain as a result of the whiplash he experienced in the accident.

    e)   Due to the snow storm and to the number of electrical outages it caused elsewhere in the City, the interruption of electrical services to southwest Edmonton caused by John's collision with the transformer lasted over ten hours. A major Boxing Day food promotion that the Bestway supermarket, which is located on Calgary Trail, had long planned had to be cancelled. The supermarket can prove that it lost $250,000 in profit. It also sustained a loss of $200 in food spoilage and an expense of $2,500 in labour costs paid in overtime to a number of its employees to move frozen foods from its store to an unheated building next to the supermarket.

The student will be asked to prepare a *legal opinion* on the facts of the hypothetical through a question which generally reads something as follows: "a) Identify the parties to, and grounds for, all causes of action to which these facts give rise; b) Identify and discuss the issues associated with each ground". Though some law teachers have innovated with essay and multiple-choice questions, questions of legal opinion on hypothetical facts remains, and must remain, the dominant method of law school examination. This is so because what law school teaching and learning is finally about — and what law school testing has therefore to be about — is professional preparation. The professionalism of lawyers resides first in their craftsmanship, in their "mastery", as Langdell put it, of applying the rules of law to "the ever-tangled skein of human affairs". Law school exams present instances of those affairs with the intention of testing the student's mastery of the lawyer's craft of culling legal issues from social facts and of identifying and applying the relevant rules.

E.   THE CHARACTER OF THE LEGAL COMMUNITY: FREEDOM AND INDEPENDENCE

Law societies alone may award the privileged status of lawyer, and they may do so on whatever grounds they see fit. These basic institutional facts determine the character of the practising branch. That the bar may do as it wishes with respect to the conditions of membership means first that, as an institution, it is characterized above all else by freedom. But freedom of this sort, positively to do as it pleases, implicates freedom of another sort. The freedom of absolute self-governance requires that the bar be free from interference from all other institutions of communal life and from interference from the state especially. This negative freedom, which alone makes self-governance possible, means that the practising branch is characterized as well by independence.

The character of the rest of the legal community — of the judicial and academic branches alike — derives from, and replicates, the freedom and independence of the practising branch. As the bar is free to set the conditions of membership, judges are free to decide cases as they see fit; as the bar is independent from outside interference and especially from the state, so too are judges; and appointment to the judicial branch, like admission to the practising branch, is secured for life subject only to the condition of good behaviour. In consequence, though judges are appointed by the state, once appointed they obey, and can be made to obey, no ruler in declaring the law save their own consciences. All of this is so precisely because judges were first lawyers and were appointed as lawyers, as members of a free and independent profession. The freedom and independence of the judicial branch depends upon there being a free and independent bar. Were there no such profession, there could be no judiciary of the sort that is characteristic of societies such as ours.

The same logic applies to the academic branch. The obligations of professional preparation and criticism require that the academic branch be free and independent simply because the profession for which it prepares students and the profession which it criticizes is itself free and independent. The character of the law school, that is, is a consequence not of its place in the university, but of its membership in the legal community. And the content of that character is determined not by general principles of academic freedom, but by the specific obligations the academic branch owes to the profession. Since the content of those obligations is defined by and contingent upon the character of the practising branch, the character of the law school is derivative from and depends upon the character of the profession.

FURTHER READINGS TO CHAPTER 2

1.   The Judiciary

Abraham, H.J. *The Judicial Process*. 6th ed. Oxford: Oxford University Press, 1993.

Aldridge, H. *History of the Courts of Law*. London: Wildy & Davis, 1835.

Bushnell, I. *The Captive Court: A History of the Supreme Court of Canada*. Montreal & Kingston: McGill-Queens University Press, 1992.

Carrington, P.D., and D.P. Marshall, special eds., "Special Issue: Judicial Independence and Accountability". (1998), 61(3) Law & Contemporary Problems 1-126.

DeCoste, F.C., guest ed. "Special Issue on Judicial Appointments" (2000), 38(3) Alberta L. Rev. 603-940.

Friedland, M. *A Place Apart: Judicial Independence and Accountability in Canada*. Ottawa: Canadian Judicial Council, 1995.

Greene, I., *et al. Final Appeal: Decision-Making in Canadian Courts of Appeal*. Toronto: Lorimer, 1998.

Griffith, J.A.G. *The Politics of the Judiciary*. London: Fontana Press, 1977.

Laskin, B. *The Institutional Character of the Judge*. Jerusalem: Magnes Press, 1972.

Lee, S. *Judging Judges*. London: Faber, 1988.

McCormick, P. *Canada's Courts*. Toronto: Lorimer & Co., 1994.

McCormick, P., and I. Greene. *Inside the Canadian Judicial System: Judges and Judging*. Toronto: Lorimer & Co., 1990.

Ontario Law Reform Commission. *Appointing Judges: Philosophy, Politics & Practice*. Toronto: Ontario Law Reform Commission, 1991.

Pannick, D. *Judges*. Oxford: Oxford University Press, 1987.

Russell, P.H. *The Judiciary in Canada: The Third Branch of Government*. Toronto: McGraw-Hill Ryerson, 1987.

Snell, J.G., and F. Vaughan. *The Supreme Court of Canada: History of the Institution.* Toronto: University of Toronto Press, 1985.

"USC Symposium on Judicial Election, Selection, and Accountability". (1988), 61 S. Calif. L. Rev. 1555-2220.

Ziegel, J.S. "Merit Selection and Democratization of Appointments to the Supreme Court of Canada". (1999), 5(2) Choices: Courts and Legislatures 3.

2.   The Bar

Abel, R., ed. *Lawyers: A Critical Reader.* New York: The New Press, 1997.

Baker, J.H. *The Legal Profession and the Common Law.* London: Hambledon Press, 1986.

Brand, P. "The Origins of the English Legal Profession". In Brand, P. *The Making of the Common Law.* London: Hambledon Press, 1992. At p. 1.

Christian, E.B.V. *A Short History of Solicitors.* London: Reeves & Turner, 1896.

Chroust, A.H. *The Rise of the Legal Profession in America.* 2 Vols. Norman: University of Oklahoma Press, 1965.

Cocks, R. *Foundations of the Modern Bar.* London: Sweet & Maxwell, 1983.

Cohen, H. *A History of the English Bar and 'Attornatus' to 1450.* London: Sweet & Maxwell, 1929.

Forsyth, W. *The History of Lawyers, Ancient and Modern.* Boston: Estes & Lauriat, 1875.

Frier, B.W. "Autonomy of Law and the Origins of the Legal Profession". (1989), 11 Cardozo L. Rev. 259.

Gordon, R.W. "The Independence of Lawyers". (1988), 68 Boston U. L. Rev. 1.

Haliday, T.C. *Legal Professions and the State.* Chicago: American Bar Foundation, 1988.

Hall, K.L. *The Legal Profession: Major Historical Interpretations.* New York: Garland, 1987.

Hurlburt, W.H. *The Self-Regulation of the Legal Profession in Canada and in England and Wales.* Edmonton: Alberta Law Reform Institute, 2000.

Kelley, B.W. *A Short History of the English Bar.* London: Swan Sonnenschein & Co., 1908.

Stager, D.A.A., and H. Arthurs. *Lawyers in Canada.* Toronto: University of Toronto Press, 1990.

Wilkin, R.N. *The Spirit of the Legal Profession.* New Haven: Yale University Press, 1938.

Wilkins, D.B. "Who Should Regulate Lawyers?" (1992), 105 Harvard L. Rev. 801.

3.   The Law School

Brooks, C.W., and M. Lobban. "Apprenticeship or Academy? The Idea of a Law University, 1830-1860". In Bush, J.A., and A. Wiiffels, eds. *Learning the*

Law: Teaching and the Transmission of Law in England 1150-1900. London: Hambledon Press, 1999. At p. 353.

Burke, J.J. *Letters to a Law Student*. Toronto: Carswell, 1887.

Carrington, P. "Hail! Langdell!". (1995), 20 Law & Social Inquiry 691.

―――. "Butterfly Effects: The Possibilities of Law Teaching in a Democracy". (1992), 41 Duke L.J. 741.

―――. "The Revolutionary Idea of University Legal Education". (1990), 31 Wm. & Mary L. Rev. 527.

―――. "Of Law and the River". (1984), 34 J. of Legal Education 222.

Dvorkin, E., *et al. Becoming a Lawyer: A Humanistic Perspective on Legal Education and Professionalism*. St. Paul: West Publishing, 1981.

Edwards, H.T. "The Growing Disjunction Between Legal Education and the Legal Profession". (1992), 91 Michigan L. Rev. 34.

Field, D.D. "Study and Practice of Law" (1844). In Sprague, A.P., ed. *Speeches of David Dudley Field*. New York: D. Appleton & Co., 1884.

Frankfurter, F. "On Entering the Law". In Frankfurter, F. *Of Law and Life*. Cambridge, MA: Harvard University Press, 1965. At p. 70.

Fulbeck, W. *Direction or Preparative to The Study of Law* (1599). Aldershot: Wildwood House, facsimile ed., 1987.

Goldring, J., *et al. New Foundations in Legal Education*. Sydney: Cavendish Publishing, 1998.

Hildesley, M. *Religio jurisprudentis: or, The Lawyer's Advice to His Son*. London: J. Harrison & R. Taylor, 1685.

Hoffman, D. *A Course of Legal Study*. Baltimore: Joseph Neal, 1836.

Holmes, O.W., Jr. "The Use of Law School". In Holmes, O.W., Jr., *The Occasional Speeches of Justice Oliver Wendell Holmes*. Cambridge, MA: Harvard University Press, 1962. At p. 34.

Kalscheur, G.A. "Law School as a Culture of Conversation". (1996), 28 Loyola U. Chicago L. J. 333.

King, D.B., ed. *Legal Education for the 21st Century*. Littleton, CO: Rothman & Co., 1999.

Leighton, P., *et al. Today's Law Teachers: Lawyers or Academics?* London: Cavendish Publishing, 1995.

Levine, M.L., ed. *Legal Education*. New York: New York University Press, 1993.

Llewellyn, K.N. *The Bramble Bush: On Our Law and Its Study*. New York: Oceana Publications, 1930.

Lord Mansfield. *A Treatise on the Study of Law* (1797). In Vol. 26 of *Classics of Legal History*. Buffalo, NY: William S. Hein & Co., 1974.

MacCrate, R. *Legal Education and Professional Development*. Chicago: American Bar Association, 1992.

Matas R. J., and D. J. McCawley, eds. *Legal Education in Canada*. Montreal: Federation of Law Societies of Canada, 1987.

Raithby, J. *The Study and Practice of the Law*. Portland: Thomas B. Wait & Co., 1806.

Sandalow, T. "The Moral Responsibility of Law Schools". (1984), 34 J. of Legal Education 163.

Sheppard, S., ed. *The History of Legal Education in the United States*. 2 Vol. Hackensack, NJ: Salem Press, 1999.

Stevens, R. *Law School: Legal Education in America from the 1850s to the 1980s*. Chapel Hill: University of North Carolina Press, 1983.

Twining, W. *Blackstone's Tower: The English Law School*. London: Stevens & Sons/Sweet & Maxwell, 1994.

Wright, C.A. "Law and the Law Schools". (1938), 16 Can. Bar Rev. 579.

Chapter 3

The Source and Resources of Law

In the last analysis, the law is what lawyers are. And the law and the lawyers are what the law schools make them.

Felix Frankfurter

Judges ... decide what the law is by interpreting the practice of other judges deciding what the law is.

Ronald Dworkin

A. INTRODUCTION

In Chapter 1, we found that, from the lawyer's point of view, law is best described as the practice of identifying, interpreting and applying legal rules and that, from this point of view, the law is therefore the practice of the legal community. It is time now to explore that conclusion. What is it about law in societies such as ours which makes the legal community the law?

B. LEGAL RESOURCES

The legal community constructs the rules of law, but it does not do so willy-nilly or out of whole cloth. Its construction of law is constrained because certain materials only are properly the object of interpretation and application. This set of resources may be described in a number of ways. It would be accurate to include in such a description all of the resources which we deem to be legal, including rules, statutes, constitutions, judicial decisions, maxims and various conventions and understandings. But an all encompassing description of this sort lacks precision. Most importantly, it obscures the fact that what makes certain resources authentic legal resources is their *pedigree,* which is to say, their institutional origin or genealogy. Viewed in this fashion, the legal community uses materials from two sources only to construct the rules of law, namely, *legislation*, which emanates, directly or indirectly, from elected assemblies of a variety of sorts; and *case law*, which emanates from the courts themselves. Before we can explore what it is about these resources which compels identifying the legal community and not the resources themselves as the source of law, we will want to describe each in some detail. And though they are not by reason of their pedigree legal resources *per se*, we will also consider certain secondary resources which members of the legal community sometimes use as aids in the practice of constructing the rules of law.

(i)   Legislation

Until fairly recently, legislation was not a significant resource simply because the body of statute law was not that sizable. Over the past 100 or so years, however, there has been a tremendous growth in legislation. In consequence, in most matters, members of the legal community look first to statutory materials which, at any moment, will concern whatever matters capture the imagination and will of legislators. Simply stated, a *statute* is an act of some legislature which declares, commands or prohibits something and which otherwise conforms with the procedures required by the rules constituting the legislature. Typically, statutes begin with words of enactment (as in "Her Majesty, by and with the advice and consent of the Legislative Assembly of Alberta, enacts as follows") which are followed first (but not always) by a section containing the short title of the act, next (and almost always) by a section containing the definition of certain words as they are used in the act, and then (always) by the parts, sections, subsections and paragraphs which comprise the body of the act. We will begin with the matter of procedure before going on to the identity of legislatures.

In Canada, a federal state, the authority to legislate is divided as between the federal Parliament and the provincial legislatures. By virtue of ss. 91 and 92 of the *Constitution Act, 1867*,[1] each is given exclusive authority over certain matters and shared authority over other matters. For instance, authority to legislate on matters such as national defence, currency, trade and commerce, patents and copyright, marriage and divorce and criminal law resides exclusively in the federal Parliament, and on matters relating to education, health, direct taxation and property and civil rights with the provincial legislatures. In addition, legislative power with respect to a number of matters is shared between the levels of government. If either level of government invades, directly or indirectly, a jurisdiction reserved for the other level of government, the legislation is beyond the competence of the legislature and if it is challenged in the courts, will be declared *ultra vires* — beyond the powers of — the legislating body and of no force or effect. If a provincial and federal law are both valid yet deal with the same subject matter in an inconsistent manner, then the provincial law is of no force or effect to the extent of the inconsistency. These constitutive rules, however, do not adequately describe the process of legislation. For even where a legislature has substantive authority over a matter, it still must exercise that authority in conformity with a complex of rules and conventions which lawyers know as parliamentary procedure.

---

[1]   (U.K.), 30 & 31 Vict., c. 3.

Proposals for new statutory law are called "bills". A bill becomes law — a statute — when it is passed by a majority vote of a competent legislative body. Bills are transformed into law in three stages. Generally,[2] it is the government, federal or provincial, which introduces a bill to its legislature through a process called "first reading" which makes the proposal available in printed form for public commentary. For a variety of reasons — not least of which is negative public reaction — many bills die at first reading. Those which do survive proceed to "second reading" at which stage the bill is reintroduced by the minister whose department is responsible for the subject matter of the bill and becomes a matter of full parliamentary debate particularly as regards the reasons for and consequences of the proposal. Second reading culminates in a vote, and if the bill passes, it is considered approved in principle and is generally then sent to the appropriate standing committee of the legislature/Parliament for further study and sometimes public hearings. Often, a committee will recommend amendments to the bill which are then debated when the bill is reintroduced for final approval at "third reading."

In the provinces, if a bill passes final reading, it becomes law — and is henceforth called an "act" or an "enactment" — immediately upon receiving Royal Assent which, in Canada, means approval by the Lieutenant Governor of the province. Royal Assent is, of course, a formality, and never delays the coming into force of a statute. Some statutes have a provision that delays their coming into force until a particular date or grants the government discretion as to the date of coming into force. Where the latter sort of provision governs, the act will have force and effect only from the date at which the government formally proclaims its coming into force. Federally, matters are somewhat more complicated since bills passed by the House of Commons have then to go to the Senate where the entire process of readings is repeated. If a bill passes in the Senate, it becomes law upon receiving Royal Assent, in this case from the Governor General. If the bill fails to pass or if the Senate amends it, the bill is referred back to the House of Commons.

All federal and provincial statutes are publicized, first in the respective government's "gazette" — *Canada Gazette, Alberta Gazette*, and so on — and subsequently in annual volumes, both of which are printed by the Queen's Printer, an office created by provincial and federal statute. The gazette is the official publication of the government, federal or provincial, which records all acts of state including especially the passage of bills into law. Acts appear in the annual volumes as numbered chapters (for example, in Alberta, the *Interpretation Act* is identified as c. I-7). Since many statutes are in fact amendments to existing acts,

---

[2]   Though not exclusively since individual members also may introduce a bill. Unless the government supports these private member bills, their fate is to die on the order paper without having once been read to the assembly. See: D.C. Marsh and M. Reed, *Private Members' Bills* (Cambridge: Cambridge University Press, 1988). Also, in the case of Canadian federal law, bills may be introduced in the Senate as well as in the House of Commons, though this is rare.

provincial and federal Queen's Printers periodically consolidate revisions in volumes which are called revised statutes (as in the *Revised Statutes of Ontario* or the *Revised Statutes of Canada*). Since the period between consolidations is often lengthy, in order correctly to identify statutory law, it is often necessary to consult several annual volumes. Many provinces now issue looseleaf editions of statutes in force which are ongoing consolidations and in most jurisdictions, consolidations are also accessible electronically.

Though "the legislature" is initially the legislature of a province or Parliament, either assembly may by statute identify some other body or office or officer as its delegate and authorize it to legislate further on its behalf with respect to some matter. This process is known as *statutory delegation*, the act as a *statutory instrument*, and the delegated or indirect legislation which results as *regulation*. In the simplest case, legislation will identify a minister of the Crown as its delegate and authorize the minister to issue regulations without further legislative debate. More complex cases involve the creation of some body or commission or tribunal — say, a school or university board or a human rights commission or a regulatory tribunal like a labour relations board — with authority over some matter, including sometimes adjudicative authority. Like statutes, regulations are first published in the federal or provincial gazettes and subsequently in annual volumes and consolidations. In many jurisdictions, regulations also are available electronically.

With the proliferation of statutes, regulations have permeated very nearly every aspect of contemporary life. Though statutory delegation makes intuitive sense — legislatures are spared having to deal with the details which in any event might only emerge through experience — there is the danger that statutory delegates will insinuate themselves improperly into the lives of citizens. For just this reason, the age of legislation has compelled the development of a new body of law called *administrative law* which seeks to constrain the powers of the state when it acts through statutory delegates. Like the legislatures who parent them, statutory delegates can only properly act within the grant of their authority. If they act *ultra vires* or beyond their authority, then their actions have no legal validity.

(ii) Case Law

DEFINITION, IDENTITY AND STRUCTURE

Case law is the aggregate of written judicial decisions, most of which are reported, on the law as it exists and applies to particular facts. Cases have been reported for the past 500 years of Anglo-North American legal history. Though the methods of reporting have varied, cases have always been identified and structured in a certain ways. They are identified according to the names of the parties. In private law litigation, the parties are the persons, individual or corporate, whose relations gave rise to the case. In the court of first instance, they are called the *plaintiff* (the party that brought the action) and the *defendant* (the party against whom the action is brought and who is defending against the action) and their names — the last names of persons and the names of companies and corporations — constitute what lawyers call the *style of cause*. Some famous private causes with which every law student becomes familiar are *Carlill v. Carbolic Smoke Ball Company*, *Rylands and Horrocks v. Fletcher*, and *Donoghue v. Stevenson*.[3] When the trial court's determination of the matter is appealed, the parties are known, depending upon which initiated the appeal, as the *appellant* and *respondent*.

The style of cause is different in criminal matters. In Canada, the parties are identified as "The Queen" and "the accused" — though when speaking, lawyers refer to "The Crown" and never to "The Queen" — and the style is "Regina v. X" (last name of the accused) or "R. v. X". When an accused appeals a trial decision, the style of cause becomes "X v. The Queen". The practice is different elsewhere. In the United States, the accused is called a defendant and the style of cause is "The People of [name of state] v. X" or sometimes "The Commonwealth of [name of state] v. X". In England, the accused remains the accused, but the accuser is not "The Queen" but the "D.P.P." or "Director of Public Prosecutions".

So far as their structure is concerned, cases always contain a recitation of the relevant facts, a statement of the law governing those facts, and an application of the law to the facts, all of which then results in a statement of the court's judgment in the matter.

MECHANICS

Case law is found in law reports. Though at one time many cases remained unreported because they involved no significant or novel point of law, with the proliferation of specialized law reports,[4] a great many decisions — and very

---

[3] The complete style of cause would include the year of the report in which the case appears and the page at which it begins. Fully cited, the style of cause of these cases would be: *Carlill v. Carbolic Smoke Ball Company*, [1892] 2 Q.B. 484, [1893] 1 Q.B. 256, 8 T.L.R. 680 ("Q.B." stands for "Law Reports, Queen's Bench" and "T.L.R." for "Times Law Reports"; the first reference is to the trial court decision and the second two to the decision on appeal which is reported in two places); *Rylands and Horrocks v. Fletcher* (1865), 11 Jur. N.S. 714, 34 Ex. 177, 3 H. & C. 774, 159 E.R. 737 (Court of Exchequer); (1866), 12 Jur. N.S. 603, L.R. 1 Ex. 265, 35 L.J. Ex. 154 (Exchequer Chambers); (1868), L.R. H.L. 330 (House of Lords) (which cites the case from trial through to final appeal to all law reports in which the decisions appear); *M'Alister (or Donoghue) v. Stevenson,* [1932] A.C. 562, 101 L.J.P.C. 119 (House of Lords). Note that when it is not otherwise clear from the name of the report, the court which rendered the decision is identified in parentheses at the end of the citation. Note as well that lawyers very often refer to leading cases in a manner different from the formal style. For instance, *M'Alister (or Donoghue) v. Stevenson* is commonly referred to as "*Donoghue v. Stevenson*" and sometimes merely as "*Donoghue*"; and *Rylands and Horrocks v. Fletcher* as "*Rylands v. Fletcher*" or simply as "*Fletcher*".

[4] There are now separate reports for many areas of substantive laws, including for example, administrative law, criminal law, family law, bankruptcy, insurance law, torts and environmental

nearly all the decisions of superior courts — are now reported. In Canada, there are reports that publish the decisions of the courts in both the federal and provincial court systems. Decisions of both the Supreme Court and the Federal Court are reported in official reports called *Canada: Supreme Court Reports* and *Canada: Federal Court Reports* which are published by the Queen's Printer for Canada. Supreme Court decisions and important decisions of the federal courts also appear in national reporting series, such as the *Dominion Law Reports* and the *National Reporter*, which are published commercially.[5] Decisions of the provincial superior courts appear in provincial law reports, in regional law reports, in the *Dominion Law Reports* and in specialized reports, all of which are commercially produced. Examples of the provincial reports are the *Alberta Law Reports* and the *Ontario Reports* and of the regional reports, the *Western Weekly Reports* and the *Atlantic Provinces Reports*. Decisions of the inferior provincial courts and of federal and provincial tribunals, boards and commissions are generally reported, if at all, in specialized reports. This massive case law is accessible, in a variety of different reports, through a variety of manual and electronic means which will not be recounted here. Anyone contemplating the study of law should note, however, that mastering those means — with which so much of their later professional lives will be occupied — is a central burden and obligation of law students, particularly in first year.

SUBSTANCE

So far as its substance, case law may concern either legislation or judge-made law. Where the former is the case, case law most often concerns the competence or the interpretation or the application of some statute. When no statute is at play, cases report judicial decisions as regards the identity, interpretation, or application of some area of judge-made law. In the Anglo-North American system, judge-made law is itself divided into two bodies of law, common law and equity, to which we must now turn in some detail.

COMMON LAW

Common law is that body of law which owes its authenticity and authority to the judgments of courts recognizing, over time, certain rules as rules of law.[6] These rules give rise to causes of action which do not depend upon statute.

---

law. There is even a series which reports cases dealing with practice matters. These reports are commercially produced and include cases from all jurisdictions and from every level of court.

[5] Maritime Law Book Co. and Canada Law Book Ltd. are the main commercial publishers of law reports, though Carswell Legal Publications has been a player in the appearance of the specialized reports.

[6] The sense of the term "common law", however, is not exhausted in this contrast to statute. It resides as well in the contrast to equity, that other body of judge-made law which will concern us shortly. A third sense is found in the contrast to civil law systems which, unlike our own, arose

Common law remains a central resource for both legal practice and education. First-year law students undertake a systematic study of the common law canon, and the practices of most lawyers and virtually all judges would be unthinkable without the common law. The categories of the common law concern the most basic of social relations. The common law of torts governs which harms to persons and property give rise to an entitlement for remedy. The common law of contract governs which failed promises give rise to entitlement. The common law of property determines who may and may not use resources and under what conditions. The common law also includes other categories of law which govern, both substantially and procedurally, other aspects of our relationships. At one time, it included categories of law which in Canada are now governed by statute.

The fact that many areas of law now governed by statute were once common law categories is as good a place as any to start addressing the question of the relationship between common law and statute law. Take for instance the law of crimes which in Canada, since 1892, has been governed by the *Criminal Code*,[7] a federal statute. Among other things, the first *Code* sought to codify and thereby to systematize and, it was hoped, to perfect the common law of crimes. This reformatory ideal was forged in England in the 18th and 19th centuries, but the 1892 Canadian enactment was the first comprehensive codification of criminal law in what was then the British Empire. Nor was this ambition, then or now, confined to the common law of crimes. Many other enactments are like the *Code*: above all else, their purpose is to encode and perfect common law rules. And when, as inevitably happens, codifications of this sort are later amended, those amendments will be controversial to the extent that they diverge from settled common law rules and understandings. But what of legislation which is novel in the sense that its purpose is not the codification of existing common law: do statutes of that sort bear a different relationship to the common law?

---

from Roman law, are usually codified, and are not so dependent upon judicial decision-making. In yet another usage, common law refers to the law common, that is, to all extant statutory and case law. A final sense of common law lies in its relation to the community whose law it is. Under this understanding, common law is the law of the community itself — and not of some ruler — because it embodies the community's whole way of life and originates not in the will of the legislator, but in the traditions and practices of the community. These last two senses are particularly important in Canadian legal history. Though English law was received in Canada at various dates depending, among other things, on the patterns of colonial settlement, by declaring that the new country was to have "a Constitution similar in Principle to that of the United Kingdom", the preamble to the *Constitution Act, 1867* makes it clear both that the law common of Canada was to include common law, equity and statute and that the law common so received constituted a reception of English legal traditions and values. For the normative view of the common law as tradition, see: R. Cotterrell, *Law's Community* (Oxford: Clarendon Press, 1995); L. Farmer, *Criminal Law, Tradition and Legal Order* (Cambridge: Cambridge University Press, 1997); and G.J. Postema, *Bentham and the Common Law Tradition* (Oxford: Clarendon Press, 1995). See also the readings for Lord Coke, Sir Mathew Hale and Sir William Blackstone in the appendix.

[7]   Now R.S.C. 1985, c. C-46.

Statutes presuppose the common law. And because they do, statutes add to the existing law and do not generally supplant it in any dramatic way. On the contrary, in most cases, statutes seek merely to fill in gaps or to add in order to address new developments. But this understanding raises some fundamental issues. If the common law is basic, what quantum of legislative change is then permissible? And does not any answer we give to that question compromise legislative supremacy and democracy, practices which appear also very much a part of our legal inheritance?

It is often claimed that because Canada — unlike the United States — is a direct heir to the constitutional history of the United Kingdom, the power of Canadian legislatures, like the British Parliament, is unlimited. Provided only that they have constitutional competence, under this view of legislative supremacy, the provincial legislatures and the federal Parliament may enact any laws they wish. It is also often claimed[8] that with the constitutional adoption of the *Canadian Charter of Rights and Freedoms*[9] in 1982, Canada adopted an American approach which limits legislative supremacy. Both of these claims are true in a very limited sense. Legislative supremacy is indeed a truth in the sense that, other things being equal, where a rule of common law and a statutory provision conflict, the statute and not the common law prevails just because the statute is an act of an electorally accountable assembly. And it is true that the provisions of the *Charter* constrain legislative power in ways which exceed the confinement provided by ss. 91 and 92 of the *Constitution Act, 1867*. But neither of these claims about our legal history ought or can be true in any sense which really matters to the question of the limits of legislative power as regards the common law.

As a normative matter, it is silly to propose that, absent some constitutional instrument like a bill of rights or a charter, a legislature in a liberal democratic society can legislate in ways that violate liberal democratic values. Such a proposal would be saved from silliness only if legislative supremacy were the chief constitutive feature of societies such as ours and that is itself a silly notion which no person of influence in Anglo-Canadian legal history has ever endorsed. What distinguishes liberal democratic societies is that they are governed by principles of law and not by the will of those men and women who happen, at any point in time, to hold power.

EQUITY

Equity is also judge-made law, but it expresses its own distinct tradition. Where common law is a tradition of governance by rules which are sovereign to the

---

[8]   Most notably by the present membership of the Supreme Court of Canada: see, for instance, *Vriend v. Alberta*, [1998] 1 S.C.R. 493, 156 D.L.R. (4th) 385.

[9]   Part I of the *Constitution Act, 1982*, being Schedule B to the *Canada Act 1982* (U.K.), 1982, c. 11.

interests of power and to the power of particulars, the equity tradition, which is traceable to the ancient Greeks, authorizes judges to depart from legal rules to meet the requirements of justice in particular cases.

In English legal history, these traditions took shape institutionally in two separate court systems, the various common law courts and the courts of Chancery which comprised the court of equity. Originally, equity was applied by the King and later by the Lord Chancellor, neither of whom was bound by the common law, to cases which were not covered by the law of the time or to cases where the technicalities of the law were somehow abused to the detriment of fairness. A party disappointed by the outcome of litigation for either of these reasons could petition the King and later the Chancellor for relief from the law. For a time, this equitable authority was so entirely discretionary that John Selden, a leading 17th-century lawyer, quipped that equity varied with "the length of the Chancellor's foot".[10] Gradually, however, the practice of the courts of equity produced rules which not only cabined equitable discretion, but by the 19th century had the effect of making equity an even more technical and rigid system than the common law. The *Judicature Act*[11] of 1875 brought to an end the institutional division between law and equity in England. Thereafter, common law courts and the courts of equity were merged and a single court of general jurisdiction became, and remains, the court of law and equity. Beginning with the 1881 Ontario *Judicature Act*,[12] Canadian jurisdictions followed the English example with the result that our superior courts are courts of both law and equity. Though these enactments merged the courts of law and equity, they did not fuse law and equity and, in consequence, common law rules remain defeasible by equitable doctrine.

Two of the most important modern equitable doctrines are the trust and certain remedies. The common law did not always deem wrong conduct which was otherwise offensive to good conscience. Most importantly, it did not provide a cause of action or remedy for situations, say in a will, in which one party conveys property to another on the understanding that the latter would hold the property for benefit of a third party. If in such a case, the party to whom the property was conveyed for this purpose instead used the property for his or her own purposes and benefit, no grounds for complaint existed at common law. Rather, the party entrusted with the property was as its legal owner thought entitled to do whatever it wished with the property. The courts of equity constructed the doctrine of trusts to deal with cases of this sort. A *trust* exists where a right of property is held by one party (the trustee) for the benefit of another (the *cestui que trust* or beneficiary). Where it is found to exist, a trust creates a *fiduciary* relationship as regards the property which places the trustee under the equitable obligation to deal with the property for the benefit of the *cestui que trust*. As

---

[10]   J. Selden, *The Table Talk of John Selden* (1689) (Oxford: Clarendon Press, 1892).

[11]   38 & 39 Vict., c. 7.

[12]   S.O. 1881, c. 5.

were many common law rules, the equitable doctrine of trusts has been codified in any number of statutes. Modern lawyers use trusts to permit their clients to dispose of property in the most advantageous ways. And modern courts often use the doctrine to avoid what they take to be the injustice worked by statutes in particular cases.[13]

At common law, the primary remedy was damages. Damages consist of monetary compensation — in an amount calculated and ordered by the court — payable by a defendant to a plaintiff for unlawfully violating the plaintiff's rights. Of course, in some cases, this remedy proved inadequate. An award of damages for breach of contract might be inadequate because permitting the defendant to continue in the conduct which constituted the breach might wreak ongoing harm on the plaintiff or because requiring the defendant to do what it promised to do alone might remedy the situation in which the plaintiff finds itself. And in torts, where a party is threatened by a violation, damages which will follow on the tort taking place are inadequate to the alternative of preventing the tort in the first place. The equitable remedies of *injunction* and *specific performance* were constructed by the courts of equity to deal with cases of just these sorts. An injunction restrains a defendant from doing or from continuing to do some act which is causing or would cause a plaintiff legal harm, and is available in a wide variety of cases. Specific performance is an equitable remedy for breach of contract which requires the defendant to make good the promise made to the plaintiff. For instance, under an order of specific performance, a party to a contract which concerns the delivery of goods would be compelled to deliver the goods or a party which promised to convey land would be ordered to execute the conveyance and thereby to transfer the land to the plaintiff. Like the equitable doctrine of trusts, these equitable remedies are used by lawyers and judges alike whenever the application of rules of law would appear reasonably to be unfair.

(iii) Other Resources

In addition to the legislation and case law on which it primarily relies, the legal community often utilizes certain other resources. These resources are secondary because their institutional pedigree, unlike the pedigree of legislation and case law, is not authoritative. Legal encyclopedias and digests and scholarly works, the two main categories of these secondary resources,[14] arise from disparate institutional sources, none of which shares the authority of the legislatures or of the courts.

---

[13] *Becker v. Pettkus* (1978), 20 O.R. (2d) 105 (C.A.); aff'd [1980] 2 S.C.R. 834 is perhaps the most famous Canadian case of this sort. On the law of trusts more generally, see: J.E. Penner, *The Law of Trusts* (London: Butterworths, 1998).

[14] Other secondary resources on which we will not pause include indexes, annotations, law dictionaries, handbooks and encyclopedias of legal terminology (words and phrases and maxims), and statute and case law citators.

Encyclopedias and digests both summarize, or abridge, the law under subject headings which appear in alphabetical order. Digests provide summaries of individual cases, the facts and the judgment, along with their citations. Encyclopedias cover both statute and case law and, instead of summaries, contain articles with footnotes identifying the cases and statutes on which their summaries of the law depend.

If they use them at all, lawyers look to two sources of this kind for Canadian law. The *Canadian Encyclopedic Digest*, despite its name, is a looseleaf encyclopedia containing articles on a broad range of legal subjects such as evidence, civil actions, negligence and bankruptcy.[15] The *Canadian Abridgment* is a digest which provides summaries of cases organized by subject heading. Both are produced commercially by Carswell, a publishing house specializing in law. For English law, lawyers refer to *Halsbury's Laws of England*, an encyclopedia, and to *The Digest* (formerly the *English and Empire Digest*), both of which are published by Butterworths, another leading legal house. Summaries of American law are found in the *Corpus Juris Secundum*, *American Jurisprudence*, *American Law Reports* and *West's Key Number Digests*. The first two are encyclopedias and the second two digests. Like the Canadian and English series, the American series are published commercially.

In law as elsewhere, scholarly works come in two genres, treatises and articles. Generally speaking, *treatises* are books which provide an exposition of the principles of some subject. In recent years, a host of Canadian textbooks have appeared. And though this is a great improvement on the former situation, there is a considerable range in the ambition and quality of these works. Those which are authored by practising lawyers and judges tend to offer simple summaries of the law in a fashion akin to the essays which appear in encyclopedias though of course at greater length. Though some of the textbooks authored by academic lawyers are also of this sort, the more accomplished ones proceed from some scholarly thesis and offer sustained and sophisticated critical inquiries of their subject matter. Since the value of textbooks of the former variety is exhausted by the state of the case law at the time at which they were written, those written by academic lawyers of some ambition alone have the chance of making a lasting impact on the law and the legal community.

Articles concerning law appear, for the most part, in legal periodicals, which are variously named "review", "journal" or "quarterly". Law periodicals vary by kind and origin. Most are generalist and publish articles on any legal topic. Others are specialist and confine themselves to certain areas of law (for instance, criminal, constitutional or family law) and occasionally to certain courts (especially final courts of appeal such as the Supreme Court of Canada). Legal periodicals are published by law schools, by bar associations and by certain other groups and organizations. In Canada, as in the United States, the majority of legal periodicals are published by law schools under law student editorship.

---

[15] The C.E.D. appears in two editions — the C.E.D. (Ontario) and the C.E.D. (West).

Examples of these are the *Alberta Law Review*, the *McGill Law Journal* and the *Dalhousie Law Journal*. The *Canadian Bar Review* is published by the Canadian Bar Foundation. To name a few others, the *Canadian Journal of Family Law* is published commercially by Carswell; the *Criminal Law Quarterly* by the Canada Law Book Company and the *Review of Constitutional Studies* by the Centre for Constitutional Studies at the University of Alberta. Unlike textbooks, which are authored by practising and academic lawyers and judges, most law articles are written by academic lawyers, though essays by practitioners, judges and law students sometimes appear. Law articles, finally, appear in three formats — *essays* (which are no different in law than elsewhere), *case comments* (these scholarly commentaries on recently reported decisions are indigenous to law) and *book reviews* (which may consist of short reviews or, more frequently, of review essays).

In the United States, there exists a widely accepted hierarchy among legal periodicals. Generally speaking, those which are published by private law schools are thought superior to those published by state schools and among the former, the *Harvard Law Review* and the *Yale Law Review* are thought superior. Despite the fancy of some, no such hierarchy exists among Canadian periodicals, though at one time, the *Canadian Bar Review* was thought by many to be Canada's pre-eminent journal. In Britain, the *Modern Law Review* and the *Law Quarterly Review* are considered superior, though their status resides on quality scholarship and not on institutional association.

A great many articles are published every year in a plethora of legal periodicals. These articles join all of those which have appeared in the past, and they in turn will be joined by all those which will appear in the future. The result is a massive body of literature to which lawyers require, no less than to case law, easy access. Not surprisingly, access is provided by various indexes. Access to American periodical literature is provided by the *Index to Legal Periodicals*, now published commercially, and by the *Legal Resource Index*, published by the American Association of Law Libraries. The most current form of the first is the *Current Index to Legal Periodicals* and of the second the *Current Law Index*. Begun in 1981, the *Index to Canadian Legal Literature* is published as part of the *Canadian Abridgment* and also in a standalone library edition. Beginning in 1986, British literature is available through the *Legal Journals Index*. The *Index to Foreign Legal Periodicals* provides access to a wide variety of journals, including especially those published in Commonwealth countries with a common law system. All of these indexes are published several times a year and are consolidated in annual volumes. Entries are indexed by subject, by author name, and by publication. In addition, some indexes include a table of cases which have been commented upon in articles. Most of the indexes are accessible electronically.

As indicated, none of these secondary resources is an authentic source of law. But that does not mean that they are equal in value or in authority. Unlike scholarly treatises and articles, which are routinely cited by courts and lawyers, neither encyclopedias nor digests are ever cited as authority for any argument or proposition of law. This is the case, obviously, because the legal community considers scholarly works to have authority whereas it thinks of encyclopedias and digests merely as aids to finding law. But this does not explain why scholarly works are thought to be authoritative. That explanation is to be found in the history and traditions of the legal community which since its inception, has both produced and relied upon distinctively legal works of scholarship. Since the transfer of legal education from the practising branch to the university law schools, it has to do as well with the view that it falls to the academic branch of the legal community particularly to maintain this tradition of scholarly work.

C. NO RULE BOOKS

Though they are found in books, legislation and case law do not for that reason comprise rule books to which lawyers and judges may simply refer to ascertain what the rules are and when and how they apply. Indeed, that the resources of law are distinctly *literary* resources teaches just the contrary lesson: because they are found in books and conveyed in words, they cannot ever, separately or combined, constitute a book of rules. Cases and statutes do not, and cannot, interpret and apply themselves. Their meaning is neither transparent nor self-recommending, and their application is not self-executing. Rather, their meaning is a matter of interpretation and their application a matter of skill. We shall deal with the application of legal rules in the next chapter. Our concern in the remainder of the present is their interpretation. We shall start with the overall character of these legal resources and then the meaning and significance of interpretation as such.

(i)   Stare Decisis: Abiding by the Past

Statutes and case law share one central defining characteristic: in order for them to serve as resources for the legal community, they must already exist, and they are therefore, of the past. Statutes record and express past decisions of competent legislative assemblies; case law records the past judgments of courts of a variety of sorts and authority. That the resources of the legal community are *historic* resources is fundamentally important to the nature of the legal community and its practices. We must discern the implications which legal history in this special sense has for those practices.

It means, first of all, that our law depends upon and is limited by the past. No advice may be proffered by counsel, no case may be heard by courts and no action may be pursed, except where legal history expressly mandates such advice, authority or action. The legal community is in this very direct way a community which abides by the past. Lawyers use the Latin expression *stare decisis* to describe this institutional phenomenon and limitation.

Stare decisis also defines the nature of legal practice, the obligations of the legal community and the relations between legislatures and the courts. Because its resources are historic, the labour of the legal community may be aptly described as archeological. Lawyers and judges excavate the meaning and current influence of our legal past. Because that past is recorded in books, they are archeologists of the word, bibliophiles whose first home is the law library and whose culture resides strewn among the case reports, the statutes, the treatises and the law reviews.

Stare decisis also erects an obligation to the past. Not only may nothing happen in law without the past's mandate, because this is so, lawyers and judges are bound to the past. Lawyers refer to this obligation as the *doctrine of precedent* which has two aspects. First, the rules of law articulated in the past govern all present and future cases to which they authoritatively apply. This is no mean measure since it compels lawyers and judges to conform their arguments and proposals and, in the case of courts, their judgments to the contours of the past. Second, since the rules of law are finally found in judicial decisions, this compulsion is peculiarly judicial and turns, therefore, on the authority of the court whose decision, whose rule, is at issue. This second judicial sense of precedent is especially important. It binds courts to follow the decisions of higher courts and it requires all courts, save perhaps courts of last resort, to follow their own previous decisions.

Judicial precedent may oblige or merely persuade. To say that a court's ruling is obligatory is to declare it authoritative, and the nature of that authority is a function of the court's place in the hierarchy to which it belongs. In Canada, for instance, the decisions of the Supreme Court of Canada are authoritative in all cases to which they apply and in all courts, federal and provincial. Within the provincial court systems, the rulings of the various courts of appeal are authoritative in all cases and courts within their respective jurisdictions, but not elsewhere. Their decisions — and indeed the decisions of courts inferior to them — might, however, prove persuasive beyond their jurisdictions, depending upon the overall state of legal doctrine at any given time (and particularly upon how extensive and settled the doctrine on any given matter happens then to be) and otherwise upon the reputation of any individual court (or judge) in the wider legal community.

The authority of the past resides in the authority which the legal community accords to statutes and case law. However, case law and statute are not equal in their authority to govern the present. First of all, statute law has priority over common law (though not equity) and, in consequence, where a statute governs, it entirely displaces common law rules and governs absolutely. However, although this is indisputably true, case law is yet ascendent because it is there that the rules of law, including those which arise from statutes, finally reside. This is a consequence of the bald fact of interpretation. Since statutes neither interpret nor apply themselves, the rules of law which depend on them are unavoidably those which the courts construct from them.[16] The practice of lawyers reflects this fact. When a statute governs a case, lawyers will first determine whether the statute has been *judicially considered*. This practice makes sense only because lawyers know that, in the final analysis, the meaning of the statute is its judicially determined meaning.

That case law is in this special way dominant to statute means much as regards the relationship which, as a matter of fact, must pertain between courts and legislators. Legislatures are very much at the mercy of the courts. Though statute is a superior source of law, its authority is nonetheless subject to the authority of the courts to determine what legislation means and entails. Yet, because statute is superior, courts are required to temper their authority with a measure of deference. We shall see that this requirement of judicial restraint has everything to do with the way the legal community has traditionally approached the interpretation of statutes.

The doctrine of precedent, then, devolves from the legal community's commitment to remain faithful to — to stand by — the past, and it takes its final and most important form in the practice of judicial precedent. However, neither the doctrine of precedent nor *stare decisis* more generally is a straightjacket which slavishly binds either the legal community or the society which it serves. Because they are themselves open to interpretation, the precedents which communicate the rules of law are porous and properly the object of criticism and contestation. Moreover, the doctrine of precedent is necessarily twinned with a *doctrine of mistake* which allows precedents to be excised from the body of the law.

(ii)   The Fact and Force of Interpretation

Interpretation is a communal practice, and virtually every body of texts in our culture has an interpretive community devoted to it. The interpretation of the Bible, for instance, falls to a certain community of theologians and clerics whose occupation it is to discuss and discern the religious (and social) meaning of scripture. The works of Shakespeare too have an interpretive community, one composed of English scholars and critics devoted to discussing and discerning the manifold meanings of Shakespeare's plays and poems. Communities of this sort share certain characteristics which together constitute the conditions of interpretation.

Every interpretive community depends upon an appraisal by its members that the works to which they are devoted are worthy of devotion. Indeed, there can

---

[16]   That this is so is neither controversial nor novel. Some time ago, John Chipman Gray put the matter thus: "statutes" remain "merely ... a source of law" until "their meaning is declared by the courts, and it is with this meaning declared by the courts, and with no other meaning, that they are imposed upon the community as law". See: J.C. Gray, *The Nature and Sources of Law* (New York: Columbia University Press, 1916), at p. 162.

be no interpretive community at all unless this appraisal is first made and then shared among those who claim to be part of the community. How this appraisal is made, individually and collectively, is a matter of much importance. Clearly, exposure to the works which comprise the community's canon is necessary. Consequently, in most cases, one becomes devoted to a body of works through exposure to an interpretive community which already exits. For instance, one becomes a member of the interpretive community devoted to Shakespeare, not by striking out on one's own, but by becoming initiated gradually through an exposure which typically takes place in university English departments. But matters do not end there. So far as any individual is concerned, the decision to join an interpretive community is premised upon *an act of faith.* That is, having been exposed to the community's work, what is then necessary is a decision, which can only be a matter of faith, that this work on these works is worth the devotion of one's life.

That interpretive communities are typically joined rather than established points to two other conditions of interpretation. First, since the community already exits, one joins on the understanding that the works which are the community's concern have a significance which will exceed whatever turns out to be one's own contribution to them and that the community which existed before one joined will continue after one has left the community. Interpretive communities are ongoing traditions whose purposes, so long as they survive, cannot be exhausted. Traditions have as their purpose not tasks which can be completed or problems which can be solved, but questions with which each generation of their practitioners engage.

The practices of all traditions, and perhaps none more so than those of interpretive communities, consist minimally of paradigms about how to proceed. Part of "the entire constellation of beliefs, values, techniques, and so on shared by the members of a given community", paradigms have been aptly defined as "models or examples ... as exemplary past achievements" which show us how to go about things.[17] In the case of interpretive communities, paradigms are examples of how to proceed with the practice of interpretation.

The legal community *is* an interpretive community. Like all other such communities, the legal community's purpose, its point, is to construct meaning for the texts — legislation and case law — to which it is devoted. And like those communities too, the legal community is an ongoing tradition which depends upon the faith of its members and upon their initiation into and observance of the paradigms of interpretation which constitute its tradition. Finally, because paradigms are not rules, but practices premised upon examples, the tradition of the legal community is a tradition of constructing the meaning of law.

---

[17]   T.S. Kuhn, *The Structure of Scientific Revolutions,* 2nd ed. (Chicago: University of Chicago Press, 1970), at p. 175.

D.   CONSTRUCTING THE RULES OF LAW

The interpretive paradigms which comprise the legal community's ways of proceeding are easily identified. Two concern the legal community's understanding of legal meaning, and a third concerns how properly to excavate meaning of those sorts from cases and from statutes. But before we proceed to the meat of the matter, it is important to note that these paradigms are indigenous, indeed they are unique, to the legal tradition. In consequence, it would make no sense at all to approach texts from other traditions — say, a Shakespeare play or a biblical book or passage — in the way lawyers approach legal texts. Likewise, the ways of reading developed in other traditions for their particular canons are not transferable to law.

(i)   Paradigm No. 1: Ratio Decidendi and Obiter Dicta

The doctrine of precedent prescribes that the legal present be governed by antecedent rules. Lawyers proceed on the conviction that judicial precedents express these rules of law. This conviction takes form in the distinction which lawyers make between *ratio decidendi* and *obiter dicta*. According to this distinction, the "*ratio*" of a case is the rule of law treated by the judge as the basis for decision, and the "*obiter*" is everything else which the judge may have conveyed but which is unnecessary to the result. This distinction between reasons which are binding and opinions which are not has critical implications for judicial and lawyerly practice.

To believe that cases are decided on ascertainable grounds is to believe that it falls to courts to render judgment according to rules of law which are discernible to others, other courts and lawyers particularly. This is a most important matter since it provides grounds for criticizing courts for failing to give reasons at all or for providing reasons which are either weak or unacceptable on doctrinal or other grounds. It also prohibits courts from rendering judgment on any ground other the rules of law which are discernible in antecedent cases. So far as lawyerly practice is concerned, this belief means that reading cases and discerning their "ratios" is a foundational occupation. We shall come shortly to how lawyers discern judicial reasons, what lawyers call briefing the case. We have now only to note that for lawyers, case briefing cannot be optional simply because the doctrine of precedent makes it very much obligatory. Nor is it avoidable. No good lawyer will mistake the reading of headnotes or case comments or textbooks for fulfilment of the obligation to know the rules of precedent which govern client advice and advocacy.

(ii)   Paradigm No. 2: Principle and Policy

Lawyers also proceed on the conviction that the rules of law discernible in precedents are instantiations of higher order principles of law and that they are not the result of judicial views of what is best overall. This conviction claims that there exists a distinction which counts between principles and policies and between principles and rules. Accordingly, lawyers think that principles concern the rights of individuals whereas policies concern general societal goods such as efficiency or wealth distribution. They also think that legal principles are distinct from legal rules in being less self-contained and complete and more general and open-ended as compared to the fact and consequent specificity which is characteristic of rules.

If legal rules are instantiations of legal principles, then the proper business of courts is the development of principle and not of social policy. In *McLoughlin v. O'Brian*,[18] a torts case concerning recovery for nervous shock, the House of Lords dealt with just this obligation and limitation:

> The distinguishing feature of the common law is this judicial development
> and formulation of principle. Policy considerations will have to be weighed;
> but the objective of judges is the formulation of principle. And, if principle
> inexorably requires a decision which entails a degree of policy risk, the
> court's function is to adjudicate according to principle, leaving policy cur-
> tailment to the judgment of Parliament.[19]

In *McLoughlin*, the defendant argued that liability should be limited because of certain social and financial consequences. The House declared that policy matters such as these fall to the legislature and not to the courts:

> Why then should not the courts draw the line [using policy]? Simply be-
> cause the policy issue as to where to draw the line is not justiciable. The
> problem is one of social, economic, and financial policy. The considerations
> relevant to a decision are not such as to be capable of being handled within
> the limits of the forensic process.[20]

According to the lawyerly conviction that there exists a distinction between principles and policies, the courts are a forum of principle whose exclusive concern it is to adjudicate as between the rights of parties and not to set social or economic policy. In discussing the institutional implications of the doctrine of precedent, we saw that, though case law necessarily dominates and subsumes statute law, it fell to judges to defer to the legislatures just because statute is yet a superior source of law. We can now add that deference requires judges to know and to respect the limits of their role and, in so doing, not to claim for the judicial branch matters of policy that are properly the concern of legislatures.

The institutional implications of the principle/policy distinction, however, are not exhausted in this separation of the role of courts from the role of legislatures. The distinction also has implications with respect to the entire structure of the law. Lawyers think that the rules of law express the application of higher order principles to particular facts. They also think that these higher order principles

---

[18]   [1982] 2 W.L.R. 982 (H.L.).
[19]   *Ibid.*, at 997 (*per* Lord Scarman).
[20]   *Ibid.*, at 998 (*per* Lord Scarman).

relate both to one another and to principles of still higher order and indeed that the whole of our law descends from an ultimate ordering principle to which all rules and principles of law finally relate. Lawyers, that is, think that the law is an edifice with deep structural integrity. And it is just this view of matters which explains the lawyerly metaphor for law as a potentially seamless web of rules woven from the "golden thread" of legal principle.[21] Law is indeed a seamless web — and not a hodge-podge of rules — but only if the tissue of principle connects and girds the whole. If law fails this test of integrity, it *perforce* is nothing but a jumble, and if law is that, we study it in vain.

(iii) Paradigm No. 3: Practices of Construction

The legal community believes that the rules of law resident in case law are ascertainable and that statutory law is properly an object for legal interpretation. Consonant with this conviction, it has developed traditions of interpretation for constructing legal rules from case law and statutes. So far as case law is concerned, lawyers pursue one practice for constructing the *ratio* of any particular case and another for construing the wider doctrines and principles of which any given case is but a part. As for statutes, lawyers have developed a set of practices they know as "canons of construction". We shall consider both.

CONSTRUING CASE LAW

Lawyers call the practice of determining the *ratio decidendi* "briefing the case". The object of briefing is to determine the rule of law for which a case is authority.

A *case brief* is a written summary of a reported judicial judgment, most often an appellate judgment. Briefs typically contain a summary of the facts and procedural history of the case, a statement of the issue, the holding or *ratio*, the judgment, and a summary of the court's reasons for decision. The summary of facts normally identifies the parties, the plaintiff's cause of action and the defendant's defence, as well as all facts relevant to both the cause and the defence. The purpose of the procedural history is to identify the procedural status of the case through a specification of its past, including the trial court's disposition of the

---

[21] So far as I can discover, lawyers owe the web metaphor to Frederic William Maitland (1850-1906), longtime Downing Professor of the Laws of England at Cambridge University. Maitland was somewhat of a phrase-smith for the law. One of his most apt is law as a living body: "[L]aw is a body, a living body, every member of which is connected with and depends upon every other member". See: V.T.H. Delany, ed., *Frederic William Maitland Reader* (New York: Oceana Publications, 1957), at p. 157. The "golden thread" metaphor has been used by countless generations of lawyers. See for example *Woolmington v. D.P.P.*, [1935] A.C. 462 where, at 481, the House of Lords offers the following description of Crown onus in criminal matters: "Throughout the web of the English Criminal Law one golden thread is always to be seen, that is the duty of the prosecution to prove the prisoner's guilt ..." (*per* Viscount Sankey L.C.).

matter and the background to the appeal (which party appealed, to which court, and the relief sought). The statement of issue specifies the issue(s) in controversy on appeal and the matter(s) which had to be decided by the appellate court to resolve the appeal. The holding, the *ratio*, is the rule of law which the court used to resolve the issue on appeal. The judgment is the legal result of the application of the rule of law to the relevant facts and it disposes of the issues between the parties by declaring who won and lost what in the matter. The reasons for decision is a summary of the court's explanation and justification of the *ratio* and the result of its decision. Because courts defend their decisions by invoking precedent, this part of the brief typically summarizes the precedents — rules and principles — upon which a court relied in formulating the *ratio* it used to dispose of the matter.

Without more, this description fails to disclose either how lawyers formulate the *ratio* of the case or how briefing contributes to that formulation. This is provided by the relationship between the statement of facts, the *ratio*, and the judge's conclusion. To brief a case is to formulate its *ratio* only because lawyers *deduce* the *ratio* from the facts treated by the judge as material together with the judge's conclusion and, of course, because briefing is the practice of identifying the facts and the conclusion. To take a famous example, in *Rylands v. Fletcher*,[22] the facts of the case were: a) the defendant had a reservoir built on his land; b) the contractor who built it was negligent; c) water escaped and injured the plaintiff. The judge treated only facts a) and c) as material, and concluded that the defendant was liable to the plaintiff. Because fact b) was omitted, *Fletcher* established the doctrine of strict liability in tort and this has been the case's widely influential *ratio* ever since.

Lawyers take just the opposite approach in constructing the principles of case law. For their practice in this endeavour is not to deduce from the facts and result of a particular case, but to *induce* from the facts and results of a body of case law. This is so even in those cases whose *ratios* directly state and establish a legal principle rather than a legal rule, since the principles there enunciated are themselves a result of just such a process of judicial review of a body of legal doctrine. To take one very famous example, in *Donoghue v. Stevenson*,[23] the House of Lords was confronted with the issue whether there existed "in English law ... some general conception of relations giving rise to a duty of care, of which the particular cases found in the books are but instances".[24] The House, of course, found that there was, and the "neighbour principle" for which *Donoghue* has since stood was crafted by the Lords from a meticulous exploration of the body of relevant precedents.

How lawyers go about this formulation of principle will vary, as do most things in law, according to their individual mastery of the lawyerly craft.

---

[22]   (1868), L.R. 3 H.L. 330.
[23]   [1932] A.C. 562 (H.L.).
[24]   *Ibid.*, at 580 (*per* Lord Atkin).

Nonetheless, it is possible to identify some of the rudiments. In *Home Office v. Dorset Yacht Co. Ltd.*,[25] Lord Diplock provides a rough outline of the process which lawyers follow in attempting to draw from precedents the principles which govern any body of case law. In *Dorset Yacht*, the issue was "whether the English law of civil wrongs should be extended to impose legal liability to make reparation for the loss caused to another by conduct of a kind which [had] not hitherto been recognized by the courts as entailing any such liability".[26] Since that matter turned upon whether the relevant principles of the law of torts gave warrant, it fell to the House to formulate the principles which properly govern cases of the sort at issue in *Dorset*.

According to Lord Diplock, the formulation of principle is a two-stage process. The first stage is "analytical and inductive".[27] Proceeding from "some general conception of conduct and relationships which *ought* to [govern]", the lawyer analyzes "the characteristics of the conduct and relationship involved in each of the decided cases" and induces from this analysis, a preliminary statement of the conduct and relationships which have so far guided the courts. In a second stage, which his Lordship describes as "deductive and analytical", the lawyer converts the preliminary statement into a positive open-ended statement of principle which would then govern the legal significance of the conduct and relationship in the case at hand.

CONSTRUING STATUTES

The lawyer's first resource in interpreting statutes is case law. Where a statutory provision has been judicially considered, a lawyer will use the interpretive practices just canvassed to construe the case law which construes the provision. Where a provision has not been considered or where a case raises a novel question, lawyers are confronted with the problem of statutory interpretation. And though in such cases, they will often seek guidance from arguably relevant case law, they will necessarily resort to their community's traditions governing statutory interpretation. Here, too, everything finally depends on the individual lawyer's mastery of these traditions.[28]

There are two traditions of lawyerly argument concerning the interpretation of statutes, namely, *argument from the ordinary meaning of the statutory words* and *teleological argument from the ultimate purpose of the statute*. Sometimes called the literal rule, the former tradition would have lawyers follow the ordinary meaning of the words in which statutory provisions are expressed. This the

---

[25] [1970] 2 All E.R. 294 (H.L.).

[26] *Ibid.*, at 324 (*per* Lord Diplock).

[27] *Ibid.*

[28] Lord Diplock puts this nicely: "The interpretation is just part of the process of being a good lawyer; a multi-faceted thing, calling for many varied talents; not a subject which can be confined to rules". Cited in Sir Rupert Cross, *Statutory Instruments*, 3rd ed. (London: Butterworths, 1995), at p. 39.

lawyer does by making three inquiries: first, what is the meaning of the statutory words when read alone; second, what is their meaning when read together with the rest of the statute; and finally — and because words take their meaning not only from the words with which they are used, but also from the background in which they are used — what is their meaning when read against the subject matter of the enactment.

To answer the first question, lawyers turn first to the interpretation section of the statute under consideration and to the general Interpretation Act of the jurisdiction. If meaning eludes those resources, they will then resort to standard English dictionaries and sometimes to legal dictionaries. To answer the second question, the lawyer resorts not only to other enacting portions of the statute, but to every printed part, including the enactment's long title, its preamble, if any, and the marginal notes and headings. It is within the context of this second inquiry that lawyers often use and refer to certain, peculiarly legal, grammatical rules of construction denoted by the Latin *"noscitur a sociis"*, *"ejusdem generis"*, and *"expressio unius, exclusio alterius"*.[29] In answering the third question, lawyers seek to particularize and refine the meanings of words in terms of the qualities of human conduct with which the enactment deals. For instance, the construction of the word "issue" in the context of an Intestate Succession Act will be different from its construction in a Bills of Exchange Act.

Teleological or purposive interpretation is an even more complex matter. For the longest time, purposive interpretation was confined to the rule in *Heydon's Case*[30] according to which statutory provisions were to be interpreted in terms of the "mischief" which the legislation was intended to cure or avoid. However, since legislative intention is not really ever accessible — and even if it were, it would itself become a matter of interpretive contest — lawyers gradually came to view the so-called "mischief rule" and the easy solution of "the intent of the legislature" as masks for pure policy discretion and for judicial legislation. And since both of these matters are beyond judicial (and lawyerly) competence, whether purposive interpretation is ever a proper means of construction has become itself a matter of much controversy.

Given both this controversy and the persistence of ordinary meaning and purposive interpretation as active traditions, it falls to every lawyer to come to a view on how the traditions properly relate and what constitutes proper purposive interpretation. Regarding the first matter, the view that ordinary meaning has priority is itself a long-standing legal tradition. Sometimes called the "golden rule," this tradition prescribes that except where the result would be absurd, the ordinary meaning of statutory words ought to govern. With a caveat for

---

[29] Respectively, the rule that a general word takes its meaning from the preceding specific words with which it is used; the rule that general phrases take their meaning from the preceding specific words or phrases; and the rule that a general word or phrase takes its meaning as well from specific words or phrases which follow it.

[30] (1584), 3 Co. Rep. 7a.

constitutional documents, such as the *Canadian Charter of Rights and Freedoms*, this understanding has merit because it confines judicial discretion and accords with the deference which judges owe to statute as a superior source of law. However, when ordinary meaning cannot govern, lawyers and judges are confronted with the question of proper purposive interpretation.

We have seen that legal rules consist of a factual predicate, a consequent and a background justification. Purposive interpretation must be confined to consideration of background justification. Otherwise it can very easily and very quickly degrade into interpretation according to personal views and convictions. We cannot pause on the particulars of construing the background justification. Suffice it to note that construing background justification is a treacherous undertaking which characteristic speaks well of the legal community's tradition of according priority to ordinary meaning.

Constitutional documents are special in two ways which require that they not be subject to the normal rule concerning the priority of ordinary meaning or to normal processes of purposive interpretation. First, constitutional documents by their very nature are expressed in words which are much more abstract than the words used in ordinary statutes. We need only think of words and phrases such as "freedom of conscience", "the principles of fundamental justice", and "equal protection" — which such documents typically contain — to realize that seeking guidance in ordinary meaning in the normal sense is inappropriate. For this reason alone, constitutional provisions cannot reasonably be subject to the priority of ordinary meaning. Nor may such provisions be interpreted according to ordinary purposive interpretation. A constitution provides the background justification of last resort for a society's legal structure and the ends and purposes of all of its law. But though constitutional interpretation is for that reason by nature purposive, it need not be a matter which falls to the discretion of personal conviction and ideology. To interpret constitutions properly requires a fine appreciation of the background justification which the constitutional provisions express.

E.   RESTATEMENT NO. 1

There exists a distinction between "law" and "laws". From an external point of view, the laws of a jurisdiction are the rules in force at any given point in time. However, from the internal point of view, from the lawyer's point of view, the law is always something more than the sum of such rules. This is so not only because those rules exist as part of a coherent whole and relate to one another and to the whole in certain ways, but also because what those rules are depends finally upon the ongoing practices of the legal community. In consequence, *from the lawyer's point of view, statutes and case law are legal resources and not themselves the source of either law or laws. The source of law, rather, is the legal community itself since, in societies such as ours, it alone is authorized to construct the laws. Its practices, that is, are the law and the outcome of those practices are the laws, the law and the laws by which we all must live.*

But neither the law nor the laws is thereby committed to the preference or power of those who happen to be lawyers and judges. Just the contrary. Because the past is its resource, it falls to the legal community to identify, interpret and apply *only* past authoritative decisions. Though this necessarily means that most of the time the legal community will be concerned with excavating its own past as found in case law, it also means that its excavations are authoritative only on condition that they are faithful to that past. *In societies such as ours, that is, the legal community's identification with the law and its construction of the laws is saved from raw power by reason of constraint by the past. The past alone has force in law and the laws constructed by the legal community are bound by and to that force.*

FURTHER READINGS TO CHAPTER 3

1. Sources of Law

Generally

Allen, C.K. *Law in the Making*. Oxford: Clarendon Press, 1927.

Brunner, H. *The Sources of the Laws of England*. Edinburgh: Clark, 1888.

Fuller, L.L. *Anatomy of the Law*. New York: Praeger, 1968.

Gray, J.C. *The Nature and Sources of the Law*. New York: Columbia University Press, 1909.

Holdsworth, W.S. *Sources and Literature of English Law*. Oxford: Clarendon Press, 1925.

Jenks, E. *Short History of English Law*. London: Methuen, 1912.

Pound, R. *Interpretations of Legal History*. New York: MacMillan, 1923.

Silving, H. *Sources of Law*. Buffalo: Wm. S. Hein & Co., 1968.

Watson, A. *Sources of Law, Legal Change, and Ambiguity*. Philadelphia: University of Pennsylvania Press, 1984.

Zane, J.M. *The Story of Law*. Garden City, NY: Garden City Publishing, 1927.

Legislation

Allan, T.R.S. "Legislation and the Common Law". In Allan, T.R.S. *Law, Liberty and Justice: The Legal Foundation of British Constitutionalism*. Oxford: Clarendon Press, 1993. At pp. 79-108.

Bennion, F.A.R. *Statute Law*. 2nd ed. London: Oyez Longman, 1983.

Bentham, J. *Theory of Legislation*. London: Trubner, 1864.

Brown, W.J. *The Underlying Principles of Modern Legislation*. 3rd ed. London: J. Murray, 1912.

Calabresi, G. *A Common Law for the Age of Statutes*. Cambridge, MA: Harvard University Press, 1982.

Hayek, F.A. *Law, Legislation and Liberty.* 2 Vols. Chicago: University of Chicago Press, 1973.

Iibert, P.C. *The Mechanics of Law Making.* New York: Columbia University Press, 1914.

Lightwood, J.M. *The Nature of Positive Law.* London: Macmillan, 1883.

Luce, R. *Legislative Principles: The History and Theory of Lawmaking by Representative Government.* New York: Da Capo Press, 1930.

Strauss, P.L. "The Common Law and Statutes". (1999), 70 U. Colorado L. Rev. 225.

Taylor, H. *The Science of Jurisprudence.* New York: MacMillian, 1908.

Tussman, J., and J. ten Brock. "The Equal Protection of the Laws". (1949), 37 Calif. L. Rev. 341.

Waldron, J. *The Dignity of Legislation.* Cambridge: Cambridge University Press, 1999.

Zander, M. *The Law Making Process.* 4th ed. London: Butterworths, 1994.

Common Law

Beaton, J. "Has The Common Law A Future?". (1997), 56(2) Cambridge L.J. 291.

Broom, H. *Commentaries on the Common Law.* 9th ed. London: Sweet & Maxwell, 1896.

Buckland, W.W., and A.D. McNair. *Roman Law and Common Law.* Cambridge: Cambridge University Press, 1936.

Cantor, N.F. *Imagining The Law: Common Law and the Foundations of the American Legal System.* New York: Harper Collins, 1997.

Cardozo, B.N. *The Growth of Law.* New Haven: Yale University Press, 1924.

———. *The Nature of the Judicial Process.* New Haven: Yale University Press, 1921.

Delany, V.T.H. *Frederic William Maitland Reader.* New York: Oceana Publications, 1957.

Eisenberg, M.A. *The Nature of the Common Law.* Cambridge, MA: Harvard University Press, 1988.

Goodhart, A.L. *Essays in Jurisprudence and the Common Law.* Cambridge: Cambridge University Press, 1931.

Holdsworth, W.S. *Some Lessons From Our Legal History.* New York: MacMillan, 1928.

———. *A History of English Law.* 17 Vols. London: Methuen, 1903f.

Holmes, O.W., Jr. *The Common Law.* Boston: Little, Brown & Co., 1881.

Hudson, J. *The Formation of the English Common Law.* New York: Longman, 1996.

Indermaur, J. *Principles of the Common Law.* London: Stevens & Haynes, 1909.

Jelf, E.A. *Fifteen Decisive Battles of the Law.* London: Sweet & Maxwell, 1921.

Llewellyn, K.N. *The Common Law Tradition.* Boston: Little Brown, 1960.

Lord Cooke of Thorndon. *Turning Points of The Common Law.* London: Sweet & Maxwell, 1997.
McEldowney, J.F., and P. O'Higgins, eds. *The Common Law Tradition.* Dublin: Irish Academic Press, 1990.
Odgers, W.B. *The Common Law of England.* 2 Vols. London: Sweet & Maxwell, 1911.
Pollock, F. *The Genius of the Common Law.* New York: AMS Press, 1967.
Postema, G.J. *Bentham and the Common Law Tradition.* Oxford: Clarendon Press, 1986.
Pound, R. *The Spirit of the Common Law.* Boston: James, 1921.
Simpson, A.W.B. *Leading Cases in the Common Law.* Oxford: Clarendon Press, 1995.
Twinning, W., ed. *Legal Theory and Common Law.* London: Basil Blackwell, 1986.

Equity

Keeton, G.W. *An Introduction to Equity.* London: Pitman & Sons, 1938.
Penner, J.E. *The Law of Trusts.* London: Butterworths, 1998.
Pollock, F. *Essays in the Law.* London: MacMillan. 1922. Chapter VII.

2.   Interpretation

Generally

Dworkin, R. *Law's Empire.* Cambridge, MA: Harvard University Press, 1986.
Lieber, F. *Legal and Political Hermeneutics.* Boston: Little & Brown, 1839.
Marmor, A. *Interpretation and Legal Theory.* Oxford: Clarendon Press, 1992.

Case Law

Cross, R. "The *Ratio Decidendi* and a Plurality of Speeches in the House of Lords". (1977), 93 Modern L. Rev. 378.
Delaney, J. *How to Brief a Case.* New York: J. Delaney Pub., 1983.
Goodhart, A.L. "Determining the *Ratio Decidendi* of a Case". In Goodhart, A.L. *Essays in Jurisprudence and Common Law.* Cambridge: Cambridge University Press, 1931. At p. 1.
———. "Case Law — A Short Replication". (1934), 50 Law Q. Rev. 196.
Hunter, D. "No Wilderness of Single Instances: Inductive Inference in Law". (1998), 48 J. of Legal Education 365.
Simpson, A.W.B. "The *Ratio Decidendi* of a Case". (1957), 20 Modern L. Rev. 27 & (1958), 21 Modern L. Rev. 155.
Summers, R.S. "Two Types of Substantive Reasons: The Core of a Theory of Common Law Justification". (1978), 63 Cornell L. Rev. 707.

Zimmermann, R. "*Statuta Sunt Stricte Interpretanda?* Statutes and the Common Law: A Continental Perspective". (1997), 56(2) Cambridge L.J. 315.

Legislation

Bennion, F. *Statutory Interpretation*. 3rd ed. London: Butterworths, 1997.

Cross, R. *Statutory Interpretation*. 3rd ed. London: Butterworths, 1995.

Driedger, E.A. *The Construction of Statutes*. 2nd ed. Toronto: Butterworths, 1983.

English Law Commission, The. *The Interpretation of Statutes*. Law Com. No. 21 London: Her Majesty's Stationery Office, 1969.

Eskridge, W. *Dynamic Statutory Interpretation*. Cambridge, MA: Harvard University Press, 1994.

Frankfurter, F. "Some Reflections on the Reading of Statutes". (1947), 47 Columbia L. Rev. 527.

Llewellyn, K.N. "Canons on Statutes". In Llewellyn, K.N. *The Common Law Tradition*. Boston: Little, Brown & Co., 1960. At pp. 521-535.

MacCormick, D.N., and R.S. Summers, eds. *Interpreting Statutes: A Comparative Study*. Aldershot: Darthmouth, 1991.

Miers, D. "Legal Theory and the Interpretation of Statutes". In Twining, W., ed. *Legal Theory and Common Law*. London: Basil Blackwell, 1986. At p. 115.

Mikva, A.J., and E. Lane. *An Introduction to Statutory Interpretation and the Legislative Process*. New York: Aspen Law & Business, 1997.

Sullivan, R. *Statutory Interpretation*. Toronto: Irwin Law, 1997.

Summers, R.S., and G. Marshall. "The Argument from Ordinary Meaning in Statutory Interpretation". (1992), 43 Northern Ireland Legal Q. 213.

Willis, J. "Statutory Interpretation in a Nutshell". (1938), 16 Can. Bar Rev. 1.

3.   Precedent

Alexander, L. "Constrained By Precedent". (1989), 63 S. Calif. L. Rev. 1.

Becker, D.M. "Debunking the Sanctity of Precedent". (1998), 76 Washington U. L. Q. 853.

Brenner, S., and H.J. Spaeth. *Stare Indecisis: The Alteration of Precedent on the Supreme Court, 1946-1992*. Cambridge: Cambridge University Press, 1995.

Cross, R. *Precedent in English Law*. Oxford: Clarendon Press, 1961.

⸻. "The House of Lords and the Doctrine of Precedent". In Hacker, P.M.S., and J. Raz. *Law, Society and Morality*. Oxford: Clarendon Press, 1977. At p. 145.

Ellenbogen, H. "The Doctrine of *Stare Decisis* and the Extent to Which It Should be Applied". (1947), 20 Temple L.Q. 503.

Gely, R. "Of Sinking and Escalating: A (Somewhat) New Look at *Stare Decisis*". (1998), 60 U. Pitt. L. Rev. 89.

Goodhart, A.L. "Precedent in English and Continental Law". (1934), 50 Law Q. Rev. 40.

———. "Precedents in the Court of Appeal". (1947), 9 Cambridge L.J. 349.

Kocourek, A., and H. Koven. "Renovation of the Common Law Through *Stare Decisis*". (1935), 29 Illinois L. Rev. 971.

Llewellyn, K.N. "The Rule of Law in Our Case-Law of Contract". (1938), 47 Yale L.J. 1243.

Lord Denning. *From Precedent to Precedent*. Oxford: Clarendon Press, 1959.

Lord Wright. "Precedents". (1943), 8 Cambridge L.J. 118.

Mason, G.F.P. *"Stare Decisis* in the Court of Appeal". (1956), 19 Modern L. Rev. 136.

Paton, G.W., and G. Sawer. *"Ratio Decidendi* and *Obiter Dictum* in Appellate Courts". (1947), 63 Law Q. Rev. 461.

Postema, G.L. "On the Moral Presence of Our Past". (1991), 36 McGill L.J. 1153.

Salmond, J.W. "The Theory of Judicial Precedents". (1900), 16 Law Q. Rev. 376.

Schauer, F. "Precedent". (1987), 39 Stanford L. Rev. 571.

Simpson, A.W.B. "The *Ratio Decidendi* of a Case and the Doctrine of Precedent". In A.G. Guest, ed. *Oxford Essays in Jurisprudence*. Oxford: Oxford University Press, 1961.

4.   Legal Research

Banks, M.A. *Banks on Using a Law Library: A Canadian Guide to Legal Research*. 6th ed. Toronto: Carswell, 1994.

Castel, J.R., and O.K. Latchman. *The Practical Guide to Canadian Legal Research*. Toronto: Carswell, 1993.

Cohen, M.L., and K.C. Olson. *Legal Research in a Nutshell*. St. Paul: West Publishing Co., 1996.

Kwaw, E.M.A. *The Guide to Legal Analysis, Legal Methodology, and Legal Writing*. Toronto: Emond Montgomery, 1992.

Yogis, J.A., *et al. Legal Writing and Research Manual*. 5th ed. Toronto: Butterworths, 2000.

Chapter 4

Legal Argument and Law's Craft

The actual life of the law has not been logic; it has been experience.

Justice Oliver Wendell Holmes (1881)

A knowledge of practice is a very necessary knowledge, but can only be acquired by practice.

Lord Mansfield (1797)

A. INTRODUCTION

Neither the world nor legal rules themselves can tell us which meanings or applications of any given rule are proper. This does not however imply that a choice among possible meanings and applications is arbitrary. Over the centuries, lawyers have developed traditions of interpretation, and it is mastery of the competencies defined by those traditions which provide the measure of interpretive propriety and save legal interpretation from caprice. To interpret legally is to participate in that community's way of life and to subject oneself to both the possibilities and constraints of which it is composed.

The same holds for application. Lawyers stretch rules to fit novel situations, reconfigure events to fit the factual predicate, reformulate the factual predicate to fit events and otherwise ignore features and events in order to make rules applicable. They also do all of this for the opposite effect, to render rules inapplicable. And sometimes they go even further and argue that a rule must no longer ever apply, that because it is mistaken, it should be removed from the body of rules which govern our conduct. As in interpretation, in applying rules, lawyers follow certain practices — what we have been calling "paradigms" — defined by lawyerly tradition. These paradigms of application will be among our concerns in the present chapter. Another will be to provide an overview of lawyering as a *craft* which includes, among other matters, all of the traditions identified in this chapter and in Chapter 3. Before we can begin, two preliminary matters warrant our attention.

Identification, interpretation and application are conceptually distinct moments of legal practice. However, they often overlap as do the "paradigms" that lawyers enlist and follow. In consequence, though the paradigms which we canvassed in Chapter 3 are as a conceptual matter most related to identification and interpretation, lawyers will nonetheless sometimes use them when applying rules. Likewise those which we will explore in this chapter. Though they are typical of practice at the application moment, these paradigms will sometimes be deployed for purposes of interpretation. With that caution in mind, our purpose in this chapter will be to segregate and explore those practices which are typical of the moment of application.

There is another matter. Lawyers distinguish between *law* and *fact*. According to this understanding, facts are the events out of which a question of law arises. Questions of law concern the identity and meaning of the legal rule; questions of fact concern whether the facts which trigger the rule — the factual predicate — obtain. Generally, questions of fact fall to the jurisdiction of trial courts and questions of law to courts of appeal. Two corollaries follow from this division. First, at trial, if there is a jury, fact determination is exclusively its concern, though on grounds of the trial judge's instructions on the law.[1] Second, because their concern is law, appellate courts are obliged to defer to the findings of fact made at trial. However, this distinction between law and fact is fraught with all manner of difficulties, both conceptual and practical, and has been the subject of ongoing debate, especially among academic lawyers and judges. Nonetheless, it is provides a vitally important orientation to the whole of legal practice, especially inasmuch as it differentiates between the point of legal practice at the application and interpretation moments in terms which accord with the structure of legal rules. Because the distinction links rule application inextricably to proof and therefore to trial, we shall have to begin our present investigations with a brief overview of the elements of proof.

B. PROOF

Proof implicates any number of very important matters. Our modest concern at this stage will be the rudiments, those central elements which constitute the concept and context of proof at law — namely, the *lis*, evidence (and trial procedure and consequence), burden of proof and standard of proof. We shall briefly consider each before turning our attention to the arguments which lawyers typically mount concerning the application of legal rules.

(i) *Lis*

Lawyers use the Latin word *lis* to express "the conception of an issue joined between two parties". Accordingly, an adjudicative decision is a decision of a *lis*, and "the decision of a *lis*, in the ordinary use of legal language, is the decision of

---

[1]   If there is no jury, then the judge acts both as trier of fact and as custodian of law and must in consequence instruct him- or herself as regards the law which properly governs the facts which he or she, as the trier of facts, is obligated to determine.

that issue".[2] The *lis* at trial is the application, and especially the proof, of a legal rule which defines and governs the issue between the parties. But the notion and importance of the *lis* is not exhausted by this simple description. The *lis* also determines what it means to apply legal rules.

Clients come to lawyers with a host of information. One of the skills required of lawyers is competence in filtering that information through their community's understanding of the law, its overall architecture and the proper reach of its various parts. In this process, which lawyers know as *characterization*, only some of the information which clients provide will be deemed legally relevant. What has to concern us at this point is the significance of this dependence on client information.

The *lis* is defined by the rule which governs the case, but which rule governs depends on the particular situation of the client. That everything finally depends on the circumstances of the client is fundamentally important. For it means that legal judgment and practice is, from its inception at the moment of application, permeated by context. Rule application is a complex matter simply because the rules which govern must, for this reason, always contend with circumstances of the concrete case. This contextuality forecloses any view of application as purely mechanical enterprise. Lawyers cannot, with logical precision, merely identify and then apply and prove the rule. Though rules do rule over facts, they are yet dependent upon and vulnerable to facts. Particular legal rules and governance by rules more generally are vindicated through the negotiation of past and present which this vulnerability requires of judges and advocates.

(ii) Evidence

The factual predicate triggers governance by a rule. For instance, in Canada, the murder rule reads in part as follows:

> Culpable homicide is murder
> (a) where the person who causes the death of a human being
>   (i) means to cause his death, or
>   (ii) means to cause him bodily harm that he knows is likely to cause his death,
> and is reckless whether death ensues or not ... .[3]

In order for that rule to govern a case of homicide — and in order for the homicide to constitute the form of culpable homicide which is termed at law murder — either of the rule's two factual predicates must be proven.

Lawyers tender three types of evidence to prove that rules apply. Evidence may prove the conditions specified in the factual predicate of a rule in either of

---

[2] *Johnson & Co. (Builders) Ltd. v. Minister of Health*, [1947] 2 All E.R. 395 at 399 (*per* Lord Greene M.R.).

[3] *Criminal Code*, R.S.C. 1985, c. C-46, as amended, s. 229. Whether a homicide is culpable — and only if it is, is it an offence — is governed by s. 222(5).

two ways. Whether evidence proves in either sense turns on what lawyers call its overall probative value which is assessed by the trier of fact. All three matters are important.

(iii) Kinds of Evidence

Evidence may be *testimonial* (*viva voce*), *physical* or *documentary*. Testimonial evidence may be drawn from either lay or expert witnesses and, in the case of expert witnesses, it will generally concern the identity, interpretation and significance of physical and documentary evidence. Rules of evidence, which are sometimes contained in codes and which always involve case law which it falls to lawyers to interpret, govern both the admissibility of evidence generally and the qualification of witnesses as experts in particular.

The major criterion for the admissibility of evidence, including testimonial evidence, is *relevance*. Relevance is a matter of law which falls to the discretion of the judge, and it concerns the character of the evidence as such and not its weight or probative value as proof. Generally, evidence is admissible if it is reasonably relevant, and it will meet that threshold if it relates to, and tends at all to prove, some fact or point at issue. However, not all evidence which is relevant in this minimal sense is admissible simply because our law of evidence has erected a number of exclusionary rules which place restrictions on the admissibility of evidence which, though relevant, is inherently unreliable, untrustworthy or prejudicial. The *rule against hearsay*, for instance, is a major restriction on the admissibility of relevant testimonial evidence. According to this rule, witnesses may only testify to that which they have actually perceived with their own senses, and are prohibited from testifying about information which they have gathered from other sources. Consequently, a witness may not testify about oral statements made by others who are not themselves testifying if the testimony is meant to prove the truth of those statements.

Witnesses then are required, and are only permitted, to testify about facts actually experienced firsthand. Questions about the meaning or significance of those facts are left to the trier of facts, and witness opinion and belief about those matters is generally excluded. In consequence, our law generally prohibits what is called "oath-helping", which is direct evidence to buttress the credibility and reliability of testimony. This rule against opinion evidence does not apply to witnesses who qualify, and are then permitted to testify, as experts. Whether expert testimony is admissible turns on whether the matter on which the expert opinion is proffered is one which is beyond common understanding. If the opinion will not in that sense aid the trier of fact, it will be inadmissible. In consequence, expert witnesses are generally called either to aid the judge and jury in understanding some technical or scientific issue or to interpret and draw inferences from technical or scientific evidence such as DNA evidence.

Even if expert opinion is admissible, the witness called as an expert must yet qualify as an expert. The test for this is the witness' knowledge and experience in the field being examined. Generally, experts are qualified by evidence of formal training, but experience alone may suffice.

Evidence which is addressed to the trier of fact without the intervention of testimony is called *demonstrative* evidence. Real evidence comes in two forms — physical evidence (*e.g.*, a gun at a homicide trial) and documentary evidence (*e.g.*, a contract). Like testimonial evidence, physical and documentary evidence are admissible only if relevant. Statutory exceptions aside, the identity and authenticity of demonstrative evidence must be proved by prior testimonial evidence before it will be admitted. For example, a gun will be admitted in a homicide trial only with the assistance of testimonial evidence, say a police officer's, which establishes that this gun was indeed the one used in the homicide.

Sometimes, during jury trials, a decision on the admissibility of evidence will require the judge to make determinations of fact. The most famous example is the question of the admissibility of confessions at criminal trials. Because statements by the accused to persons in authority are admissible only if they were made voluntarily, in order to decide admissibility, the judge must first determine whether, as a matter of fact, the accused's confession was voluntary. Because the jury and not the judge is the trier of fact, and because were it present for evidence on the matter, it might hear material which is later ruled inadmissible, in such cases, the factual determination will be made in the absence of the jury in a proceeding called a *voir dire*. In this "trial within a trial", the judge is trier of both fact and law and all of the elements of the trial process which are canvassed below obtain.

(iv) Kinds of Proof

Admissible evidence may prove a point in issue either *directly* or *indirectly*. Direct evidence is evidence which, if it is believed, without more and by itself, proves the fact at issue. Indirect or circumstantial evidence, on the other hand, is evidence which proves or tends to prove a fact in issue by inference drawn by the trier of fact. In *R. v. John*,[4] the trial judge illustrated the distinction in his instructions to the jury in the following way:

> If a witness gives evidence that he saw A stab B with a knife, that is direct evidence that A stabbed B. If a witness gives you evidence that he found a dagger with an unusually long blade in the possession of A and another witness testified that such a dagger could have caused B's wound, that is circumstantial evidence tending to prove that A did in fact stab B.

The trial judge went on to add:

> The two forms of evidence are equally admissible but the superiority of direct evidence is that it contains only one source of error, namely the unreliability of human testimony, where circumstantial evidence in addition to the

---

[4]   [1971] S.C.R. 781, 15 D.L.R. 18.

unreliability of human testimony suffers from the difficulty of drawing an inference from the circumstantial evidence.[5]

This addition is important. While direct evidence is indeed superior to indirect evidence for just these reasons, good direct evidence is rare and the reliability of most direct evidence is open to well-founded dispute. Take, for instance, *eye-witness testimony*, long thought the paradigm of reliable direct evidence: recent research has shown that the testimony of eye-witnesses is, instead, incorrigibly unreliable. Most matters turn on a myriad of circumstantial evidence which proves only through the inferences drawn from it by the trier of fact. Well-instructed triers of fact in civil cases draw only those inferences which are reasonable and probable; in criminal cases, they will draw only those which are beyond doubt.

(v) Probative Value and Weight

The significance and impact of evidence, what lawyers call its *probative value*, is a matter for the trier of fact. The value of any particular piece of evidence turns on the degree to which it establishes or contributes to proof of a fact in issue, and that will turn on a number of factors including whether the evidence is direct or indirect, its overall weight in the scheme of things and, in the case of testimonial evidence in particular, on its credibility. Weight is particularly important in civil trials, and credibility is central to proof in all trials, civil and criminal.

Lawyers use the phrase "weight of evidence" to indicate the inclination of the preponderance of credible evidence tendered at trial towards one side of the issue or the other. If on weighing the whole of the evidence, the trier of fact in a civil[6] trial finds that the evidence on balance favours one side rather than the other, then that party is entitled to its verdict. "Weight", of course, is metaphor and not mathematics, and where the balance lies is always and necessarily a matter of informed judgment by, and of the good sense of, the trier of fact.

Lawyers also use the term "weight" in a more limited way when assessing the significance of any particular piece of evidence. When used in this way as regards testimonial evidence, the assignment of weight will always turn minimally on the witness' credibility, which is to say, on whether the witness' testimony is believed. Credibility presumes that the witness is competent to testify, turns on a number of factors including the witness' demeanour (and sometimes the witness' character and reputation) and, more generally, implicates the evidentiary structure of trials as such. We will pause briefly on each.

A witness may be seized of relevant evidence and, were the evidence received, the witness' testimony might be highly credible; yet just such a witness

---

[5]   *Ibid.*, at 788.
[6]   The weight of evidence, in this sense, does not determine matters in criminal trials.

might be prevented from testifying because certain personal characteristics or a certain status renders the witness legally unfit and unqualified. For instance, because of their status, a judge or a juror may not testify in a trial in which either serves as trier of fact. Disqualification due to status is, however, a narrow category and rather rare in practice. More important and certainly more frequent is disqualification due to personal characteristics, the most important category of which is mental incompetence. Witnesses may be found unfit due to mental incompetence by reason of age or of mental infirmity or deficiency. Our law of evidence contains a host of rules with respect to the fitness of children, the mentally ill and the mentally deficient.

The trier of fact, jury or judge alone, has a wide discretion in assessing the credibility of witnesses — and, therefore, in accepting or rejecting their testimony — but that discretion is not entirely unfettered. First, our law presumes that witnesses are telling the truth until there are indications to the contrary. Second, whether in any case the presumption ought to be rebutted turns on a number of firmly established factors which govern and confine the trier's discretion. This law of credibility has been summarized as follows:

> [I]t cannot be said without limitation that a Judge [trier of fact] can refuse to accept evidence. I think he cannot if the following conditions are fulfilled:
> (1) That the statements of the witness are not in themselves improbable or unreasonable;
> (2) That there is no contradiction of them;
> (3) That the credibility of the witness has not been attacked by evidence against his character;
> (4) That nothing appears in the course of his evidence or of any other witness tending to throw discredit upon him; and
> (5) That there is nothing in his demeanour while in Court during the trial to suggest untruthfulness.[7]

These factors are, of course, still subject to the trier's judgment and much discretion therefore remains. That demeanour, for instance, includes matters such as the witness' physical appearance and carriage, tone of voice, gestures and eye contact makes this plain. Nonetheless, the trier of fact is bound by law to presume truth and to consider only certain factors as indicative of witness reliability and untrustworthiness.

(vi) Trial Procedure and Verdict

This rendition of the law of credibility includes a number of factors — attacks on credibility and character, for instance — which implicate the structure of trials, a matter to which we must now briefly turn.

A trial is a judicial examination and determination of the issues, of law and of fact, between the parties to an action. The conduct of civil and criminal actions

---

[7]   *R. v. Covert* (1916), 28 C.C.C. 25 at 37 (*per* Beck J.).

is prescribed by the law of criminal and civil procedure. Civil actions are generally commenced with the plaintiff's filing a "statement of claim" with the clerk of the court and subsequently by serving the statement of claim on the defendant. Among other things, the statement of claim contains a summary of the facts upon which the plaintiff relies for its claim. Normally, and within the time limit prescribed by the rules of court, the defendant will file and serve a "statement of defence" which sets out the grounds and the material facts which are relied upon by the defence. The criminal process begins with an "information" or an "indictment", depending upon whether the offence is handled in provincial court or in superior court, which charges the accused with an offence and sets out the facts which the Crown alleges satisfies the elements of that offence. The indictment triggers a complex process about which, for our purposes, the less said the better.

Though civil and criminal trials differ in a number of very important ways, they are structured the same way. The plaintiff and the Crown have what lawyers call the "burden of proof" and they are, therefore, obliged to present their case first. This portion of the trial is called the "case in chief" and, through its case in chief, the plaintiff or the Crown must present sufficient evidence to prove each element of the cause of action or offence alleged in the statement of claim or in the indictment. Plaintiffs and the Crown attempt to discharge this burden by tendering physical, documentary and testimonial evidence.

When a witness is called by a plaintiff or by the Crown during the case in chief, the plaintiff's counsel or the Crown counsel questions the witness first. This part of the questioning is called the "examination-in-chief" or "direct examination". When the examination-in-chief is complete — and lawyers signal this using a variety of phrases — the defendant's or accused's counsel is given the opportunity to conduct what is called a "cross-examination" of the witness. Cross-examining counsel may ask the witness any question provided it is relevant to the matter. The wide scope afforded cross-examination is particularly important with respect to witness credibility, a matter which is always very relevant: counsel may ask a host of wide-ranging and leading questions designed to compromise or challenge the witness' credibility. When the cross-examination is complete, which is generally signalled by counsel saying "no further questions", the direct examiner may conduct a "re-examination" or "redirect" which is limited to explaining or to refuting matters raised by the cross-examination, including matters having to do with credibility. At the completion of the redirect, cross-examining counsel may conduct a "recross-examination" of the witness, which is limited to matters raised during the redirect.

The case in chief for the plaintiff or the Crown finishes when all of the plaintiff's or the Crown's evidence has been tendered. Counsel signal this by saying "no further evidence" or "that is the close of the case for the plaintiff [or Crown]". Generally, the other side is then expected to open its case in chief.

Though it has the same testimonial structure as the plaintiff's and Crown's case, the defendant's or the accused's case in chief has a very different purpose.

Whereas plaintiff or Crown counsel leads evidence in order to make out each of the elements in either the cause of action alleged in the statement of claim or the offence alleged in the indictment, defence counsel leads evidence either to refute the plaintiff's or Crown's case or to prove affirmatively some defence or counterclaim. Counsel for the defence does this by calling witnesses (who are then open to cross-examination and subsequently to redirect and recross-examination) and by introducing physical and documentary evidence.

When defence counsel advises the court that no further evidence will be called, the defence's case in chief is closed, and counsel for the plaintiff or the Crown, in the absence of the jury, may move for a directed verdict on any of the defence's affirmative defences or counterclaims. The judge must then review the evidence to determine whether the defence led any credible evidence in support of the defence or counterclaim. If it did, then the matter must be left to the jury.

After the determination of such motions, if any, the plaintiff or Crown may seek the court's permission to lead additional evidence. The court will permit such evidence only to rebut a matter which could not reasonably have been foreseen at the outset of the trial. Permission to lead additional evidence will not, therefore, be forthcoming where the plaintiff or the Crown merely wishes to take another kick at the can in order supplement its case. If "rebuttal" evidence is permitted, the court will often also permit the defence to lead what lawyers call "surrebuttal" evidence. In the event rebuttal evidence is permitted, at its close, plaintiff or defendant counsel or defence counsel in a criminal case, may again move for a directed verdict.

The next stage of the trial is usually *closing arguments* by counsel for all parties. In their closing arguments, counsel will summarize the evidence for the jury, and explain how the evidence relates to the law and why the evidence and the law together require a verdict for counsel's client. After closing argument and before the judge charges the jury on the applicable law, counsel are sometimes invited — and sometimes request permission — to make submissions on the content of the charge. In civil cases, the charge includes questions which it falls to the jury to answer. Often, counsel will submit an agreed-upon statement of jury questions for the judge's approval. Jury questions generally concern both liability with respect to each cause of action and, if liability is found, damages. None of this pertains in criminal trials where juries return general verdicts of "guilty" or "not guilty".

Once the judge has delivered the charge, the jury retires to the jury room for its deliberations. The only instructions given to jurors is that they should first elect a foreperson and that, in civil cases, they must answer all of the questions put to them in the judge's charge. In consequence, the conduct of the jury's business is left entirely in its own hands. When the jury reaches a *verdict*, it signs the required forms and signals to the judge, through the judge's bailiff, that it is prepared to return its verdict. Counsel, the judge and the jury, in that order, then return to the courtroom. When all are present, the judge asks the jury whether it has reached a verdict and the foreperson responds with a simple "yes" and is then directed by the judge to give the verdict to the bailiff who gives it to the judge. After checking the verdict forms to ensure they are properly completed, the judge gives the verdict to the court clerk who reads the verdict aloud. After the verdict is read, the judge will ask counsel whether they wish to "poll" the jury. If any party wishes to poll, the clerk asks jurors individually whether the verdict read is their verdict. If the number of jurors who answer "yes" is sufficient to satisfy the requirement for verdict, either a majority or unanimity depending on the law which governs, then the jury's duties are spent and it is dismissed. If, however, the number of affirmative replies fails to meet the requirement, the jury must continue to deliberate. If in the fullness of time a jury cannot reach a verdict — because, as lawyers say, it is "hung" — then the judge will dismiss the jury and declare a mistrial. The matter will then have to be retried before a freshly impaneled jury.

There are several matters which arise after the verdict. Though rarely successful, counsel for the losing party may move for judgment notwithstanding the verdict. Certain other matters must be addressed at the conclusion of every civil and criminal trial. Most important in civil cases is the matter of costs and in criminal cases, where the accused has been found guilty, sentencing. These matters may be dealt with immediately, but are more often "set over" to a future date. After all such matters have been concluded, judgment is entered and the case ends so far as the trial court is concerned. If the losing party wishes to appeal the trial judgment, counsel must file a notice of appeal in a timely fashion.

Though matters may be resurrected by appeal, the trial verdict in a civil trial remains centrally important since it has the effect of disposing, once and for all, all of the issues between the parties arising from the facts. In consequence, the parties are thereafter forbidden — lawyers say "estopped" or "barred" — from again litigating those issues and those facts. Lawyers know this effect as *res judicata*:

> No Court shall try any suit or issue in which the matter directly and substantially in issue has been directly and substantially in issue in a former suit between the same parties, or between parties under whom they or any of them claim, litigating under the same title, in a Court of jurisdiction competent to try such subsequent suit or the suit in which such issue has been subsequently raised, and has been heard and finally decided by such Court.[8]

Since parties have only one go at matters, it is most important that they exhaust all potential claims and defences.

---

[8]   *Re Ontario Sugar Co.; McKinnon's Case* (1910), 22 O.L.R. 621 at 623 (C.P.); affd. (1911), 24 O.L.R. 332 (C.A.), leave to appeal to S.C.C. refused (1911), 44 S.C.R. 659.

(vii) Burden of Proof

Ei qui affirmat, non ei qui negat, incumbent probatio. So, traditionally, have lawyers put the principle of burden of proof at law: "the burden lies on him who affirms, not on him who denies". This principle comprises a fundamental *evidentiary agnosticism*, aptly captured by the child's phrases "saying so, doesn't make it so" and "prove it".

The "legal" burden always[9] rests with the party, the plaintiff or the Crown, that is making a claim against the party who denies, the defendant or the accused. It falls to the plaintiff or the Crown to prove each of the elements of the cause of action alleged in the statement of claim or of the offence alleged in the indictment. This burden remains with both throughout the trial and is properly described as "ultimate". As a matter of law, nothing falls to the accused or the defendant: neither has to prove anything and each may remain silent throughout the affair.

Most often, defendants and accused persons do speak. Defence counsel not only cross-examine the other side's witnesses, typically they also call their own evidence either to rebut the plaintiff or Crown case or to establish an affirmative case of their own. When the defendant or the accused does the latter, the burden of proving the required elements properly falls to each since it is they who are then affirming a case against the other side. Suppose, for instance, a defendant has been sued for negligently causing a traffic accident and, in its statement of defence, claims that the plaintiff contributed to the accident through its own negligence. In such a case, no violence is done to the *ei qui affirmat* principle by requiring the defendant to prove that case at trial. Just the contrary: the principle requires that it do so. Likewise in a criminal case in which, for instance, the accused claims that its actions should be excused because of self-defence. For the accused to carry the burden with respect to that matter is to apply and not to abandon the principle.

That, however, does not tell us why the common defence practice of cross-examining witnesses and adducing rebuttal evidence does not violate the principle governing burden. Lawyers make a distinction between "legal" burden and "tactical" (or "secondary") burden to explain this riddle. The legal burden not only is exclusively the plaintiff's and the Crown's, it cannot be shirked by either of them. Were the plaintiff or the Crown not to tender any evidence, matters would end, without more, in the defendant's or accused's favour.[10] Because the legal burden never visits the defence, it can, as we have seen, simply sit on its hands. And were the plaintiff or the accused not to adduce any evidence or, for that matter, not to cross-examine any of the witnesses, judgment against them

---

[9]   Always, absent some statute which shifts the burden to the defendant or the accused. These so-called "reverse onus" clauses are relatively rare and, with respect to criminal law, are by and large a nullity.

[10] The same result would follow were the defence not to call evidence in support of an affirmative defence or a counterclaim.

would not necessarily follow — as it would against the plaintiff or Crown — simply because the legal burden would yet remain on the plaintiff or the Crown and it would still fall to the trier of fact to decide whether that burden had been successfully discharged by the uncontradicted evidence led by either.

Judgment against a silent defendant or accused is not compelled as a matter of law. However, as a practical matter, such an outcome is highly likely and, in the vast majority of cases, very nearly inevitable. This follows from the very nature of evidence and of trial process. We have seen that ultimate proof, evidence which is final and conclusive, is the rarest of legal commodities. Trials typically progress through the adducement of much more modest evidence, evidence which is never entirely conclusive and which, if it proves at all, does so on basis of the inferences which the trier of fact draws from it. When the plaintiff or the Crown has led evidence of this middling sort, evidence which would permit — but would not require — the trier of fact to find in its favour with respect to the issue to which it is directed, it falls to the defence, if it wants to avoid that unnecessary result, to seek to compromise and, wherever possible to contradict, the implication. Competent defence always wants to avoid that result, and is compelled by the nature of evidence and trial process to take up this "tactical" burden, first through cross-examination and then by adducing rebuttal evidence during its case in chief. One court, in commenting on "the confusion which is often occasioned by not distinguishing between the two different senses in which the term "burden of proof" is employed," aptly drew the distinction between legal and tactical burden as follows:

> The expression 'burden of proof' means (1) the burden of establishing the case which never changes throughout the trial and (2) the burden of going forward which shifts from time to time during the trial of a cause.[11]

For the plaintiff and the accused, to choose not to go forward is to choose not to overcome the effect of the plaintiff's and Crown's evidence and, most often, to choose to have the trier of fact decide in the other side's favour. That evidence and trial process compels the defence to reply does not, however, diminish the critical distinction between the two burdens, nor does it derogate from, let alone contradict, the principle of *ei qui affirmat*.

(viii) Standards of Proof

Determining which party has the legal burden is different from knowing what the party must do to discharge the burden successfully. That the plaintiff must prove each element of the cause action alleged in the statement of claim or that the Crown must prove each element of the offence alleged in the indictment tells us nothing about the degree of probability which the plaintiff's or Crown's evidence must meet in order for either to succeed. The requirements of proof in this

---

[11]   *Re Barter; Corbett v. Wall*, [1939] 2 D.L.R. 201 at 207 (N.B.C.A.).

second sense raises a separate matter which lawyers call "the standard of proof". The standard of proof specifies for the trier of fact the degree of agnosticism which the law requires and that agnosticism varies according to whether the case before the trier of fact is civil or criminal.

What are often called the "civil onus" and the "criminal onus" are easily stated. In civil cases, the party having the legal burden — generally the plaintiff, but respect to affirmative defences or counterclaims, the defendant — must establish its case on a "balance of probabilities". In contrast, in criminal cases, the Crown must prove its case "beyond a reasonable doubt"; with respect to its affirmative defences, the accused, however, is held to the civil standard. Easily stated, certainly; but understanding what they mean is somewhat more complicated.

It is sometimes said that whereas "beyond a reasonable doubt" requires proof to a moral certainty, "balance of probabilities" requires only that the case be more likely than not. And if "moral certainty" means clear, precise, and indubitable and if "more likely" means overbearing, to some degree, the weight of the evidence going the other way, then no fault can be found with these definitions. Still, they are not precise enough for they fail to relate the finer detail, and the different nuance, of the standards.

In *R. v. W. (D.)*,[12] the Supreme Court of Canada provides a glimpse of this detail. Speaking for the majority on the issue of the proper charge to the jury on the matter of the accused's credibility, Cory J. offers the following:

> First, if you believe the evidence of the accused, you must acquit. Secondly, if you do not believe the testimony of the accused but you are left in reasonable doubt by it, you must acquit. Thirdly, even if you are not left in doubt by the evidence of the accused, you must ask yourself whether, on basis of the evidence which you do accept, you are convinced beyond a reasonable doubt by that evidence of the guilt of the accused.[13]

This is to declare that the criminal standard entitles the accused to the finding of fact most favourable to acquittal.[14] And it is just this, and not any formulaic contrast of certainty and probability, which distinguishes the standard in criminal cases from the standard in civil cases. In the latter, the standard is indeed a contest as between which party's evidence, the plaintiff's or the defendant's, is on balance more believable. While in criminal cases it is, of course, necessary that the trier of fact believe the Crown's evidence, such a belief is not sufficient for a finding of guilt since the trier of fact must even then ask itself whether that evidence establishes guilt beyond a reasonable doubt, to a certainty. And this in turn means that, unlike the defendant in a civil trial whose evidence contests with the plaintiff's for preponderance overall, the accused's evidence need be

---

[12] (1991), 63 C.C.C. (3d) 397 (S.C.C.).
[13] *Ibid.*, at 409.
[14] And it is for this reason too that, with respect to affirmative defences, the accused is held to the civil and not the criminal standard.

tendered not in the interest of proof but, more modestly, for the purpose of raising reasonable doubt.

C. APPLYING LEGAL RULES

We come then to the arguments which lawyers typically muster with respect to the application of legal rules. However, because it is often claimed that rule application is a matter of a peculiarly legal form of reasoning — and not, as will be claimed here, of lawyerly traditions concerning argument — we shall attend briefly to two preliminary matters, the claim for legal reasoning and the nature of argument generally. We will then identify and explore those paradigms of argument which are characteristic of the moment of application.

(i) Legal Reasoning or Reasoning Legally

Panic is a common experience among third-year law students. The long-anticipated convocation by then a nearly accomplished fact, articles impending, their lives in law about to begin, a great many students start anxiously to question their readiness: to think that whatever it is they know, it is neither special nor readily retrievable or particularly useful, to feel that something is missing, something which they should but do not know, something that without more would permit them to act as lawyers. At its core, this anxiety is about knowledge or, more accurately, about its absence.

Through their three years of law school, a great many law students come — and are sometimes led — to the view that there exists some form of reasoning which is unique to law, that legal reasoning, to use a lawyer's phrase, is *sui generis*. Yet, having adopted, or at least absorbed, that view, near the end of their legal education, with practice confronting them, they discover that they at least are seized of no system of reasoning which they can identify as legal and which, as promised, can be applied to problems to produce legal solutions. Happily, later on, they will also discover that their anxiety was for naught. If they stay with the law, they will learn that the lawyers from whom they learn, those senior lawyers with whom they work and those judges before whom they appear, are possessed of no such special system of reasoning either. They will discover, instead, that law is about certain kinds of reasons and not about a special kind of reasoning and that, in the final analysis, lawyering is a craft of argument about those reasons and not an exercise in some specialized logic.

We will briefly explore the qualities of those reasons which are so often, and mistakenly, viewed as constituting a form of reasoning unique to law. Joseph Raz defines "legal reasoning" as "an instance of moral reasoning" more generally: [15] "Legal reasoning is a species of normative reasoning. It concerns norms, reasons for action, rights and duties, and their application to general and specific situations".[16] Two things follow from this view: first, what is called "legal reasoning" is not, nor can it ever be, *sui generis*, some form of thought that is unique to law; and second, an acceptable account of whatever distinguishes legal reasoning, so understood, from other instances of moral reasoning must not depend upon a revival of any element of the *sui generis* view. We will pause briefly on each matter.

That "legal reasoning" is not an autonomous form of reasoning and is instead a localized form of normative reasoning more generally would surprise no one who knows what lawyers in fact do *and* has had the opportunity to observe the argumentative practices of children. Simply, that we hear from children the same sorts of arguments we hear from lawyers should disabuse anyone — including law students — of the notion that lawyers reason in some unique and specialized way. James Penner puts the matter well:

> The basic intellectual manoeuvres of what we call 'legal reasoning' are understood and practised from a very young age. Anyone who has ever raised children knows that almost from the time they speak their first words, children will argue from precedent ('But you let us have sweets before dinner last night'), understand the application of rules (e.g., bedtime at 7:30), know that rules may not apply in certain circumstances (e.g., staying up late when guests are over), expect reasons for a decision which makes sense to them, and place great weight on the principle that like cases must be decided alike ('You let Madeleine go out without boots on'). It is even the case that general justifying principles may be and are, on occasion, derived from a body of decisions, for example that the overarching guidance of the precedents is founded upon the authority of one's parents to 'take care' of one, to maintain health and in particular, to avoid physical harm. Finally, it is also apparent that children employ concepts ('That's not fair') which to the tutored mind appear to be extremely abstract.[17]

Of course, children are not lawyers. What distinguishes the arguments of children from those of lawyers cannot, however, be found in any difference in the form of reasoning each employs with respect to rules and their application. Both argue using the same, and very ordinary, moral categories, and each does so with the intention of articulating reasons regarding the propriety of rule governance in specific situations. The difference between a child's argument and the lawyer's argument with respect to these matters resides, rather, in style and in context.

---

[15] Raz, "On the Autonomy of Legal Reasoning" in J. Raz, *Ethics in the Public Domain* (Oxford: Clarendon Press, 1994), at p. 324.

[16] *Ibid.*, at p. 310.

[17] J. Penner, "Incomplete Theorisation in Legal Reasoning: Political and Cognitive Explanations" (unpublished manuscript on file with author). See also his: "Common Law Cognition and Judicial Appointment" (2000), 38(3) Alberta L. Rev. 683.

Though children and lawyers share a form of argument, the arguments made by lawyers are yet distinct in a number of very important ways. First, legal arguments are not only generally more complex and nuanced than moral arguments made by non-lawyers (children not only included), they also are standardized in a way and to an extent that is not apparent in common moral argument. The lawyer's arguments are standardized precisely because they are instances of the paradigms of legal argument which we shall explore shortly. Second, legal argument is distinguished from common moral argument by institutional context and purpose. Lawyers alone are permitted to argue in those places — the courts — in which arguments, if successful, have not just persuasive but institutional force. And unlike common moral argument about rules, legal argument is disciplined by purpose. Where common argument most often is directed to appraising the virtue of a rule overall, the object of legal argument is most often to determine what precisely the rule is and what precisely the rule requires *according to law*. Unlike common moral reasoning about legal rules, that is, "legal reasoning" about legal rules concerns, in the moment of identification, "what authoritative decisions have been made for society" and, in the moment of application, "what they entail or require in a given case".[18]

(ii)   The Nature of Argument

We began this chapter with the declaration that the application of legal rules is a matter which is made possible and constrained by certain traditions of practice developed over time by the legal community. To interpret and to apply legal rules, we said, is therefore to participate in the legal community's way of life and to subject oneself to governance by its traditions. This claim implies, and requires, a certain, very important premise, namely, that, descriptively at least, "legal knowledge *is* a matter of convention".[19] This view, in turn, depends upon a certain understanding of the meaning of argument which requires a brief overview.

According to this understanding, the word "argument" denotes "a form of social interaction ... a social relationship" and "arguments" are "social interactions having many of the characteristics of social interactions in general".[20] This means that argument generally, and not just legal argument, is grounded, not in some set of rules, but in the different social situations which create and sustain various instances of the argument relationship and that the arguments characteristic of each such situation arise, not from some form of reasoning, but from the social demands and institutional history and traditions of that situation.

---

[18]   A. Altman, *Arguing About Law* (New York: Wadsworth Publishing, 1996), at p. 224. See also: C.L. Black, Jr., *Decision According to Law* (New York: W.W. Norton & Co., 1981).

[19]   C.A. Willard, *Argumentation and the Social Grounds of Knowledge* (University, AB: University of Alabama Press, 1983), at p. 188 (emphasis in original).

[20]   *Ibid.*, at p. 21.

As applied to law — which, incidentally, many non-legal theorists believe to be the paradigmatic case of both argument and interpretation[21] — this understanding compels the conclusion that "the ongoing practices of lawyers are what make up" legal argument and the law more generally.[22] And as is the case in other "institutions of discourse", those practices are a consequence not of rules, but of "traditions built out of recurring definitions of situation".[23] When persons come to law, "they take up pre-established lines of action" because "to enter an argument field is to adopt a starting point with a willingness to abide" with those traditions.[24]

This view of argument reveals a fundamentally important question: What would lead one to such a willingness to abide? Since traditions of argument are just that, and not specialized forms of reasoning or systems of rules, willingness cannot be a consequence of utility or of truth. Willingness, rather, has to be a matter of faith and trust in the point of the ongoing practice. Having situated "argument", we will turn to the traditions which comprise the situation of argument which is our law.

(iii) Paradigms of Application

In Chapter 1, we discovered that rules are essentially syllogisms. They state a major premise (the factual predicate) which, if it obtains in the "instant" case (the minor premise), compels a certain legal result (the consequent). In Chapter 2, we saw that, regardless of their source, the meaning of legal rules is a result of lawyers inducing generalizations from the body of relevant case law. It is sometimes said that this inductive process at the moment of interpretation is paralleled by a deductive process at the moment of application. According to this view, once the meaning of a rule is determined, and its minor premise proved, applying the rule is a matter of simple deduction. This view, which is false, raises an important issue regarding the relationship between the rules of reason and the traditions of legal (and other) discourse to which we must attend.

That all human discourse must satisfy the requirements of rationality does not mean that human discourse is consumed and defined by those requirements. Rationality is a condition of intelligibility, and all human discourse, law included, is subject to what might be termed the rules of reasoning. But what is special about any discourse is its subject matter and its practice, not logic. Indeed, the requirements of rationality generally, and of logic particularly, are best viewed as "nothing more than a backdrop": "like all scenery, [they] support the action, contribut[e] to the mood, but suppl[y] little of the dialogue".[25] As we

---

[21] See for example: Willard, *supra*, note 19, at pp. 178-96; and H.-G. Gadamer, *Truth and Method* (New York: Crossroad Publishing, 1986), at pp. 289-305.
[22] Willard, *supra*, note 19, at pp. 187-88.
[23] *Ibid.*, at p. 84.
[24] *Ibid.*
[25] *Ibid.*, at p. 186.

have seen, the action and dialogue is supplied by the traditions of the particular discourse which are imparted to participants through socialization.

The application of legal rules shows this dramatically. A trial is not, as the deductive view would have it, a special instance of some general rule. Trials, rather, are where legal rules, formulated through past inductive argument, meet the hard reality of new facts and, as such, every trial is in a very real sense unique. To understand what happens when rules confront facts at trial, "we turn not to the language of the law so much as to the understandings among legal actors".[26] And when we do that, we discover that, instead of being a tidy process of deduction, "law is a loose framework" which is "of necessity diffuse because it is brought to life through the ongoing practices of legal actors".[27] We discover that "the rules change from case to case and are remade with each case".[28]

More particularly, the ongoing practices of the legal community disclose the purpose, process and import of legal argument. When a rule confronts facts, what is at issue is whether the rule *ought* to govern those facts and determining that issue depends upon certain traditions of moral argument concerning "what facts will be considered similar to those present when the rule was first announced".[29] Legal argument is about justifying an existing rule's governance of the present, and that justification minimally involves "the finding of similarity or difference" between the rule and the present case.[30]

This understanding is much richer than the mechanistic deductive view on four important counts. First, it requires us to confront the fact that "legal reasoning" is a species of moral reasoning and forbids us to reduce what lawyers do to mere technique or logical manoeuvre. Second, it allows us to discern what is really important about the form of rules, namely, that their syllogistic structure, though not determinative of matters in the way the deductive account alleges, does provide a fund of very legal arguments. We will discover that the primary arguments of application — analogy, difference and mistake — flow directly from the structure of rules. Third, it permits us to view deductive reasoning as just another means of justification. In consequence, when judges, as they sometimes do, deliver their opinions in the form of a simple syllogism, we will not confuse the form with the substance of the matter. On the contrary, we will know that the opinion does not depend upon its form — but instead, minimally and typically, on the judge's having found the requisite similarity — and that the form is meant to justify that finding. Finally, it discloses the "logic of the law" to be a grander and more elegant affair than mere syllogism. We referred earlier

---

[26] *Ibid.*, at p. 184.
[27] *Ibid.*, at p. 188.
[28] E.H. Levi, *An Introduction to Legal Reasoning* (Chicago: University of Chicago Press, 1949), at p. 2.
[29] *Ibid.*
[30] *Ibid.*

to Maitland's famous metaphor of law as "a living body".[31] When not only the interpretation but the application of legal rules as well is viewed as a practice of lawyerly tradition, then, as Maitland thought, "every member" of the law's body indeed becomes "connected with and depends upon every other member".[32] So viewed, the rules which at any given moment govern our lives will be seen to depend upon lawyerly arguments of induction concerning what the legal past justifiably supports and upon the ongoing justification of those rules as new facts about our lives emerge. The deeper "logic of the law" consists in this symmetry between the sedimented rules produced by past argument and the openness of those rules to reformulation and challenge by arguments in the present.

Similarity and difference do not exhaust the arguments of justification offered by lawyers with respect to application. We shall explore the following six paradigms of argument, each of which figures — though to different degrees — in the ongoing practices of the legal community: argument from choice of rule (*characterization*); argument from similarity (*analogy*); argument from difference (*distinguishing*); argument from mistake (*overruling*); argument from consequence *(slippery slope/floodgates)*; and argument from *public policy*. Once again, it is important to note that, though we will approach these arguments separately as ideal types, in practice, they overlap and, in any given case, lawyers may join them in ways which are limited only by their skill, imagination and ingenuity.

CHARACTERIZATION

Rules do not, without more, apply to facts. This is not just a consequence of the notorious slipperiness of facts. Nor is it solely a matter of the requirement that lawyers translate social facts into legal facts, a process which involves them in constructing and not merely in reporting the facts. Facts are indeed slippery and lawyers, in interviewing and counselling clients, do indeed reconstruct their personal tales into legal tales. However, even where the parties agree about which facts are legal facts, they might yet disagree about their legal significance in a very fundamental way: they might disagree about which legal rule properly governs those legal facts. And because this is so, lawyers have available to them arguments with respect to which rule properly governs. Arguments of this sort are fundamentally different from arguments concerning whether any rule, which the parties agree governs, properly applies to the facts of the case. Whereas the arguments of the latter sort are directed to issues of proof, arguments of the former sort concern issues of classification or characterization.

---

[31] V.T.H. Delaney, *Frederic William Maitland Reader* (New York: Oceana Publications, 1957), at p. 157.

[32] *Ibid.*

Take, for example, the facts which were before the Supreme Court of Canada in the case of *Norberg v. Wynrib*.[33] There the plaintiff had agreed to engage in sexual relations with her doctor on the condition that the doctor would prescribe a drug to which she was addicted. The question for the Court was whether her consent was good and whether — because consent is a complete defence to battery — the plaintiff patient was barred from recovery in her cause of action in the intentional tort of battery. The "threshold" issue before the Court was whether the plaintiff's action was, as lawyers say, properly "framed" in battery. That is, the issue was the proper characterization, or classification, of the agreed facts. The majority held, in opposition to the findings at trial and on first appeal, that because the plaintiff's consent was not genuine and had no force or effect at law, her cause in battery was good. There were, however, two minority judgments which took the view that the cause was improperly framed in battery. Justice McLachlin (as she then was) characterized the facts as giving rise to a breach of the fiduciary duty that doctors owe to patients and, on that ground, held the defendant liable despite the fact that the sexual relations were consensual. Justice Sopinka too thought the consent good, but characterized the facts as grounding a cause for breach of the doctor's duty to treat his patient with due competence.

Cases like this raise two questions — whence this divergence on a matter as fundamental as the definition of the case; and can we judge, on legal grounds, different characterizations? The answers to these questions reveal much about argument from characterization and we will pause briefly on each.

To say that lawyers frame cases in whichever fashion best serves the interests of their clients is roughly true, but it does not tell us anything about how they go about serving their clients in that fashion. Whatever its motivation, a lawyer's framing of a case depends upon the view which the lawyer adopts of the facts of the matter overall. This view is generally referred to as the lawyer's "theory of the case". In *Norberg*, for instance, the lawyers who sat in final judgment of the matter turned out to have profoundly different theories of the case as obviously did the lawyers who argued the case before them. A theory of the case is simply the lawyer's approach to all of the evidence, undisputed and disputed. The theory of the case grounds the cause of action which the lawyer thinks is proper to the facts. Subsequently, the theory will also inform the lawyer's strategy at trial, including especially how properly to approach the evidence favouring the other party. Framing cases in this way is very much a legal art which defies easy revision into a how-to list. Indeed, facility and judgment in this matter is one of the things which distinguishes junior counsel from senior counsel and, over the length of their lives in law, great lawyers from middling and inferior ones.

Though from the lawyer's point of view choice of characterization is informed by the interests of the client, there are grounds at law on which to appraise characterizations. What might be called "classificatory reasons" are

---

[33]   [1992] 4 W.W.R. 577, [1992] 2 S.C.R. 226.

reasons for or against the applicability of a cause of action in a particular fact situation. Classificatory reasons are reasons why certain facts belong to a certain cause *and* they are reasons for classifying facts as belonging to that cause. Reasons of the first sort have less to do with characterization in the sense which concerns us here because they have more to do with whether the facts at play are consistent with the element or elements of the cause at issue than with the second order concern, which does concern us, about whether the facts, as lawyers say, might possibly "sound" in a certain body of law. When the second matter is at issue, the classificatory reason which governs is *coherence*. Coherence requires that characterizations conform with legal values embedded in general legal principles. And if a proffered characterization violates, compromises or otherwise does damage to those values, it must be rejected as a matter of law: those facts cannot sound in that body of law because they would disfigure the law.

Norberg is a good, if unfortunate, example. It is an undisputed value of our law that persons are free and responsible actors and that, because they are, others might reasonably rely on the choices freely made by them. In *Norberg*, the Supreme Court was faced with a characterization of the law of consent which would profoundly violate the value of autonomy. Yet, rather than rejecting that characterization on grounds of incoherence, the majority of the Court chose instead to change the law of consent and, in so doing, seriously to undermine the value of responsible freedom and the social practices which depend upon it.

ANALOGY

When there is no contest regarding the rule which governs a case, the issue is solely proof of the conditions in the factual predicate. However, when the rule is contested or uncertain, matters become considerably more complex. In such cases, the judge has to decide whether to extend an existing rule to cover the case, or to distinguish the instant case from governance by the proffered rule or, sometimes, even to overrule a rule which might otherwise apply. And it is with respect to those decisions that the tripartite structure of legal rules — the factual predicate, the consequent and the background justification — comes critically into argumentative play. This is so because arguments from *analogy* (which would extend a rule), arguments from *difference* (which would distinguish a rule), and arguments from *mistake* (which would overrule a rule) depend entirely upon this structure. We shall consider each category of argument, though it might be prudent to caution that the structure of rules typically supports arguments from analogy and from difference and much less frequently arguments from mistake.

We have already discovered that lawyers induce rules from case law. In doing so, they are raising general propositions of law from the legal particular. Analogy, too, is a matter of induction except that it induces from the particular to the particular. Argument from analogy in law is grounded on the factual predicate. Suppose a rule states that "if a, b and c facts obtain, then legal result r follows" and that the instant case is either an "a, b" case or an "a, b, c and q" case: in such cases, it makes sense to ask whether the rule may be either expanded or shrunk to suit and therefore to govern the facts. Whether a rule will be applied analogously to a case which in either sense fails to satisfy the conditions stated in the factual predicate will depend on whether the instant case sufficiently resembles cases in which the conditions are satisfied. Some cases of argument by analogy may appear easy. For instance, it might make intuitive sense that a rule which forbids dogs in the airport ought to apply analogously to other animals. But the appearance is deceptive since resemblance at law is a rather complicated affair.

What is required are *legal* reasons for finding similarity. We might think that precedent provides the answer. So with respect to our "dog rule" facing a "cat case", if there were other prior cases which extended the rule — to other animals generally, to some other animal or to cats specifically — we might be inclined to think, on grounds of *stare decisis* alone, that the precedents would settle the matter. But we would be deceived. We still would not know what grounded the similarity in those other cases nor would we have any basis for arguing by analogy in any novel case. So the problem persists: what constitutes similarity at law?

From the lawyer's point of view, at least initially, similarity is entirely facial. Lawyers will argue any similarity which is at all relevant and which serves their clients. However, facial similarity of this kind cannot satisfy judges because the issue for the court is whether any of those facial similarities ought to count *as a matter of law*. Legal similarity is assessed with respect to three factors, each of which may constitute a reason for extending by analogy the application of a rule to a case which otherwise fails to satisfy the rule's conditions.

First, a rule may be extended if the instant case falls under the rule's background justification, the rule's purpose or the value which it protects. Take for instance our "dog rule" and "cat case". If the background justification of that rule is quiet use and enjoyment of the airport, then arguably the cat is caught by the rule. On the other hand, if the justification is patron safety, then arguably the cat is excluded. As we shall see when we discuss mistake, a rule's background justification is itself a matter of legal argument. Second, that the extended rule would be consistent with other existing rules is a good reason to count similarities and to extend the rule. On the other hand, analogies which point to inconsistencies supply good reasons for not extending a rule. Third, that litigants in one area of law are not treated the same as litigants in other, yet analogous, areas of law is good reason for extending a rule. On the other hand, analogies which reveal that extension would work unfairness are good reasons for not extending the rule.

A very famous decision of a very renowned judge illustrates these matters. In *MacPherson v. Buick Motor Company*,[34] Buick sold an automobile to a retail dealer which in turn sold it to the plaintiff MacPherson. While the plaintiff was in the car, it collapsed — one of its wheels was defective — and the plaintiff was thrown from the car and injured. Though Buick had purchased the wheel from another manufacturer, the defect could have been discovered had Buick inspected the wheel which it had the opportunity, but failed, to do. The plaintiff's case in negligence against Buick turned on whether the defendant owed a duty to anyone besides the immediate purchaser, that is, the retailer. Prior to *MacPherson*, it was settled law that liability in negligence was limited to the immediate purchaser except where the manufacturer's negligence put human life in "imminent danger". The defendant argued that, though a car was "inherently dangerous", "inherently dangerous" was different from "imminently dangerous"; that, in consequence, the facts of the case failed to satisfy the rule's conditions; and that, therefore, liability did lay against Buick. Judge Cardozo had before him then a issue of extension by analogy: was "inherently dangerous" sufficiently similar at law to "imminently dangerous" to warrant extending the rule of liability in negligence? In answering this question, Cardozo meticulously and exhaustively analyzed the facts in prior cases concerning manufacturer liability to non-immediate purchasers and articulated the similarities and dissimilarities held relevant. In deciding to extend the rule to favour the plaintiff, Cardozo found: a) that the defendant was a manufacturer was a similarity going to liability; b) that the car was designed for speeds up to 50 m.p.h. and that, unless its wheels were sound, injury was certain, were similarities going to liability; and c) that the "inherent/imminent" distinction was of no force – "[T]he case does not turn upon these restricted niceties. If danger was to be expected as reasonably certain, there was a duty of negligence, and this whether you call the danger inherent or imminent". In consequence, it was proper to extend the existing rule to the instant case. Cardozo's decision in *MacPherson* turned out to be "momentous" because it subsequently led courts in the United States and in the United Kingdom to induce a general principle of liability for negligently manufactured goods.[35]

This discussion of argument from analogy has at least three very profitable lessons. First, we may be able to see why lawyers are famous nitpickers. Because very nearly always everything turns on the presence or absence of some fact or facts, the labour of lawyers is by definition enmeshed in detail and, in consequence, lawyers are committed to rigorous analysis and detailed mastery of the facts of the case.

Second, we may be able to conceive of legal argument and practice more generally as "experimental" because they are experiential.[36] "The rules and principles

---

[34] 217 N.Y. 382, 111 N.E. 1050 (1916).
[35] See J.G. Fleming, *The Law of Torts*, 8th ed. (Melbourne: The Law Book Co., 1992), at p. 482.
[36] M. Smith, *Jurisprudence* (New York: Columbia University Press, 1909), at p. 21.

of case law" cannot ever be "treated as final truths". Rather, because case law and legal argument ineluctably rely upon, and must always contend with, facts from the world, these rules and principles must be considered "working hypotheses" which are vulnerable to "retest[ing] ... in every new case".[37]

Argument from analogy is one way of "determining the rules by which law shall be governed".[38] Our consideration of the remaining arguments will add to this description and to our understanding of "how the rules change as the rules are applied".[39] But mere description will not suffice. At some point, we shall have to explain how this diffuse, not very deductive and always very open process might yet constitute decision according to law. However, on basis alone of our discussion of analogy, it should be clear — and this is the third lesson — that, though the legal community creates new legal rules, it does so conservatively. Argumentative proposals for new rules may only succeed on condition that they do not introduce new and discordant values or purposes into the body of the law, and that they instead serve values and purposes already extant in the law.

DISTINGUISHING

Distinguishing is the obverse of analogy: to distinguish a rule is to find a reason why the rule should *not* govern the instant case. Oftentimes, the reason is factual difference. Suppose that a rule's predicate states "if a, b and c" and that the present case is either an "a, c" case or an "a, b, c and q" case. In cases of these sorts, lawyers will argue that the facial differences are good reason, to distinguish the instant case from governance by the "a, b, c" rule on grounds, as is in analogy, of background justification, consistency and fairness. But rules are sometimes distinguished when there are no such facial differences. It is cases where an "a, b, c" rule is distinguished notwithstanding the instant case otherwise appears to be an "a, b, c" case that reveal distinguishing as a category of argument independent from analogy.

In *Hedley Byrne & Co. Ltd. v. Heller & Partners Ltd.*,[40] the plaintiffs, an advertising company, had their bank contact the defendant bank concerning the credit-worthiness of company X, one its customers. The defendant advised that X was a good credit risk and, in reliance on that advice, the plaintiffs entered contracts for television and newspaper advertising for X under which the plaintiffs became personally responsible for payment. Subsequently, X went into liquidation and the plaintiffs lost a large amount of money on the advertising contracts. The plaintiffs sued the defendant bank for that loss on grounds that its advice regarding X's credit was given negligently. Though, in the final appeal of the matter, the House of Lords found against the plaintiff, its decision on the

---

[37]   *Ibid.*
[38]   Oliver Wendell Holmes, *The Common Law* (Boston: Little Brown, 1881), at p. 2.
[39]   Levi, *supra*, note 28, at pp. 3-4.
[40]   [1964] A.C. 465, [1963] 2 All E.R. 575 (H.L.).

rules governing situations of this sort had profound implications with respect to liability in negligence for purely economic loss. The decision is also important for our purposes since it demonstrates how courts and lawyers may distinguish a rule which otherwise appears perfectly triggered by the facts.

Prior to *Hedley*, it was established law that A had a right to damages for economic losses arising from A's reliance on B's false statement only if the statement was wilfully or recklessly made. The rule in *Derry v. Peek*[41] — the case in which this rule was first declared — excluded, therefore, liability for negligent misstatements. The misstatement in *Hedley* was neither wilful nor reckless and, in consequence, the rule in *Derry* would appear to govern. Nonetheless, the House of Lords distinguished *Derry* by ruling that proof of actual intention to deceive or of wilful recklessness as to truth was required only in an action for damages for the intentional tort of deceit. In so doing, the House opened negligence as a cause of action for pure economic loss in the absence of contract, and the creation of this legal freedom established *Hedley* as a monument in the common law of tort. Thereafter, A has a right to damages against B where A reasonably relies on B's false statement and where B had grounds to foresee that A would rely but failed to take reasonable care to be accurate.

The House did not distinguish *Derry* on the facts because there were in *Hedley* no distinguishing facts. Instead, the House ruled that *Derry* "did not establish any universal rule that in the absence of contract an innocent but negligent misrepresentation cannot give rise to an action" and, on that ground, it confined the rule in *Derry* to actions for deceit.[42] Now, note: the Lords did *not* overrule *Derry* — they distinguished it. This they did by characterizing the rule in such a fashion that it became confined to one body of law (the tort of deceit) and excluded from another (the tort of negligence). In its most extreme form, distinguishing by category can lead courts to define the category in terms of the facts of the ruling case and thereby to confine the case to those precise facts. However, even in that event, the case is not overruled and will continue to govern those facts to which it exactly applies.

Arguments for distinguishing by reason of category, like arguments for distinguishing by reason of facts, depend ultimately on background justification, consistency and fairness. Consistency, however, is especially important as witness the ruling in *Hedley*. Between 1889, when *Derry* was decided, and the 1960's, when *Hedley* was heard, the law of negligence had developed tremendously. In 1932, in *Donoghue v. Stevenson*,[43] the House of Lords had freed the law of negligence from strict factual precedent. "The categories of negligence", it held, "are never closed" because negligence finally depends, not upon the facts in which it has been found, but upon the legal principle of neighbourhood

---

[41]   (1889), 14 App. Cas. 337.

[42]   *Hedley Byrne, supra*, note 40, at 484 (*per* Lord Reid).

[43]   [1932] A.C. 562. In *Donoghue*, the House of Lords cites with approval Cardozo J.'s decision in *MacPherson v. Buick Motor Co., supra*, note 34.

which governs those facts.[44] In consequence, after *Donoghue*, plaintiffs had no longer to fit their cases into the facts of past decisions, and could argue instead that the neighbour principle was engaged because they were "persons ... so closely and directly affected by [the defendant's] act that [the defendant] ought reasonably to have [had] them in contemplation as being so affected when [it] was directing [its] mind to the acts or omissions" of which the plaintiffs complain.[45] *Donoghue* gave lawyers cause to argue that no area of negligence, including pure economic loss, should be closed and that the whole of negligence should be governed by the principle of reasonable foreseeability of harm. *Donoghue* sealed *Derry*'s fate: when the occasion arose in *Hedley* for the court to make the law of negligent economic loss consistent with the law of negligence more generally, it seized the opportunity by distinguishing *Derry* and thereby by removing it entirely from the body of rules governing liability for inadvertent harm to persons, their property, *and* their finances.

There are lessons here as well. In Chapter 3, we discussed the doctrine of precedent and concluded that, just because precedents have necessarily to be interpreted, our law is more porous than the doctrine might otherwise lead us to believe. We can now add that, in fact and in theory, the doctrine of precedent does not just mean that a precedent must be followed; fully stated, it means that a precedent must either be followed *or* distinguished. On the other hand, as we discovered to be the case with analogy, courts are seriously constrained in deciding that a precedent does not apply to facts to which it otherwise clearly applies. First — and this is what distinguishes "distinguishing" from "analogy" — in distinguishing courts can only narrow rules, they cannot extend them. This follows by definition since to distinguish is to modify a rule so as to avoid its application. Not only that: as in the *Hedley* modification of *Derry*, the modified rule must replicate the entire factual predicate of the old rule together, of course, with the new restrictive condition. Nor only that: the new condition must be consistent with the conditions expressed in the factual predicate of the old rule so that the new rule could have justified the outcome in the case in which the old rule was articulated. We may conclude that while the doctrine of precedent does not prescribe our enslavement to the past, nor does it permit whole cloth abandonment or alteration of the past. The doctrine of precedent is too fine and nuanced a practice to be captured by either extreme.

OVERRULING

In the vast majority of cases, lawyers argue that legal rules should be either followed or distinguished. Sometimes, however, they will argue that a standing legal rule is mistaken and that the court should, on that account, overrule the rule. Arguments of this sort constitute the *doctrine of mistake* which, in Chapter

---

[44]   *Ibid.*, at 619 (*per* Lord Macmillan).
[45]   *Ibid.*, at 580 (*per* Lord Atkin).

3, was described as the twin of the doctrine of precedent. The doctrine of mistake permits precedents to be excised from the body of the law. But to understand how and why this is accomplished requires that we be especially precise in locating the doctrine.

In some countries — Canada and the United States, for instance — lawyers can argue that legislated rules ought to be struck down because they unacceptably offend some value which is entrenched in a constitutional document. Specialized arguments of that sort are not our present concern because they sound in constitutional law and not in the doctrine of mistake. Nor are we concerned with simple cases of what lawyers call *per incuriam*, cases in which a higher court finds that a lower court has inadvertently misapprehended the law. Nor are we concerned with ordinary "overturning" or "reversing" of lower court decisions. When a higher court reaches a different decision on the law or the facts, it is said to overturn or to reverse the lower court. The higher court might overturn the result (X now loses) or it might uphold the result yet reformulate the law or adopt or approve only a part of the lower court decision. But none of this is an instance of the doctrine of mistake.

What we want to examine are those lawyerly arguments which attempt to persuade, independently from any constitution, that a standing rule of law is mistaken. Arguments of this sort seek to convince the court expressly to overrule a standing rule of law and, where successful, their effect is a declaration that an extant rule is, properly considered, no rule at all. Arguments from mistake come in two varieties and we shall briefly consider each.

Among Justice Holmes, many justly famous declarations about law and life is the following: "It is revolting to have no better reason for a rule of law than that so it was laid down in the time of Henry IV. It is still more revolting if the grounds upon it was laid down have vanished long since, and the rule simply persists from blind imitation of the past".[46] In this, he was delivering a biting version of one of the arguments from mistake, namely, *the argument from changed social and cultural conditions*. The decision of House of Lords in *R. v. R.* will serve as illustration.[47]

In that case, the court had to decide whether the common law rule that a husband cannot commit a rape against his wife remained good law. The rule was longstanding — the House traces it to the 18th century — and was based on the view that, by marriage, a wife irrevocably consents to intercourse with her husband. Lord Keith, for the entire House, held that "on grounds of principle there is now no justification for the marital exception in rape".[48] His Lordship supported this ruling to overrule the marital exception on two grounds: that the rules of law must "evolv[e] in light of changing social, economic and cultural developments" and that "the status of women, and particularly of married women,

---

[46] O.W. Holmes, "The Path of the Law" (1897), 10 Harvard L. Rev. 457 at p. 469.

[47] [1991] 3 W.L.R. 767, [1991] 4 All E.R. 481.

[48] *Ibid.*, at 772.

ha[d] changed out of all recognition" from "the state of affairs ... at the time when [the rule] was enunciated".[49] Note, however, that the court's assessment of change is an assessment of legal change: the argument from cultural change is an argument about cultural change as evidenced by law as a whole.

The second argument from mistake also relies on background justification, but more directly. We have to distinguish this argument from simple cases in which a rule is not applied because application would be inconsistent with the rule's background justification. For instance, a rule which prohibits sleeping in a railway station might not be applied to a traveller who dozes while waiting for a train simply because, properly construed, the rule's purpose is to prevent people from using the station as nighttime shelter and its application to these facts is inconsistent with that justification.[50] But, in that event, the background justification supplies a reason against applying the rule in the instant case, and not a reason for declaring it mistaken in every case. It is the latter possibility which concerns us here.

This possibility relies generally on the nature of background justification in law and, more particularly, on two basic properties of rules, namely, that rules are not equal as rules and that rules exist in clusters or in families. We shall consider each and then illustrate how they may combine to establish the second argument from mistake.

Legal argument and legal interpretation proceed on the understanding that the rules of law, individually and as a whole, are not arbitrary. They assume that there are reasons for the rules, reasons which we have been calling background justifications. Now, justification — in law or anything other human enterprise — may concern either why something is the case or why something is right. Justification in the former sense concerns motivation, say, the motivation of a judge ruling against an accused (the judge is a strong "law and order" type). Justifications of this sort are not legal justifications because they attempt to explain, rather than to show what should be, the case; and arguments concerning either the application or meaning of legal rules which are founded on motivation will not be heard, nor can they have any force, in law. Justification in the second sense is normative in the required case because it attempts to disclose that a rule is right.

Though all legal rules have a background justification in this sense, the force of that justification varies according to the location of the rule. Every legal rule is part of some larger network of rules, and the law as a whole consists of the network of these networks. The force of a rule's justification is determined by the place of the rule in the network to which it properly belongs and by the place of that network in the overall network of the law. In consequence, rules are unequal in two senses: in any given body of law, some rules are more important

---

[49] *Ibid.*, at 770.

[50] This example is taken from L. Fuller, "Positivism and Fidelity to Law: A Reply to Professor Hart" (1958), 71 Harvard L. Rev. 630.

than others; and some bodies of law are more important, in the overall anatomy of the law, than other bodies of law. To add to Maitland's metaphor, in any subsystem of the law's body, some matters are more crucial than others; and, in the system as a whole, some subsystems are nearer the heart and lungs of the matter than others. For instance, in the family of rules which lawyers designate as the tort of negligence, the rule concerning reasonable care is more foundational, and its background justification more forceful, than is the rule concerning the impact of particular statutory provisions on proof. Likewise, tort law as a whole is subordinate to other areas of law, for example, the law of crimes or the law of the constitution.

It is this complex anatomy which permits a second sort of argument of mistake, what we will call *the argument from contradiction*. A rule may be overruled either because its background justification contradicts the background justification of a superior rule in the subsystem to which it belongs; and a rule of any such system, even a superior rule, may be overruled because it contradicts the background justification of a rule of a superior system or the background justification of that superior system as a whole. Lawyers often refer to this as "trumping": as is the case with cards in the game of bridge, in law, where there is irresolvable conflict, superior rules trump subordinate rules and superior bodies of law trump subordinate bodies of law.

We shall consider an example of the first, more common, sort of argument. In *Donoghue v. Stevenson*,[51] the plaintiff purchased a bottle of ginger beer from a vendor who in turn had purchased it from the defendant manufacturer. Unknown to the plaintiff — the bottle was made of dark opaque glass — the beer contained a decomposing snail and, after consuming part of the beer, she became seriously ill. The plaintiff sued in negligence claiming that the defendant owed her a duty to take reasonable care to ensure that its products did not cause her harm. The defendant responded, quite correctly, that the plaintiff's claim disclosed no cause of action since (a) the law of negligence as it then stood required plaintiffs to show cause by identifying a past decision, concerning similar facts, in which a duty was found to exist, and (b) there then existed no such authority, no "decomposing snail in an opaque bottle" case nor any case analogous to it. Yet, despite this rule, which was both clearly established and clearly applicable, the plaintiff succeeded. She succeeded because the House overruled the rule, properly invoked by the defendant, which had until then governed the matter of duty in the tort of negligence.

The House reasoned to this result first by identifying the background justification of "liability for negligence" as a whole and then by deploying the argument from contradiction to excise the "precedent" rule.[52] Lord Atkin stated: "There must be, and is, some general conception of relations giving rise to a duty of care, of which the particular cases found in the books are but

---

[51] *Supra*, note 43.
[52] *Ibid.*, at 580 (*per* Lord Atkin).

instances".[53] And he then proceeded to identify and to articulate that "conception": "You must take reasonable care to avoid acts or omissions which you can reasonably foresee would be likely to injure your neighbour".[54] But if moral proximity between the doer and sufferer of harm grounds the law of negligence, then the "precedent" rule, which would keep "closed ... the categories of negligence",[55] contradicts that higher order justification and must be mistaken.

It may appear that the doctrine of mistake leaves the doctrine of precedent in tatters, but this is itself a mistaken view. It is true that overruling is free of the restrictions attached to analogy and distinguishing. But the power to overrule exists more selectively and is used more sparingly than either of those other means of changing the rules of precedent. There exist good reasons for this. First, as an institutional matter, most courts most of the time are simply stuck with the rules as they exist because most courts most of the time are obliged to follow and to apply the rules of courts which are their superior. In Canada, for instance, no court, other than the Supreme Court itself, has the authority to overrule the decisions of the Supreme Court of Canada. And though provincial courts of appeal may overrule rules articulated by courts inferior to them in their own jurisdictions and even their own precedents, most of the time, the precedents which count are those articulated by the Supreme Court.

Even however when that is not the case — as, for instance, when the applicable precedents are those of a sister or superior court from another jurisdiction and have in consequence persuasive force only — courts are generally reluctant to overrule. Courts, at all levels, exhibit the same disinclination with respect to their own precedents. This hesitation is systemic and is a consequence of a second constraint which serves as well very much to preserve the doctrine of precedent.

We have found that, where they have the authority, courts will overrule an existing rule when such a rule is either socially incongruent or doctrinally contradictory. Which is to say, courts will overrule *only* when introducing a new rule will *improve* the law by curing the incongruities or contradictions demonstratively associated with the old rule. This was clearly the case in both *R. v. R.*[56] and in *Donoghue*[57]: excising the old rule and introducing a new rule improved the law by, respectively, making it more congruent and more consistent.

CONSEQUENCES

Sometimes judges and lawyers argue that the application of a rule, and especially a decision to amend a rule by analogy or distinguishing, properly turns on

---

[53] *Ibid.*
[54] *Ibid.*
[55] *Ibid.*, at 619 (*per* Lord Macmillan).
[56] *Supra*, note 47.
[57] *Supra*, note 43.

the consequences which would follow upon deciding the matter one way or another. For instance, in *Donoghue*, Lord Macmillan offered the following consequentialist argument in support of overruling the "precedent" rule and replacing it with the "proximity" rule:

> Suppose that a baker, through carelessness, allows a large quantity of arsenic to be mixed with a batch of his bread, with the result that those who subsequently eat it are poisoned, could he be heard to say that he owed no duty to the consumers of his bread to take care that it was free from poison, and that, as he did not know that any poison had got into it, his only liability was for breach of warranty under his contract of sale to those who actually bought the poisoned bread from him? [...] Yet the principle of the decision appealed from is that the manufacturer of food products intended by him for human consumption does not owe to the consumers whom he has in view any duty of care, not even the duty to take care that he does not poison them.[58]

Arguments of this sort — lawyers refer to them as "slippery slope" arguments — sound naturally in law since law deals with problems case by case and it therefore makes abundant sense to test present decisions against hypothetical future decisions. But we have to be careful in how we frame the authority of arguments of this sort. Unless we pay attention to their credentials as specifically *legal* arguments, there is a danger that consequentialist arguments may degrade into general sociological speculation, and our law cannot be premised upon the contingencies of armchair sociology.

Slippery slope arguments have the following form: if we allow A, B will necessarily or very likely follow; B is unacceptable; therefore, we must not allow A either. The status of a slippery slope argument as a legal argument depends upon the grounds of that acceptability. It should not surprise that coherence and consistency provide the peculiarly legal grounds on which the force of slippery slope arguments depend. To qualify as a legal argument, the hypothetical must address, not general factual consequences, but factual consequences which have to do with whether the supposed ruling will fit into the legal system and whether it is consistent with established rules. The first matter is more general and concerns coherence with background justifications either of bodies of rules or of the law as a whole; the second matter is much more strict and concerns the possibility of contradiction with the formal structure and requirements of extant rules.

There is another argument which judges especially sometimes invoke, the so-called "floodgates" argument, which has the form of a slippery slope argument but which, as usually intended, does not qualify as a legal argument at all. According to this argument, the application of a rule may properly depend upon whether the decision would lead to a "flood" of litigation. Now, whether this consequence is legally significant, turns on why the "flood" would occur. If the reason is legal uncertainty, then a floodgates hypothetical may have force, and

---

[58]   *Ibid.*, at 620-21.

especially so where the uncertainty is itself a result of incongruence or inconsistency. Often the floodgates argument is directed not to legal uncertainty but to
judicial administration. Under this view of the matter, it is a good argument
against a decision at law that the flood of litigation which it would cause would
overburden the courts. But, since it goes neither to congruence nor to consistency, this is no argument at all and would, were it ever accepted, introduce into
our law a pervasive and entirely unmanageable uncertainty.

POLICY

In *C.N.R. v. Norsk Pacific S.S. Co.*[59] — a case which deals with liability in negligence for pure economic loss — McLachlin J. (as she then was), for a majority
of the Supreme Court, held that "The question is not only one of legal doctrine,
but of where, from the point of view of individual fairness and economic policy,
the loss should ultimately fall".[60] By in this fashion segregating doctrine from
policy, Her Ladyship was contributing to a long line of cases which give cre-
dence to the view, popular among a great many law students and not a few lawyers, that decisions at law may be compelled either by legal rules or by
something called "policy". This is a profoundly mistaken view. Though "policy", properly conceived, is indeed sometimes at play in the application and
amendment of legal rules, in order for a judicial decision to qualify as a legal
decision, and not just as an exercise of power by a judge, any policy which informs it must itself be a distinctively *legal* policy.

In *Fender v. Mildmay*,[61] Lord Wright held that the term "public policy" may
only be used in a legal sense, that in that sense public policies are legal principles, and that only as legal principle does public policy justly ground a legal
decision.[62] Public policy, in consequence, like the rest of the law, "is governed
by the use of judicial precedents" and, in no event, does it visit upon a judge
(and much less a lawyer) "peculiar powers" to act "upon his individual views or
predilection".[63]

Now, this should sound familiar. In Chapter 3, we discussed how, in constructing the rules of law, the legal community proceeds from the view that the
law is a body of rules which, individually and as a whole, instantiate *legal* principles about what is right and not *social* or *economic* policies about what is best
overall. And in the present chapter, we have associated these principles with the
background justifications, not merely of individual rules, but of different bodies
of rules and of the law as a whole. The principles of which Lord Wright speaks
are background justifications in just these senses. And, if in law we ever speak

---

[59] (1992), 91 D.L.R. 289, [1992] 1 S.C.R. 1021.
[60] *Ibid.*, at 360.
[61] [1938] A.C. 1, 33 T.R. 885.
[62] *Ibid.*, at 38-40.
[63] *Ibid.*, at 39, 40.

of policy — and because the word is in standard usage, we will — it must be those senses which we have in mind. Any other sense of policy, and in particular any usage which would confuse legal principle with economic or social or any other sort of policy, is *not* a legal sense;[64] and any argument which departs from such an understanding is *not* a legal argument. Were we ever to conceive of policy in those ways, we consign our law, and the rules which govern our lives and our affairs, to "the idiosyncratic inferences of a few judicial minds".[65] If, on the other hand, we discipline policy by confining it to principle, then the matter becomes just another instance of how lawyers do lawyerly things with the tri-partite structure of legal rules and with their background justifications in par-ticular.

D. LAW AS CRAFT

In denying King James authority to interpret the law, Sir Edward Coke cau-tioned His Majesty that "law is an art which requires long study and experience, before that a man can attain to the cognizance of it".[66] Perhaps we can see, on basis of our explorations so far, that he was right. The distinctively legal activi-ties of identifying, interpreting and applying the rules of law, we have discov-ered, are not themselves rule-bound activities, but are instead enterprises defined, permitted, and constrained by the traditions of the legal community. We have also discovered that those traditions together comprise a culture, charac-teristic of societies such as ours, whose purpose it is to craft, not all at once but over the time of generations, the rules which guide and govern our lives. But though we have also encountered some of the elements of that craft, we have not addressed its nature directly or in a systematic way. This is what we must do now.

Not much is to be gained for our purposes by delaying over the concept of craft. Anthony Kroman, for instance, uses "the concept of craft" as it applies to law as imparting "the idea that law is a craft demanding a cultivated subtlety of judgment whose possession constitutes a valuable trait of character, as distinct from mere technical skill, and which therefore justifies the special sort of pride

---

[64] That loses should be "shifted" according to the size of the "pockets" of the parties is a particu-larly pernicious version of argument from economic policy which is often encountered by first-year law students. See, for example, Lord Denning's decision in *Spartan Steel & Alloys Ltd. v. Martin & Co. (Contractors) Ltd.*, [1972] 3 All E.R. 567. For a judgment which soundly (and properly) rejects such judicial legislation, see Stephen J. in *Caltex Oil v. The Willemstad* (1976), 136 C.L.R. 529 at 580-81. For a forceful theoretical rejection of economic redistribution as a ground for judicial decision, see E. Weinrib, "Legal Formalism: On the Immanent Rationality of Law" (1988), 96 Yale L.J. 509.

[65] *Fender, supra*, note 61, at 12 (*per* Lord Atkin).

[66] *Prohibitions del Roy* (1608), 12 Co. Rep. 63b-65.

that the possession of such a trait affords".[67] Yet, though he is right in this, his formulation is too grand for present purposes. On the other hand, and though it includes a number of matters to which we will come, Mary Ann Glendon's view of the craft values which are the mark of lawyerly excellence — the trained eye for the issue, the feel for common ground, the eye to the future, mastery of the apparatus of the law, a sense of legal architecture, an appreciation of procedure, inherited experience in problem solving, "strong" toleration and a commitment to incremental change — is not grand enough, not at least in terms of synthesis and organization.[68] If we need a concept as premise for the description which follows, then let's do with this: as applied to law, craft consists of those "habits of legality" which characterize lawyers as such.[69] This notion has the virtue of distinguishing the core which is properly characteristic of all lawyers from the special craft excellences associated with each of the law's sub-practices.[70] It also accords with the idea of law as community and culture from which we have been proceeding since communities and cultures are defined and sustained by the habits of their members.

Being a lawyer is not so much a matter of "thinking like a lawyer" as it is a matter of doing those things which lawyers do. To be a lawyer is to participate in a way of life and to be competent in its ways of proceeding, its patterns and constraints, and committed to its ideals. Viewed from this vantage, legal education is a process of initiating newcomers into the habits of the legal community.

There is no one single essence to the lawyerly craft. Rather, our craft is a complex of competencies which relate to one another in a coherent whole. Gaining a sense of this whole — what Karl Llewellyn termed more poetically a "vision of the Whole"[71] — therefore depends on one's having a good sense of the particulars, including especially the order of their relation, which comprise the whole. Those parts, in order of dependency, are these: *mastery of legal rules*; *mastery of legal forensics*; *legal sensibility* and *legal consciousness. Wherever lawyers are placed in law's community, their status as lawyers minimally depends on their competency in each and every of these elements of lawyerly craft.*

---

[67] A.T. Kronman, *The Lost Lawyer: Failing Ideals of the Legal Profession* (Cambridge, MA: Harvard University Press, 1993), at p. 295.

[68] M.A. Glendon, *A Nation Under Lawyers* (Cambridge, MA: Harvard University Press, 1994), at pp. 102-107.

[69] I borrow this wonderful term of phrase from Francis Allen. See: F.A. Allen, *The Habits of Legality: Criminal Justice and the Rule of Law* (New York: Oxford University Press, 1996).

[70] Consequently, the description of lawyerly craft which follows will not touch on the craft competencies associated with private practice (for instance, counselling and interviewing, and trial and appellate advocacy), with judging (for instance, practical wisdom), or with the academic branch (for instance, the craft of teaching and scholarship).

[71] "The Crafts of Law Re-Valued" in K.N. Llewellyn, *Jurisprudence: Realism in Theory and Practice* (Chicago: University of Chicago Press, 1962), pp. 316 at 322.

(i)   Legal Forensics

We have dwelt at length in this chapter on the second competency, and we need now only emphasize what should be obvious: that speaking as a lawyer requires knowledge of, and literacy in, the six traditions of legal argumentation. Though achievement and excellence in these forms of communal speech is a matter of judgment and discernment which time and experience only can muster, the process of becoming a lawyer can only begin with the adoption and use of these forms and patterns of lawyerly speech.

(ii)   Legal Knowledge

"Knowledge of the law" is "the precondition of our work".[72] So says Karl Llewellyn, and he is right. Literacy in the rules of law is, as lawyers are apt to put it, the *sine qua non* of being a lawyer. Otherwise, the remaining elements of our craft are not merely besides the point, they are also beyond reach since in law the craft appears and is accessible only in the particulars of the rules of which it is comprised. But what must lawyers know about those rules?

Lawyers must know the architecture of the law. In order to advise clients, in order to adjudicate claims, in order to teach others the law and to write about the law, in order to do any of these lawyerly tasks, lawyers must be seized of a sense of the structure which lies behind legal rules and which those rules express. Otherwise, "the torrent of laws, regulations, and decisions spilling out from legislatures, courts, administrative agencies, and private associations" — "the never-ending legal construction" which characterizes our law — must remain nothing more than "a regulatory deluge", at once unmanageable and incomprehensible.[73]

A sense of the law's architecture begins with the elemental divide between public and private law. Public law — the law of crimes, constitutional law, and administrative law, especially — governs the relationship between the state and citizens. Private law — say, the law of contracts, torts and property — governs the relations between persons.

Understanding this architecture requires understanding its point. This includes not only the point and purposes of public and private law as such, but the point and purposes as well of the bodies of law of which each is composed and of the foundational rules and principles of each of those bodies. Lawyers know the law just to the extent that they can, with competence and confidence, answer to these matters. That they may do so *only* by reading the law, by briefing, formally or in mind, the cases in which rules are forged, brings a certain elegant symmetry to the task. On the one hand, because of law's fluidity, no lawyer may ever know, nor need know, every rule of law. On the other hand, knowing what lawyers must know can only be gained by attending to the particulars of

---

[72]   *Ibid.*, at p. 318.
[73]   Glendon, *supra*, note 68, at p. 104.

individual rules as they are expressed and amended in the literature of the law. There is in law no epiphany, no point at which "the path of law"[74] becomes somehow clear. Clarity, rather, resides in the particulars of legal craft and attendance to those particulars may alone produce the sense of structure overall on which legal knowledge finally depends.

(iii) Legal Sensibility

It is not accidental that lawyers are indeed the nitpickers so many accuse them to be. That trait, which most condemn in all lawyers save their own, has rather to do with three features of our law which together elevate what may appear as an annoying affectation of lawyers to a central competency of their craft.

We have just seen that lawyers experience the legal world, including even its generalities, through the prism of particular rules and particular cases. Thinking on a large scale, in and about abstractions, is not the lawyer's way. Lawyers think, and they must think, on a small scale because the particular always rules their world. Theirs remember is a world of cases, of specific clients and parties with specific stories of complaint and defence, of concrete, individual, lived realities. And their passion must therefore reside in those particulars, in that face-to-face stuff of the world, and not in any view of what any of it might mean according to some ideological or theoretical abstraction.

So one reason lawyers are nitpicky is their orientation to the world. But matters do not end there. Remember that their work consists of translating social reality into legal norms using the lexicon of legal rules. Rules themselves are a sticky business. The facts of the case must meet the conditions expressed in a rule's factual predicate. Since everything in law turns on that, on whether the facts satisfy or fail to satisfy the conditions which trigger the law at issue, lawyers are by nature and of necessity sticklers about the facts.

There is another reason. Some rules of law are procedural. They prescribe conditions which claims must satisfy in order either to become claims at law at all or to be expressed and determined at law. These rules of evidence and procedure aim to minimize arbitrariness and to create order and, in so doing, in a more general way to permit people to live their lives with some sense of security. Rules of this sort are every bit as important as the rules of substantive law, indeed oftentimes more so. They "pervade the lawyer's world", and "love of procedure makes the most diverse members of the legal profession cousins, if not siblings, under the skin".[75] They also make lawyers, individually and as a whole, sticklers on procedural correctness.

This orientation towards and commitment to the individual case, this rigour in the analysis of the facts, and this insistence on procedural correctness together comprise the craft competence which we have here termed "legal sensibility".

---

[74] I borrow here from Holmes, *supra*, note 46.
[75] Glendon, *supra*, note 68, at p. 105.

For want of a better overall description of it, we have said that lawyers are nit-pickers. But the matter goes deeper than that. Lawyers are nitpickers because they are suspicious about human nature and about the general course of human affairs.

Suspicion attends the very need for rules. Were human experience different from what it has been, then neither rules nor the traits they require of lawyers would be necessary for the conduct of human affairs. But human history is what it is and rules and lawyers are its fellow travellers. If these insights into the human situation make lawyers, as Glendon claims,[76] strongly tolerant, it does so at the risk of pessimism, which good lawyers aim to avoid.

Bad lawyers, and one includes here, bad law students, are of course another matter. One way of being a bad lawyer (and law student) is by failing to nurture in oneself the sensibility which our law requires of its practitioners. One can fail the lawyer's craft in this way either by turning away from the particulars of individual lives and cases and towards the comforting fuzziness of abstraction or more simply by lacking the courage to insist on correctness.

(iv) Legal Consciousness

Law requires of its participants — of lawyers, judges, law professors and law students — that they view "the law as a set of rules with legitimacy and moral authority".[77] This requirement is not at all incidental to the lawyer's craft nor is it in any fashion subordinate to its other elements. The internal point of view is, rather, indispensable.

The internal point of view requires that law's participants be possessed individually, and that they share corporately, a certain, specifically *legal* consciousness. This consciousness is a consciousness of the point of the law a whole, and it is fundamental to legal craft because without it, the other requirements become impossible to perform.

To understand the point of a practice is to understand the *background agreement* which permits the practice, as a pattern of behaviours and expectations, to take place. So conceived, the point of a practice is not merely its *raison d'être*, some purpose or end which it serves, but is instead its genesis and its constitution. And if one is a practitioner in a practice, and not just an external observer, understanding a practice's point means accepting and affirming its point as authoritative and participating in the ongoing constitution of the practice. But none of this tells us how participants go about gathering what the point of a practice is.

Practitioners typically take advantage of *articulated versions of the point of their practice* which are supplied to them by senior practitioners. For instance, in

---

[76] *Ibid.*, at p. 106.
[77] D.E. Litowitz, "Internal and external Perspectives on Law" (1998), 26 Florida State U. L. Rev. 127 at p. 128.

law, serious practitioners read the great books of their tradition and keep abreast of leading contemporary articulations which just might someday become great books. But recourse of this kind cannot satisfy the practitioner. Though they will refer to the articulations of other practitioners, those articulations will serve only as a guide to their practice and it will be in their practice itself that the point of law will reveal itself to them. And it will do so incrementally and in its particulars, the particulars of specific rules.

Again then we find the particular and a correspondence and interdependence between the concrete and the general. Lawyers learn the point of their practice by being lawyers and doing the things which lawyers do. Articulating the meaning of individual cases and rules leads them to identify the contours of bodies of law and to seek their background justifications. And this endeavour in turn leads them to articulate the connections between these bodies of rules and their significance as a whole. The point of law resides not just in that final articulation but in the process which leads to it. Lawyers understand the point of being a lawyer by being lawyers.

The craft of lawyering, then, consists of reading and applying legal rules with a certain sensibility and with an affirmative understanding of the point of doing so. None of these requirements can be segregated, and none of them is incidental. They exist rather as a coherent and interdependent whole. And together not only do they make it possible for lawyers to do, with competence and commitment, the things which lawyers do, they require them to do those things in a "grand manner", a manner which accounts for and finds the purpose of the whole in the particulars of the parts.[78]

E. RESTATEMENT NO. 2

There exists no distinctive form of legal reasoning. But that does *not* mean that there is no distinctive form of legal practice or that decisions at law are not decisions according to law. Legal practice *is* distinct from moral and political deliberation more generally because it is governed by the craft traditions of the legal community. And legal decisions are lawful despite their being always legally contestable.

Legal knowledge is moral knowledge. This is so, we have found, for two reasons. Legal rules and legal principles *are* moral categories. They establish relations of right as between persons and between citizens and the state. Lawyers have, as a matter of both their *status* and their *craft*, morally to acknowledge and affirm those relations. "It follows that legal expertise and moral understanding and sensitivity are thoroughly intermeshed".[79] But there remains a fundamental

---

[78] I borrow this turn of phrase from Llewellyn. See: K. Llewellyn, *The Common Law Tradition* (Boston: Little Brown, 1960), at p. 4.

[79] A. Altman, *Arguing About Law* (New York: Wadsworth Publishing, 1996), at p. 31.

difference between "what ought to be done according to law and what ought to be done all things considered".[80] This is so because the moral knowledge which is the law is the knowledge of the legal community and because the legal community's knowledge is a knowledge received from, and bound to, the past.

Law is open textured. This is so, not because it is vague, but because it has always to contend with the diverse facts of human life. Decisions at law are not compelled, nor may they be justified (or understood), by the standards of scientific or logical certainty. Yet "law's work" is "lawfulness":[81] rules and principles do rule over facts. Decisions concerning the identity, application and meaning of law are decisions according to law because they are confined and constrained by tradition, by "the gravitational force"[82] of past decisions about which rules and principles ought govern our lives and by the conventions and commitments which comprise the craft of law. The rules of law are *not*, then, rules of thumb which merely recommend: rather, they *bind* us because we are *pledged* to them.

But law remains still porous. The lawyer's craft keeps law's past vulnerable to the facts of the present through its persistent *criticism* of those rules and principles. Lawyers may criticize the past, not only because, in the final analysis, what rules is "not the letter of particular precedents", but their "spirit",[83] but also because sometimes the past is mistaken. However, the outcome of this enduring contest between past and present is not "innovation", and still less revolution, but "renovation".[84] It falls to lawyers, that is, to negotiate a path between our past and present lives under law: neither their training nor their craft visits on them the authority — not to mention the ability — to announce a new and better way of life.

A life at law is, therefore, a life whose aspirations are cabined by the past. This does not diminish the value of such a life or of the craft which sustains it. Indeed, its value, as Llewellyn appears to have thought,[85] just might reside in that marginality to larger questions concerning what is best and proper overall. But whatever is the case in that regard, it is overwhelmingly important that those who are new to law's community recognize and acknowledge, not just the promise, but the limits of the life which they propose to live.

---

[80] *Ibid.*, at p. 317.

[81] C.L. Black, Jr., *Decision According to Law* (New York: W.W. Norton & Co., 1981), at p. 31.

[82] R. Dworkin, *Taking Rights Seriously* (Cambridge, MA: Harvard University Press, 1977), at p. 113.

[83] *Fisher v. Prince* (1762), 3 Burr. 1363 at 1364 (*per* Lord Mansfield).

[84] The opposition between renovation and innovation is longstanding among lawyers. See: *Calvin's Case* (1608), 7 Co. Rep. 1a at 27a.

[85] Many years ago Llewellyn beautifully captured the irony of law being at once critical and marginal: "Law means so pitifully little to life. Life is so terrifyingly dependent on law". See: K.N. Llewellyn, "What Price Contract? — An Essay in Perspective" (1931), 40 Yale L.J. 704 at p. 751.

FURTHER READINGS TO CHAPTER 4

1.   Legal Argument

Aldisert, R.J. *Logic for Lawyers.* 3rd ed. South Bend, IO: National Institute for Trial Advocacy, 1997.

Alexy, R. *A Theory of Legal Argumentation.* trans. Adler, R. and N. MacCormick. Oxford: Clarendon Press, 1989.

Ashley, K.D. *Modelling Legal Argument.* Cambridge, MA: Massachusetts Institute of Technology Press, 1990.

Atiyah, P.S., and R.S. Summers. *Form and Substance in Anglo-American Law: A Comparative Study of Legal Reasoning, Legal Theory, and Legal Institutions.* Oxford: Clarendon Press, 1987.

Barak, A. *Judicial Discretion.* trans. Kaufmann, Y. New Haven, CT: Yale University Press, 1989.

Bell, J. *Policy Arguments in Judicial Decisions.* Oxford: Clarendon Press, 1983.

Brewer, S. "Exemplary Reasoning: Semantics, Pragmatics, and the Rational Force of Legal Argument by Analogy". (1996), 109 Harvard L. Rev. 923.

———. ed. *The Philosophy of Legal Reasoning.* 5 vol. New York: Garland, 1998.

Burgess, J.A. "The Great Slippery Slope Argument". (1993), 19 *J. of Medical Ethics* 169.

Burton, S.J. *An Introduction to Law and Legal Reasoning.* Boston: Little, Brown & Co., 1985.

Carter, L.H. *Reason in Law.* 5th ed. New York: Longman, 1998.

Farrar, J.H., and A.M. Dugdale. *Introduction to Legal Method.* London: Sweet & Maxwell, 1984.

Feteris, E.T. *Fundamentals of Legal Argumentation.* Dordrecht: Kluwer Academic Publishers, 1999.

Golding, M.P. *Legal Reasoning.* New York: A.A. Knopf, 1984.

Goodrich, P. *Reading the Law: A Critical Introduction to Legal Method and Techniques.* Oxford: Blackwell, 1986.

Hage, J.C. *Reasoning With Rules.* Dordrecht: Kluwer Academic Publishers, 1997.

Helman, D., ed. *Analogical Reasoning.* Dordrecht: Kluwer Academic Publishers, 1988.

Hohfeld, W.N. *Fundamental Legal Conceptions as Applied in Judicial Reasoning.* New Haven, CT: Yale University Press, 1946.

Holland, J.A., and J.S. Webb. *Learning Legal Rules.* 3rd ed. London: Blackstone Press, 1996.

Horovitz, J. *Law and Logic: A Critical Account of Legal Argument.* New York: Springer-Verlag, 1972.

Hunter, D. "No Wilderness of Single Instances: Inductive Inference in Law". (1998), 48 J. of Legal Education 365.

Knight, W.S.M. "Public Policy in English Law". (1922), 38 Law Q. Rev. 207.

Lee, S., and M. Fox. *Learning Legal Skills.* 2nd ed. London: Blackstone, 1994.

Levi, E.H. *An Introduction to Legal Reasoning.* Chicago: University of Chicago Press, 1949.

Lundquist, W.L. *The Art of Shaping the Case.* Little Falls, NJ: Glasser Legal Works, 1999.

MacCormick, N. *Legal Reasoning and Legal Theory.* Oxford: Clarendon Press, 1978.

Morris, C. *How Lawyers Think.* Cambridge, MA: Harvard University Press, 1937.

Nagel, S.S. *Evaluative and Explanatory Reasoning.* Westport: Quorum Books, 1992.

Perry, S.R. "Two Models of Legal Principles". [1997] Iowa L. Rev. 787.

Raz, J. "On the Autonomy of Legal Reasoning". in Raz, J. *Ethics in the Public Domain.* Oxford: Clarendon Press, 1994. At p. 310.

Read, W. *Legal Thinking.* Philadelphia: University Pennsylvania Press, 1986.

Samuel, G.J. *The Foundations of Legal Reasoning.* Antwerp: Maklu, 1994.

Samuelson, D.R. "Introducing Legal Reasoning". (1997), 47 J. of Legal Education 571.

Saunders, K.W. "What Logic Can and Cannot Tell Us About Law". (1998), 73 Notre Dame L. Rev. 667.

Schauer, F. *Playing by the Rules.* Oxford: Clarendon Press, 1991. Ch. 8 "Rules and Law".

———."Slippery Slopes". (1985), 99 Harvard L. Rev. 361.

Schlag, P., and D. Skover. *Tactics of Legal Reasoning.* Durham, NC: Carolina Academic Press, 1986.

Sunstein, C.R. *Legal Reasoning and Political Conflict.* New York: Oxford University Press, 1996.

———."On Analogical Reasoning". (1993), 106 Harvard L. Rev. 741.

van der Burg, W. "The Slippery Slope Argument". (1991), 102 Ethics 42.

Vandevelde, K.J. *Thinking Like a Lawyer: An Introduction to Legal Reasoning.* Boulder, CO: Westview, 1996.

Wasserstrom, R.A. *The Judicial Decision.* Stanford, CA: Stanford University Press, 1961.

Winfield, P.H. "Public Policy in English Common Law". (1928), 42 Harvard L. Rev. 76.

2.   Legal Craft

Black, C.L., Jr. *Decision According to Law.* New York: W.W. Norton & Co., 1981.

Davis, J.P. "Cardozo's Judicial Craft and What Cases Come To Mean". (1993), 68 N.Y.U. L. Rev. 777.

Elkins, J.R. "Ethics: Professionalism, Craft, and Failure". (1984-1985), 73 Kentucky L.J. 937.

Field, M., ed. *Famous Legal Arguments.* Rochester: E.J. Bosworth & Co., 1897. Reprinted as Volume 6 of *Classics in Legal History.* New York: W.S. Hein & Co., 1970.

Fish, S. "Dennis Martinez and the Uses of Theory". (1987), 96 Yale L.J. 1773.

Flemming, R.B., *et al. The Craft of Justice: Politics and Work in Criminal Court Communities.* Philadelphia: University of Pennsylvania Press, 1992.

Gerwin, L.E., and P.M. Shupack. "Karl Llewellyn's Legal Method Course: Elements of Law and Its Teaching Materials". (1983), 33 J. of Legal Education 64.

Granfield, R. *Making Elite Lawyers: Visions of Law at Harvard and Beyond.* New York: Routledge, 1992. Chs. 4 and 5.

Gregg, B. "Using Legal Rules In An Indeterminate World: Overcoming the Limitations of Jurisprudence". (1999), 27(3) Political Theory 357.

Kelley, B.W. *Famous Advocates and Their Speeches.* London: Sweet & Maxwell, 1921.

Lieberman, J.K. "The Art of the Fact". [1999] J. of the Legal Writing Institute 25.

Llewellyn, K.N. "The Crafts of Law Re-Valued". in Llewellyn, K.N. *Jurisprudence: Realism in Theory and Practice.* Chicago: University of Chicago Press, 1962. At p. 316.

———. "The Normative, the Legal, and the Law Jobs". (1940), 49 Yale L.J. 1355.

———. "Appellate Judging as a Craft of Law" and "Mansfield's Methods, Reason into Sand, and Reason Resurgent". In Llewellyn, K.N. *The Common Law Tradition.* Boston: Little Brown, 1960. At pp. 213, 404.

Martineau, R.J. "Craft and Technique, Not Canons and Grand Theories: A Neo-Realist View of Statutory Construction". (1993), 62 George Washington L. Rev. 1.

Maughan, C., and J. Webb, *Lawyering Skills and the Legal Process.* London: Butterworths, 1995.

Mentschikoff, S., and I.P. Stotzky. *The Theory and Craft of American Law — Elements.* New York: Mathew Bender, 1981.

Nathanson, S. *What Lawyers Do.* London: Sweet & Maxwell, 1997.

Nivala, J. "From Bauhaus to Courthouse: An Essay on Educating for Practice of the Craft". (1989), 19 New Mexico L. Rev. 237.

Nussbaum, M.C. *Poetic Justice: The Literary Imagination and Public Life.* Boston: Beacon Press, 1995.

Teachout, P.R. "The Heart of the Lawyer's Craft". (1985), 42 Washington & Lee L. Rev. 39.

Veeder, V.V., ed. *Legal Masterpieces: Specimens of Argumentation and Expositio by Eminent Lawyers.* 2 Vol. St. Paul: Keefe-Davidson Co., 1903. Reprinted as Volumes 24 and 25 of *Classics in Legal History.* New York: Wm. S. Hein & Co., 1974.

Chapter 5

The Law Question

Law is something more than mere will exerted as an act of power. ... Arbitrary power, enforcing its edits to the injury of the persons and property of its subjects, is not law ... .

Matthews J.
Hurtado v. California, 110 U.S. 516 at 535-36 (1884)

In the matters which count most to its constitution, perpetuation and practices, the society of lawyers is subject to no regulation save its own. We have seen that the legal community uses this wide-ranging and monopolistic institutional power to impose its understanding of law on others who are not themselves members of the legal community. In so doing, it subordinates and marginalizes other views of the proper terms and conditions of communal life and takes upon itself the normative construction of society. In defining and in imposing "the general framework within which social life takes place",[1] lawyers and judges, we must now add, become *rulers*.

The enduring question of law — *the law question* — is whether this *rule by lawyers* is justifiable and, if so, how. From one perspective, this is a question about the authority of law. Is law reducible to power plain and simple? Is it a mere form in which the powerful with the connivance of the legal community dress, secure and legitimize their extra-legal victories? Is law, in that sense, an empty vessel into which are poured the products and preferences of power? Or is law, instead, seized of a moral sense and sensibility of its own, an understanding which is immanent to its institutions and practices as such? So viewed, the question is whether law is authoritative or merely authoritarian.

From another, perhaps deeper, perspective, the law question is a question about the relationship between law and life. What is and what ought to be law's contribution to social and individual life? And, just as importantly, what properly are the limits of law's contribution to the construction of the terms and conditions of human association?

To answer the "law question" is to engage both of these matters. Any answer which confines itself to one or another of them is not an answer which warrants serious consideration. Rather, views of the authority of law and of the legal

---

[1]   J. Raz, *The Authority of Law* (Oxford: Clarendon Press, 1979), at p. 120.

community must themselves be part of an overall view of the law's contribution to social life. Otherwise, a part might be mistaken for the whole.

Now, we have seen that, from the internal point of view, the authority of the legal community is a matter of convention. The identification, interpretation and application of legal rules involves not rule-following, but the observance of certain traditions. In constructing the rules of law, lawyers and judges depend upon, and claim to be constrained and justified by, the traditions which together constitute their craft. But the answer to the law question cannot consist merely of this description of lawyerly self-understanding. Convention, after all, might be casuistry or self-delusion. More is required.

The wider question of authority addresses what might be termed the issue of "public reason", namely, whether there exists a vocabulary of institutional practice and validity which does not reduce merely to power or to personal perspective and preference. Answering that question minimally requires the identification of *the grounds of validity* and *the conditions of their satisfaction*. Answering to the matter of law's contribution and limits requires *a theory of the state* since law is a state-sponsored enterprise. These two matters are intimately related. Views concerning the authority of law are part and parcel of a fuller view of the proper conduct of political affairs.

So far as law is concerned, legitimacy has been sought in two places: in the authority of certainty and in the authority of context.[2] According to the first view, the authority of judges and lawyers resides in their special knowledge of the law. Their construction of society, and their subordination of other views, is therefore justified because in both matters they are acting on, and in service to, legal truth. But we have seen that this view of legal practice cannot be sustained. Lawyers do not discover the law, they construct it. In consequence, their practices cannot be justified as a certitude compelled by expert knowledge.

According to the second view, legitimacy resides in the shared social practices and understandings of the legal community. This view depends upon the understanding that law, like most other human endeavours, is an interpretive process and that law, like the rest, is therefore necessarily communal. That community "is not just a set of ideas ... : it represents actual institutional practices, anchored in and produced by educational systems ... . Interpretation occurs within [the] community and depends on a circular process of seeking to understand [the] whole in terms of its parts, and the parts in their contribution to the whole".[3] Now, this view should sound familiar. In Chapter 3, we conceived of legal practice in just these terms and in Chapters 3 and 4, we identified the traditions of interpretation and of argument which comprise the lawyerly craft of constructing the rules of law. But, in that event, have we not simply remitted the

---

[2] For a full exploration of these, see S.J. Burton, *An Introduction to Law and Legal Reasoning* (Boston: Little Brown & Co., 1985), at chs. 9 and 10.

[3] M. Minow, "Partial Justice: Law and Minorities" in A. Sarat and T.R. Kearns, eds., *The Fate of Law* (Ann Arbour: University of Michigan Press, 1991), pp. 15 at 40.

matter of legitimacy to our description of lawyerly craft which we have admitted might itself be a matter of false or even bad consciousness.

Were we to leave the matter there, that indeed would be the unhappy, and unnecessary, result. It would be unnecessary because further exploration is both possible and required. Remember that in Chapter 4, we identified legal consciousness as perhaps the most critical element of lawyerly craft. Legal consciousness, we saw, involves the discernment by lawyers of the point of law as a whole and in all of its (major) parts. Now, to discern law's point in those senses, law's practitioners are required to adopt an articulation of law, a theory of law's practices and purposes. Such an articulation will consist of a theory of state or at the very least of its minimal requirements. And it is just this theory which alone may make of our understanding of law as community a standard of justified authority.

But not any theory will do. An articulation which proposes to disclose the point of law will have to *fit* our description of the actual practices of the legal community. Nor only that: as between different views which meet the threshold of fit, the better view is the one which shows our practices in their best light as a coherent and consistent whole.

The remainder of this book will track these requirements. Part II is devoted to an exploration of the Rule of Law as the best articulation of the point of law in societies such as ours. We will find that the legal community's right to rule is grounded on its being itself a requirement of Rule of Law and on the Rule of Law's being a rule of rights. In Part III, we shall explore the conditions which the legal community must satisfy in order to make good this promise of authority.

Our pursuit of these purposes will also uncover some fundamental truths about law and the human situation. We shall find "the discourse of law" to be an "articulated dream" about our lives and affairs both as individuals and as a community.[4] We shall find as well that the culture of law, by its very nature, provides us with ideals and practices which, if the legal community is only faithful to them, keep open our futures by destabilizing our present. And we shall find finally that what lawyers do is essential to the goodness of human government and that absent their fidelity to law, rule by law can easily become the enemy of individuals and of the cause of civilization more generally.

FURTHER READINGS TO CHAPTER 5

Friedrich, C.J. *Tradition and Authority*. New York: Praeger, 1972.

Green, L. *The Authority of the State*. Oxford: Clarendon Press, 1988.

Harris, R.B., ed. *Authority: A Philosophical Analysis*. University, AB: Alabama University Press, 1976.

Hurd, H.M. "Challenging Authority". (1991), 100 Yale L.J. 1611.

---

[4]   G. Steiner, *After Babel*, 2nd ed. (Oxford: Oxford University Press, 1922), at p. xiv.

Pennock J.R., and J.W. Chapman, eds. *Authority Revisited: Nomos XXIX.* New York: New York University Press, 1987.
Raz, J. "Authority and Justification". (1985), 14 Philosophy & Public Affairs 3.
Schmidtz, D. "Justifying the State". (1990), 101 Ethics 89.
White, J.B. *Acts of Hope: Creating Authority in Literature, Law and Politics.* Chicago: University of Chicago Press, 1994.

PART II

EXPLAINING LAW

Chapter 6

A Political Primer

Ethical thought consists of the systematic examination of the relations of human beings to each other, the conceptions, interests and ideals from which human ways of treating one another spring, and the systems of value on which such ends of life are based. These beliefs about how life should be lived, what men and women should be and do, are the objects of moral inquiry; and when applied to groups and nations, and, indeed, to mankind as a whole, are called political philosophy, which is but ethics applied to society.

Isaiah Berlin

A. INTRODUCTION

In the last chapter, we discovered that explaining law involves coming to a view on the proper relationship between law and social life, between legal practice and the burdens and benefits of living in a society such as ours. We also found that such a view must be predicated on some theory of the state since law above all else involves the state. Because theories of the state are the stuff of political philosophy, answering our questions about the relationship between law and life will require that we turn to political philosophy. It is the purpose of this chapter to provide a modest introduction to contemporary political philosophy by examining, and on occasion illustrating, certain terms and distinctions which together comprise its elemental moral vocabulary. Those terms and distinctions are the following: *personal morality* and *political morality* (and the distinctions between the *public* and the *private* realms and between *law* and *politics* which arise from that distinction), *equality, liberty, harm, rights, toleration* and *justice*.

B. PERSONAL AND POLITICAL MORALITY

The distinction between personal and political morality is fundamental to our understanding and explanation of legal practice and the public culture of which it is part just because our law *is* political morality.

Personal morality has as its object what it means to lead a good life. Political morality, on the other hand, concerns itself, not with individual good in that sense, but with the good of political community, and its objects are "the fundamental bases of political life",[1] and not the ends of a human life well lived.[2] Institutions are of course fundamental to a community's political life. It falls to political morality to tell us what those institutions should be, "how [they] should be designed, [and] how people in them should act".[3] Concerning the first two matters, conceptions of political morality have minimally: a) to identify the institutions required for a community's political life; b) to structure the relations between those institutions; c) to set standards for the treatment of members of political community by those institutions and d) to identify when those institutions may regulate the relations between members of political community and in what fashion. The third matter concerns the institutional moralities which those institutions define for, and impose upon, their officers.

In order to satisfy these requirements, a political morality must identify and expound some value (or values) which, in its view, is the proper foundation for the terms and conditions of human association in political community. Political moralities will therefore differ according to the values which they aim to serve and from which they depart. According to most contemporary conceptions, political morality "is concerned primarily with protecting and promoting the well-being of people"[4] and most therefore depart from the value of equality.

But all of this is definition, and none of it adequately captures the crucial differences which obtain between political and personal morality. To get at those differences and to illustrate their significance to the conduct of our law especially, we shall dwell on two cases in which the law's status as political morality is starkly revealed.

(i)   The Primacy of Political Morality

The first case concerns the law's relationship to religious morality. In *R. v. Lewis*,[5] the accused's six-year-old child fell ill with diphtheria. The accused was a member of the Christian Science Church which forbade treating disease by any means other than prayer. Instead of providing the child with medical help, the

---

[1]   S.M. Shumer, "Machiavelli: Republican Politics and Its Corruption" (1979), 7(1) Political Theory, p. 5 at 8.

[2]   This of course raises a question concerning the relationship, if any, between political and personal morality. About which, see S. Hampshire, ed., *Public and Private Morality* (Cambridge: Cambridge University Press, 1978). Happily, with one exception, this perplexing issue is beyond our purposes. The exception, which is discussed in the conclusion of this book, is the relationship between the public morality of law and the private morality of members of the legal community.

[3]   T. Nagel, "Ruthlessness in Public Life" in Hampshire, *ibid.*, p. 75 at 90. Also published in T. Nagel, *Mortal Questions* (Cambridge: Cambridge University Press, 1979), at pp. 75-90.

[4]   J. Raz, *Ethics in the Public Domain* (Oxford: Clarendon Press, 1994), at p. v and *The Morality of Freedom* (Oxford: Clarendon Press, 1986), at pp. 1-6. See also: R. Dworkin, *A Matter of Principle* (Cambridge, MA: Harvard University Press, 1985), at p. 370 ("concern for [their] subjects ... is the most basic requirement which political morality imposes on those who rule".).

[5]   (1903), 7 C.C.C. 261, 6 O.L.R. 132, 23 C.L.T. 257 (Ont. C.A.).

accused sought the assistance of a Christian Science demonstrator who prayed over the child. The child died and the father was subsequently charged with manslaughter for failing in his parental duty to provide the necessaries for life which duty included the provision of medical treatment. At trial, the accused admitted that were he not a Christian Scientist, he would have called in a doctor, but he pleaded that his sincere belief in Christian Science doctrine ought to excuse him from guilt. The jury thought otherwise and convicted him of manslaughter.

The issue on appeal was whether the accused's faith in church doctrine and the innocence of his motivation should constitute lawful excuse for his failure to provide his son with medical help. In rejecting sincere belief in personal morality as an excuse at law, Moss C.J.O. had this to say:

> [W]hile the merits or demerits of the Christian Science or faith are things with which we have nothing to do as long as it does not transgress or lead to a transgression of the law, the law of the land is paramount, and it is not for people to set themselves up in opposition to it; ... the law of the land must be obeyed, and it must be obeyed even though there be something in the shape of belief in the conscience of the person which would lead him to obey what in his state of mind he may consider a higher power or authority.[6]

The conviction was affirmed.

The second case, *Thomas v. Norris*,[7] discloses the relationship between law and the morality of cultural difference and identity. The Coast Salish people, along with the Kwakiutla and the Haida, are the original occupants of the Northwestern Coast of North America. The Salish occupied, and still do, those parts of the Coast now designated as northern Washington state and southern British Columbia. European settlers began arriving in the 1850s and, for a period of 67 years beginning in 1884, the Canadian government banned Salish religious practices. Despite this, the religious and ceremonial life of the Salish has survived into the present.[8]

Spirit Dancing remains the central Salish cultural practice.[9] In Salish tradition, it is through initiation to Spirit Dancing that men and women come to a vision of their place in the world. The initiation is conducted by Salish elders, and involves rites of separation and purification. The initiate is sequestered in the community's Long House for a period of from four to six days, during which time he or she abstains from all sustenance save water, and is attended by several general helpers and a special helper called a "babysitter", who, through various rites, help the initiate come to his or her vision. The vision experience is an encounter with the initiate's guardian spirit, and is signalled by the initiate's

---

[6] *Ibid.*, at 267.
[7] (1992), 2 C.N.L.R. 139 (B.C.S.C.).
[8] W. Suttles, *Coast Salish Essays* (Vancouver: Talon Books, 1987), at p. 203.
[9] *Ibid.*, esp. ch. 10 ("Spirit Dancing and the Persistence of Native Culture Among the Coast Salish").

singing his or her song. Under Salish tradition, people can be initiated to the Spirit Dance either voluntarily or involuntarily. In the latter case, the initiation is by capture, and commences with the rite of "grabbing" in which the initiate is involuntarily taken to the Long House. Grabbing, however, is only undertaken at the behest and with the consent of a member of the initiate's family, often a wife.

In the late afternoon of February 14, 1988, David Thomas, a 35-year-old Salish living off-reserve, was "grabbed" at the request of his common law wife Kim Johnny by seven Spirit Dancers, three of whom were elders, for initiation at the Somenos Long House of the Cowichan Indian Band No. 642, which is located near Duncan, B.C. Kim Johnny requested the grabbing because she hoped Thomas' initiation would help solve problems in their marriage and his excessive drinking. The Dancers, reluctant witnesses one and all, will only say that they agreed to the grabbing because Kim Johnny needed their help and because they "are there to help". They have, however, made it clear that the initiation was involuntary.

Thomas was held in the Long House for four days during which time he underwent traditional rites of purification, attended at all times by the Dancers and his "babysitter". When he began experiencing pain from a stomach ulcer — which he had prior to the initiation and which the Dancers had guarded against by having Kim Johnny deliver his medication to them — the Dancers allowed Thomas to leave the Long House, whereupon he delivered himself to the hospital in Duncan. He never returned to the Long House, and instead commenced civil proceedings for damages against the Spirit Dancers, alleging assault, battery, and false imprisonment. Thomas suffered no physical harm in the initiation save for mild dehydration and some very minor contusions; and he apparently did not sing his song prior to release.

The case was heard in September 1991, and the judge easily concluded that the initiation constituted assault, battery, and false imprisonment. His finding was easy, not only because the defendant Dancers admitted that Thomas was taken and confined against his will, but also because the defenses they raised (that they intended no harm, that they had the consent of his family) were in law beside the point. The matter, in consequence, came to turn on whether the plaintiff's and the defendants' cultural difference, their being Salish, ought to make any difference.

Counsel for the defendants cast the claim in constitutional terms. As put by the judge:

> [T]he defendants say that their right to traditional practices is an Aboriginal right protected by s. 35(1) of the *Constitution Act, 1982* and that accordingly they enjoy a form of civil immunity. In performing the Spirit Dance Tradition they are not bound by the common law, and the plaintiff's civil rights against assault, battery, and false imprisonment are subordinate, and must

give way, to the collective right of the Aboriginal nation to which he belongs, and which is protected by s. 35(1).[10]

Plaintiff's counsel argued that the defendants' rights claim was no good. Again as put by the judge:

> The plaintiff says that ever since English law was proclaimed to be the law on Vancouver Island in the mid-1800's, the defendants have been subject to the common law of the Province like any other citizens; that when participating in any Aboriginal tradition or religious practice, the defendants must abide by the common law, and in this case, the law of assault, battery and false imprisonment.[11]

The judge found that Spirit Dancing was not an existing aboriginal right within the meaning of s. 35(1); and that, even assuming that it was, it was subordinate to the plaintiff's common law rights in tort.[12] He awarded the plaintiff damages in the amount of $12,000.

What interests us is the judge's summation which aptly captures the law's attitude towards collective cultural moralities:

> In summary, making all the necessary assumptions with regard to the Aboriginal right claimed, it is my opinion that the defendants still cannot succeed. Placing the Aboriginal right at its highest level it does not include civil immunity for coercion, force, assault, unlawful confinement, or any other unlawful tortious conduct on the part of the defendants, in forcing the plaintiff to participate in their tradition. While the plaintiff may have special rights and status in Canada as an Indian, the "original" rights and freedoms he enjoys can be no less than enjoyed by fellow citizens, Indian and non-Indian alike. He lives in a free society and his rights are inviolable. He is free to believe in, and to practice, any religion or tradition, if he chooses to do so. He cannot be coerced or forced to participate in one by any group purporting to exercise their collective right in doing so. His freedoms and rights are not "subject to the collective rights of the Aboriginal nation to which he belongs".[13]

That law is a political morality has then great import. As *Thomas* and *Lewis* illustrate, not only is our law therefore distinct from the various versions of the good by which men and women guide their lives: whenever the precepts of such notions conflict with the requirements of our law, law takes precedence over those commandments of personal goodness. The rest of this book is devoted to explaining, and to justifying, this remarkable primacy of the legal. We can begin that task by exploring the distinction between the public and private spheres and the distinction between law and politics.

---

[10] *Supra*, note 7, at 151.
[11] *Ibid.*
[12] *Ibid.*, at 156 and 160 respectively.
[13] *Ibid.*, at 162.

(ii) Public Sphere/Private Sphere

Our law subordinates personal morality by relegating it to the sphere of private choice and, in so doing, it locates itself in a distinctively public sphere. For instance, when in *Thomas*, the judge held that, though the plaintiff was "free to believe in, and to practice, any religion or tradition, if he cho[se] to do so, he [could] not be forced or coerced to participate in one",[14] he was depending upon, and expressing, the distinction between the public and private realms. The public realm is the realm of political morality, of political society, of the state, law and citizenship, and of justice. The private realm, in contrast, is the realm of personal morality, of civil society, of free association, authenticity and personhood, and of moral independence and autonomy from, among other things, political interference. It turns out then that the relationship between political and personal morality, between law and life, is much more complex than it might have first appeared. Our law *does* supercede and subordinate personal morality, but only as regards matters political and, as in *Thomas*, it does so in order to preserve the private realm and to protect the social from the political. But this view of matters raises obvious questions: how then are we to set the boundary between the civil and the political? More particularly, how are we to distinguish between those aspects of our lives which are rightly subject to guidance and control by public institutions and those which must remain subject to our personal choice and preference and beyond the meter of justice?

(iii) Law and Politics

Though law and politics are both undeniably normative undertakings, law is yet distinct because it is constrained in ways and by means unthinkable in, and inappropriate to, politics. Whereas politics consists of "open-ended disputes about the basic terms of social life, disputes that people call ideological, philosophical or visionary", law is defined by "a commitment to, and therefore a belief in the possibility of, a method of legal justification that contrasts with [such] open-ended disputes".[15] How legal disputes differ from political disputes in this fashion becomes then the nub of the distinction. The distinction *cannot* depend on any view which associates the activities of lawyers, and judges especially, with the production of rationally unavoidable solutions to legal disputes. Just the contrary: legal and judicial practice have more to do with constructing than with discovering solutions, and are more a matter of cultural criticism than of some special legal rationality. Nor, put more widely, can the solution reside in any view which would construe lawyers and judges as mere rule-followers and politicians, in their legislative capacity, as rule-makers. We have found that the fact and force of interpretation makes such a tidy view of matters entirely untenable.

---

[14] *Ibid.*
[15] R.M. Unger, *The Critical Legal Studies Movement* (Cambridge, MA: Harvard University Press, 1987), at p. 1.

That lawyers and judges are professionals and not ideologues, that they are members of a distinctively legal community and not advocates of party politics, depends rather on the traditions of their community. Those traditions consist not only in the literary resources which the legal community thinks are alone relevant to legal disputes, but also in the premises and protocols of their interpretation and application. Among those traditions is one which has to do with distinguishing legal disputes from political contests. The so-called *doctrine of justiciability* consists of a body of arguments and case law concerning whether, or not, a matter is properly one for the legal community and for decision in the courts.

Very much turns then on our identifying law as part of the political morality which governs human association in the state. Not only do legal questions become segregated from a host of other political and moral questions, but the very nature of legal questions as such becomes fixed. *Legal questions are questions which concern the identity, conduct, and limits of public institutions.* And though those questions *must* leave aside questions which are in many respects more important to our public and personal lives, it is our law's answers to those legal questions which permits men and women freely to contest and to answer those other questions about their fates. That there exists, in this sense, two sovereignties in human affairs, the one legal and at once primary and limited, and the other non-legal yet more diverse and significant, means we shall find everything to law and life in societies such as ours.

C. EQUALITY

The political morality which governs in societies such as ours is a morality which departs from, and seeks to protect and promote, the *abstract ideal of equality*, that is, the ideal of treating everyone in political community with equal concern and respect. This notion of equality directly answers one of the four questions of political morality which we identified earlier, namely, how the institutions of public life must treat citizens.

(i) Moral Equality

Abstract equality is a moral category. It is therefore not a description of some existing state of affairs and much less an ontology of the human condition. It is rather a prescription, a moral claim about political and legal duties, about what we are owed as persons in political community. That claim is this: that, despite the many differences, individual and collective, which inevitably obtain between us, we are yet equal morally and we therefore deserve to be treated equally. This *moral equality* — this equality beyond and despite difference — is the end value of societies such as ours simply because, for us, persons are "the ultimate units of moral worth".[16]

(ii) Legal Equality

Formal equality is equality beyond difference and it presumes, and constructs, an undifferentiated political and legal subject. Each of us is this entity beyond the chance of difference of race, sex, and so on: so far as law and politics are concerned, we are legal persons and citizens, no more and no less. This *juridical equality* is the foundation of equal treatment because it alone founds and articulates each person's claim to be treated the same as any other person. Legal equality requires that the state treat us, every one of us, in an impartial, non-discriminatory way. Our interests must weigh the same as the interests of any other in governmental policy, and those policies must themselves accord with principles of equality. Each of us has a claim to *equal protection of the law* and to *equal application of the law*. None of us may be excluded from the protection afforded by any law by reason alone of arbitrary difference, and each of us may expect the law to apply to us without regard to any difference we may claim or others may attribute to us. Equal protection of law and equality before the law, in these senses, are the stuff of a lawyerly conception of equality.

What is often called substantive equality may concern either equality of resources or equality of welfare. Resource equality concerns the distribution of society's resources whereas welfare equality would adjust distributions in terms of the desires and preferences which people happen to have. Though the details need not concern us, the best view of distributive equality attaches equality to resources directly and not through the mediation of preferences. What must concern us is this: *in societies such as ours, distributions are a political and not a legal matter.* Though once distributions are made, it falls to lawyers (and to courts) to ensure that those entitlements are available and applied equally, defining those distributions in the first instance falls, not to the legal community, but to the legislatures.

(iii) Fidelity and Infidelity

Before we conclude our discussion of equality, we will turn to a few cases which demonstrate both the legal community's fidelity to, and its occasional abandonment of, the ideal of legal equality.

In *Re Drummond Wren*,[17] a Mr. Wren objected to a restrictive covenant on land he had purchased which required that the land "not be sold to Jews or to persons of objectionable nationality". Notwithstanding that there was no prece-

---

[16] W. Kymlicka, *Contemporary Political Philosophy: An Introduction* (Oxford: Clarendon Press, 1990), at p. 140.

[17] [1945] 4 D.L.R. 674 (Ont. H.C.).

dent on point, Mr. Justice Mackay of the Ontario High Court held that the covenant was offensive to public policy and so void. Relying in part on the *San Francisco Charter*,[18] the predecessor to the U.N. *Universal Declaration of Human Rights*,[19] which affirmed "the dignity and worth of the human person" and "universal respect for, and observance of, human rights and fundamental freedoms for all without distinction as to race, sex, language, or religion", the "policy" His Lordship invoked was nothing less than legal equality. As put by the judge:

> Ontario, and Canada too, may well be termed a Province, and a country, of minorities in regard to the religious and ethnic groups which live therein. It appears to me a moral duty, at least, to lend all aid to the forces of cohesion, and similarly to repel all fissiparous tendencies ... [...] I do not conceive that I would be breaking new ground to hold the restrictive covenant ... to be void as against public policy. Rather I would be applying well-recognized principles .... That the restrictive covenant ... is directed in the first place against Jews lends poignancy to the matter when one considers that anti-Semitism has been a weapon in the hands of our recently-defeated enemy and the scourge of the world. But this feature of the case does not require innovation in legal principles to strike down the covenant; it merely makes it more appropriate to apply existing principles.[20]

Four years later, in *Re Noble and Wolf*,[21] the Ontario Court of Appeal upheld a restrictive covenant which forbade selling summer resort property to "any person of the Jewish, Hebrew, Semitic, Negro or Colored race or blood". The court found that the covenant was imposed merely "in the interest of congenial association for summer residence", that "the public interest [was] in no way involved", and that "the judgment in *Re Drummond Wren* [was] wrong in law and should not be followed".[22]

In its landmark ruling in *Law Society of British Columbia v. Andrews*,[23] the Supreme Court of Canada addressed directly the meaning and requirements of legal equality. In *Andrews*, the plaintiff/respondent, a landed immigrant, challenged the citizenship rule, in the B.C. *Barristers and Solicitors Act*,[24] that required applicants for admission to the B.C. bar to be Canadian citizens. Andrews' case was dismissed at trial, but he succeeded on appeal. The Law Society appealed this ruling to the Supreme Court which affirmed the decision of the B.C. Court of Appeal. Now, it is no matter for our purposes that the court in *Andrews* was considering equality within the context of s. 15(1) of the *Canadian Charter of*

---

[18] *Charter of the United Nations*, 26 June 1945, Can T.S. 1945 No. 7.
[19] G.A. Res. 217 (III), UN GAOR, 3d Sess., Supp. No. 13, UN Doc. A/810 (1948).
[20] *Supra*, note 17 at 679.
[21] [1949] 4 D.L.R. 375 (Ont. C.A.).
[22] *Ibid.*
[23] [1989] 56 D.L.R. (4th) 1 (S.C.C.).
[24] R.S.B.C. 1979, c. 26.

Rights and Freedoms.[25] What we want to disclose is the court's understanding of the requirements of legal equality as such.

It is worthwhile to extract at some length the judgment of Mr. Justice MacIntyre which exhibits a fine understanding of equal protection and equality before the law and of moral equality more generally. As put by His Lordship:

> To approach the ideal of full equality before and under the law ... , the main consideration must be the impact of the law on the individual or the group concerned. Recognizing that there will always be an infinite variety of personal characteristics, capacities, entitlements and merits among those subject to law, there must be accorded, as nearly as may be possible, an equality of benefit and protection and no more of the restrictions, penalties or burdens imposed upon one than another. In other words, the admittedly unattainable ideal should be that a law expressed to bind all should not because of irrelevant personal differences have a more burdensome or less beneficial impact on one than another.[26]

A law which accords protection and benefit on basis of irrelevant personal characteristics is discriminatory and violates legal equality. Again as put by the judge:

> [D]iscrimination may be described as a distinction, whether intentional or not, based upon on grounds relating to personal characteristics of the individual or group, which has the effect of imposing burdens, obligations, or disadvantages on such an individual or group not imposed upon others, or which withholds or limits access to opportunities, benefits, and advantages available to other members of society. Distinctions based on personal characteristics attributed to an individual solely on the basis of association with a group will rarely escape the charge of discrimination, while those based upon an individual's merits and capacities will rarely so be classed.[27]

Our courts have not always been as articulate and faithful as the court in *Andrews* in their stewardship of equality. *Noble and Wolf*[28] is just one instance of infidelity, and it is important that we consider others. Suppose, for instance, that a legislature passes an act which affirms, promotes and protects the moral equality of citizens by constructing a list of prohibitions against discrimination in a number of areas including employment. Suppose that the list prohibits discrimination by reason of "race, religious belief, colour, gender, physical disability, marital status, age, mental disability, ancestry or place of origin". Suppose too that after much legislative discussion, discrimination by reason of sexual orientation is deliberately excluded from the list of prohibitions. Suppose finally that a citizen is fired from his job because he is homosexual and that when he

---

[25] Part I of the *Constitution Act, 1982*, being Schedule B to the *Canada Act 1982* (U.K.), 1982, c. 11.

[26] *Supra*, note 23, at 11.

[27] *Supra*, note 23, at 18.

[28] *Supra,* note 21.

complains to the statutory delegate responsible under the legislation for policing discrimination, he is told that he has no complaint since discrimination on grounds of sexual orientation is not prohibited. This was precisely the case that came before the Alberta Court of Appeal in *Vriend v. Alberta.*[29]

The judgment of McClung J.A., in overturning the Alberta Court of Queen's Bench disposition of the matter in Vriend's favour, is a remarkable departure from the ideal and standards of legal equality. Not only did His Lordship decide that the act neither "dr[e]w distinctions between heterosexuals and homosexuals"[30] nor "invit[ed] or promot[ed] differing social impact, or its expectation, upon homosexuals as opposed to heterosexuals", when he came to characterize the omission, he had this to say:

> I apprehend no constitutional violation flowing from the legislature's disengagement from the issue of "sexual orientation". ... I have reached this conclusion mindful of the objectives of the two schools of legitimate social concern that have forced this case. Alberta's legislative response was not disproportionate. I am unable to conclude that it was a forbidden, let alone a reversible, legislative response for the province of Alberta to step back from the validation of homosexual relations, including sodomy, as a fundamental right, thereby "... rebutting a millennia of moral teaching".[31]

In this, McClung J.A. is displacing legal equality with legal inequality. Rather than standing fast with equality, he is eager instead to assist the legislature in counting difference against a certain group of citizens and in so doing to deny to that group the equal protection and benefit of law.[32]

Infidelity can serve to aggrandize entitlements as well as to diminish them. Such is the result in *R. v. Lavallee,*[33] a famous case to which all first-year law students are now exposed. In *Lavallee,* the accused killed her abusive common law husband and successfully argued that she was defending herself. Prior to *Lavallee,* it was established law that self-defence lay only where the accused reasonably apprehended imminent danger of death or grievous bodily harm from the deceased person, and that it was inherently unreasonable to apprehend death or grievous bodily harm unless or until a physical assault was actually in progress. The rationale for this rule was simple: one will be excused of the most grievous offence at law only where taking another's life was the only alternative — the "last resort" — to having one's own life taken or one's body grievously harmed. The facts in *Lavallee* failed these requirements and this rationale simply because the accused shot the deceased in the back of the head while he was

---

[29] (1996), 181 A.R. 16 (C.A.); revd [1998] 1 S.C.R. 493.

[30] *Ibid.,* at 22-23.

[31] *Ibid.,* at 28.

[32] On further appeal, the Supreme Court of Canada overturned the Court of Appeal's decision in *Vriend,* [1998] 1 S.C.R. 493, 156 D.L.R. (4th) 385. For commentary on the Supreme Court's disposition of the matter, see F.C. DeCoste, "The Separation of State Powers in Liberal Polity: *Vriend v. Alberta*" (1999), 44 McGill L.J. 197.

[33] (1990), 55 C.C.C. (3d) 97, 1 S.C.R. 852.

leaving her room. The Supreme Court cured this evidentiary deficiency by receiving into law expert psychiatric evidence regarding both the existence and
significance of the so-called "battered woman syndrome."

The Court proceeded on the view that, "in the context of a battered wife's efforts to repel an assault", expert testimony could undermine the assumption that
"it is inherently unreasonable to apprehend death or grievous bodily harm unless
or until the physical assault is actually in progress".[34] It then received the evidence of a Dr. Shane — which had been proffered by the defence at trial and
was based in part on hearsay — to conclude that, in the case of battered wives at
least, reasonable apprehension of imminent death or grievous harm may exist
even where no assault against the accused was in progress. On basis of the expert's opinion that battered women are "helpless" and powerless" and in fashion
akin to inmates in "a concentration camp ... paralyzed with fear",[35] the Court
drew an analogy between battered women and hostages and concluded that for
them the alternative of leaving is no resort at all and that they may therefore
reasonably experience imminence where others would not.[36]

Lavallee subtracts from legal equality by creating a subclass of citizens to
whom the usual rules with respect self defence do not apply, namely, that subset
of women[37] who qualify as battered spouses.[38] Those ordinary rules do, however,
continue to govern the actions of all other women and all men. This result rends
the fabric of legal equality. In a matter as serious as self-defence, most accused
will have fully to account for the harm they cause others whereas some accused
will be held to a lower standard of responsibility. But this not only diminishes
the entitlements of the former, it also diminishes the status of the latter. Holding
battered spouses to a lower and special standard renders them less equal as morally accountable beings. And to diminish their moral equality in this way is to
treat them paternalistically, as beings less accountable for their lives and their
choices and less self-reliant. When we discuss the concept of harm, we shall
discover that paternalism is not only the mark of inequality in this sense, but a
sure signal as well of states and political communities which fail to take seriously their citizens and members.

---

[34] *Ibid.*, at 116.

[35] *Ibid.*, at 121.

[36] *Ibid.*, at 125.

[37] Though the battered women's defence may turn out be a battered spouse's defence, judging by
certain of Wilson J.'s comments in *Lavallee*, such was not the Court's intent: "If it strains credu-
lity to imagine what the "ordinary man" would do in the position of a battered spouse, it is
probably because men do not typically find themselves in that situation. Some women do, however. The definition of what is reasonable must be adapted to circumstances which are, by and
large, foreign to the world inhabited by the hypothetical 'reasonable man'." *Ibid.*, at 114.

[38] "Spouses" because, though defence counsel have tried to extent its reach, courts have cabined the
Lavallee defence to spouses. See for example, *R. v. Eyapaise* (1993), 20 C.R. (4th) 246, in which
the Alberta Court of Queen's Bench held that, though the accused was a battered woman, the defence could not save her from conviction for assault with a weapon against a stranger.

D. LIBERTY

"Part of the idea of being moral equals is the claim that none of us is inherently subordinate to the will of others, none of us comes into the world as the property of another, or as their subject. We are all born free and equal".[39] We have just explored the nature of that equality which we found to reside not in some natural state of affairs, but in a distinctively moral claim about politics and law. We have now to turn to liberty. It too is a prescription, and it also has a legal sense that is fundamental to our law (though, as we shall see, not as fundamental as equality).

What does it mean to be free? And why should we think it important that people, ourselves and others, be free? Both of these questions are critical to understanding our law. Take first the matter of definition. Though we may use the word descriptively — as in "Britain is free country" — when we do so, we are depending upon a meaning which is normative and it is that meaning which informs the assessment on which our description depends. Our concern is the normative content of individual liberty.

(i) Negative and Positive Liberty

Individuals may be free in either of two senses: they may be free *from* interference, coercion, or restraint, or they may be free *to* act or be as they will. This distinction between *negative* and *positive* liberty found its classic modern expression in Isaiah Berlin's essay "Two Concepts of Liberty".[40] Berlin explained "negative liberty" in the following fashion:

> I am normally said to be free to the degree to which no man or body of men interferes with my activity. Political liberty in this sense is simply the area within which a man can act unobstructed by others. If I am prevented by others from doing what I would otherwise do, I am to that degree unfree; and if this area is contracted by other men beyond a certain minimum, I can be described as being coerced or, it may be, enslaved. Coercion is not, however, a term that covers every form of inability. ... Coercion implies the deliberate interference of other human beings within the area in which I could otherwise act.[41]

Positive liberty is another matter entirely. Again as put by Berlin:

> The "positive" sense of the word "liberty" derives from the wish on the part of the individual to be his own master. I wish my life and decisions to depend upon myself, not on external forces of whatever kind. I wish to be the instrument of my own, not of other men's, acts of will. I wish to be a

---

[39] Kymlicka, *supra*, note 16, at p. 60.
[40] "Two Concepts of Liberty" in Isaiah Berlin, *Four Essays on Liberty* (Oxford: Oxford University Press, 1969), at pp. 118-72.
[41] *Ibid.*, at p. 122.

subject, not an object; to be moved by reasons, by conscious purposes, which are my own, not by causes which affect me, as it were, from outside. I wish to be somebody, not nobody; a doer — deciding, not being decided for, self-directed and not acted upon by external nature or by other men as if I were a thing, or an animal, or a slave incapable of playing a human role, that is, of conceiving goals and policies of my own and realizing them.[42]

Positive liberty is an *intra-personal* concept according to which one is unfree to the extent that he or she is prevented from doing something, not by other persons, but by reasons having to do with that person's self. Negative liberty, on the other hand, is an *inter-personal* concept and when we use the word in that sense, we mean to say that one is unfree to the extent that he or she is prevented from doing something, which he or she could otherwise do, by some external restraint emanating from some other person or persons.

(ii) Law and Liberty

Generally, law is about negative liberty. And because it is, law is about when others — *other persons or the state* — may prevent us from doing whatever it is we might wish to do. A speeding limit, for instance, is a restriction of our negative liberty to drive as fast as we wish. At law, positive liberty is not merely subordinate to negative liberty, it can never provide justification for the curtailment of negative liberty.

In *American Booksellers v. Hudnut*,[43] the court was faced with a conflict between negative and positive liberty. Due to the efforts of Catharine MacKinnon and other prominent feminist theorists and activists, the city of Indianapolis passed an anti-pornography ordinance which defined pornography as "the graphic sexually explicit subordination of women, whether in pictures or words ...".[44] The ordinance specified materials that depict women "as sexual objects who enjoy pain or humiliation or ... rape", or as degraded or tortured or filthy, or in "postures or positions of servility or submission or display" as falling within that definition, but it did not include an exception for artistic or literary value.[45] The plaintiff American Booksellers Association, "the major association of publishers of general books, textbooks and educational materials in the United States",[46] challenged the ordinance as a violation of First Amendment free speech guarantees. The court agreed and held that the ordinance was unconstitutional. This was affirmed on further appeal,[47] and the U.S. Supreme Court subsequently declined to review the matter. Our concern, however, is not the constitutional

---

[42] *Ibid.*, at p. 131.
[43] 598 F.Supp. 1361 (S.D. Ind. 1984).
[44] *Ibid.*, at 1320.
[45] *Ibid.*
[46] *Ibid.*, at 1319.
[47] 771 F.2d 323 (U.S. Ct. App., 7th Cir.).

details, but the court's response to the defendants' arguments, which revolved around positive liberty.

At trial, the defendants argued that pornography, as defined by the ordinance, did not deserve constitutional protection because it "victimizes all women" by contributing to their subordination in society more generally, and in particular by diminishing their ability to speak in and to be heard by society.[48] They were arguing, that is, that the plaintiff's negative liberty of free speech ought to fall to the positive liberty of women as a class. The trial judge held that the state's interest in prohibiting sex discrimination, in this sense, was not so compelling as to outweigh the negative liberty of free speech.[49] The Circuit Court of Appeal agreed. Judge Easterbrook conceded the defendants' point that "much speech is dangerous" and that "the association of sexual arousal with the subordination of women may have a substantial effect", but he reasoned that "if the fact that speech plays a role in a process of conditioning were enough to permit governmental regulation, that would be the end of free speech".[50] On this and other grounds, the judge held that the definition of pornography as graphic sexually explicit subordination of women, as detailed in the ordinance, was unconstitutional and that the plaintiff's negative liberty could therefore be neither defeated nor confined by defendants' positive liberty to a society free of sexual subordination.[51]

(iii) The Primacy of Equality

We come then to our second question: why do we value liberty in this negative sense? We value negative liberty, because leaving individuals in that sense alone is a necessary and foundational part of treating them with equal concern and respect. To treat individuals in any other way, to interfere with them at whimsy or in service to making their lives conform to some view which we may have of right conduct, is to treat them as entities whose lives are not fully their own at all; and to treat persons in that way is to treat them as less than equal and with a disrespect and lack for concern for them as equals. Though liberty is in this fashion a derivative and therefore secondary value, it remains both central and distinct. No society which fails to recognize and enforce negative liberty is an egalitarian society. Yet in a society which does, there will remain always conflicts to resolve between equality and liberty.

---

[48] *Supra,* note 43, at 1336-37.
[49] *Ibid.,* at 1342.
[50] *Supra,* note 47, at 333, 330.
[51] *Ibid.,* at 333-34.

E. HARM

In his classic essay *On Liberty*,[52] John Stuart Mill identified harm to others as the threshold of principle for collective interferences in individual lives. As put by Mill:

> The object of this Essay is to assert one very simple principle, as entitled to govern absolutely the dealings of society with the individual in the way of compulsion and control, whether the means used be physical force in the form of legal penalties, or the moral coercion of public opinion. That principle is, that the sole end for which mankind are warranted, individually or collectively, in interfering with the liberty of action of any of their number, is self-protection. That the only purpose for which power can be rightfully exercised over any member of a civilized community, against his will, is to prevent harm to others. His own good, either physical or moral, is not a sufficient warrant. He cannot be rightfully be compelled to do or forbear because it will be better for him to do so, because it will make him happier, because, in the opinion of others, to do so would be wise, or even right. These are good reasons for remonstrating with him, or reasoning with him, or persuading him, or entreating him, but not for compelling him, or visiting him with any evil in case he do otherwise. To justify that, the conduct from which it is desired to deter him must be calculated to produce evil to some one else. The only part of the conduct of any one, for which he is amenable to society, is that which concerns others. In the part which merely concerns himself, his independence is, of right, absolute. Over himself, over his own mind and body, the individual is sovereign.[53]

Accordingly, the only legitimate reason for society to restrict the liberty of one of its members is to prevent him or her from causing harm to others. This so-called "harm principle" is foundational to our political culture generally and to our law especially.

The notion of harm both marks the boundary between the public and private spheres *and* establishes the threshold of equal concern and respect. Unless they harm another, an individual's actions are private. They cannot be a proper matter for collective deliberation and control and must, instead, be left entirely to the individual's discretion. Moreover, to interfere with an individual's life for any other reason would be to treat that life as less deserving of concern and respect and, in the result, as less than equal. To restrict liberty to prevent harm serves both liberty and equality by saving all our lives from unwanted direction by others. To restrict liberty in the absence of harm, however, diminishes equality because, in that event, the course and contour of all of our lives would depend on whatever calculus of worth happens to be favoured by those who happen to have the power to impose their preferences on us.

---

[52] "On Liberty" (1859) in John Gray, ed., *On Liberty and Other Essays* (Oxford: Oxford University Press, 1991), at p. 5.
[53] *Ibid.*, at pp. 13-14.

The coercive machinery of political society will interfere with the private conduct of individual lives and the political conduct of public authority only where there is harm — where one individual has harmed another, or where the state has harmed a citizen or, yes, where an individual has harmed the state. Harm in those senses measures moral equality and limits political and personal liberty. Our law measures those harms: *the whole of our law is a practice about the nature of harm.* Not surprisingly, then, from the lawyer's point of view, the practice of law consists of the practices of *naming, defining* and *proving* harm. If no harm exists at law — either because no case has arguably recognized the harm now alleged or because a recognized harm cannot be proven on the facts of the instant case — then there is no complaint at law and the coercive force of law cannot intervene in the affairs of the parties.

It is sometimes claimed that "the word 'harm' is both vague and ambiguous".[54] But, from the lawyer's point of view, the general meaning of "harm" is not at all illusive.[55] And this lawyer's view of the matter is very much Mill's view. According to Mill, a harm exists where *other-regarding conduct causes real damage to some identifiable legal person.* This simple definition is pregnant with meaning. That self-regarding conduct is excluded as harm at law prohibits legal paternalism; that the damage caused by other-regarding conduct must be sustained by legal persons excludes constructive harms from law; and that the damage must be real, and not a matter of mere offence at the conduct, prohibits legal moralism. *Legal paternalism* is the view that prevention of physical, psychological or economic harm to an actor him- or herself is a good reason to interfere with that individual's choices and conduct. *Constructive injuries* are those which are thought to be sustained, not by "assignable" individuals,[56] but by abstractions, such as society generally or some class or category of individuals within society, say the poor or women or the religiously devout. *Legal moralism* is the view that, even where it causes neither harm nor offence to the actor or to others, individual conduct might yet be a legitimate object of interference and control if the conduct in question can be shown to be inherently immoral.

So the legal definition of harm excludes from law's domain a very large swath of human activity and complaint. Perhaps as a result, there are some who claim that this definition is a mere conception of harm and that there exist other conceptions which stand in legitimate competition with it. According to views of this sort, the notion of harm is endlessly plastic and, because it is, law may legitimately interfere with a host of activities which the Millian definition places

---

[54] J. Feinberg, *The Moral Limits of the Criminal Law, Vol. 1: Harm to Others* (New York: Oxford University Press, 1984), at p. 31.

[55] Nor indeed are the particulars. As between individuals, harm consists of injury to persons, property, and promises; as between the state and citizens (and putting aside the state's liability as a private actor for injury to persons, property and promises), injury consists of unequal treatment; and as between citizens and the state (putting again aside an individual's liability for injury to state property and for promises to the state), injury consists of sedition and treason.

[56] *Supra,* note 52, at p. 91.

clearly beyond reach. Unhappily for all of us, a growing number of lawyers and judges, especially, have, in recent years, moved towards some such plastic notion of harm; we will conclude our discussion of harm with an important illustration of just such a move.

In *R. v. Butler*,[57] the Supreme Court of Canada had before it the constitutional validity of the obscenity provisions of the *Criminal Code* of Canada.[58] Our concern is not with the case's constitutional aspects, but with the Court's construction of harm at law. And in this regard, the Court held: a) that some explicitly sexual material harms women because "materials portraying women as a class as objects for sexual exploitation and abuse have a negative impact on 'the individual's sense of self-worth and acceptance'";[59] and b) that "the proliferation of materials which seriously offend the values fundamental to our society is a substantial concern which justifies restricting the otherwise full exercise of the freedom of expression".[60] Together these views fundamentally redefine harm. The second violates the prohibition against constructive harm by investing society generally with a legal persona, and with values and views, which can suffer harm. The first violates that prohibition as well by investing women as a class with a legal personality capable of being harmed. But it also violates the prohibition against legal moralism by making one person's liberty contingent on whether some person (or class of persons) takes offence at its expression.

The Court in *Butler* turned its back on the notion of harm which alone limits the law's governance of our lives. That this turn is "ominous for liberty" should become even more apparent through our examination of the notion of rights to which we shall now turn.[61]

F.   RIGHTS

Because ours is a political morality devoted to the moral equality of individuals, each of us, as legal and political subjects, has "a back-up general right to equality".[62] That general right to equal concern and respect is made good in a "schedule of specific rights" which provides and protects the negative liberty that equality requires.[63] None of this however explains what rights are, nor in sufficient detail what they do, nor how they do whatever it is they do.

At very start of his classic *A Theory of Justice*,[64] Rawls offers the following direction about the moral status of political community:

---

57   [1992] 1 S.C.R. 452.
58   R.S.C. 1985, c. C-46. To be precise, s. 163.
59   *Supra*, note 57, at 497.
60   *Supra*, note 57, at 496.
61   R. Dworkin, *Freedom Law* (Cambridge, MA: Harvard University Press, 1996), at pp. 206-207.
62   W. Kymlicka, *Liberalism, Community and Culture* (Oxford: Clarendon Press, 1989), at p. 110.
63   *Ibid.*
64   (Cambridge, MA: Harvard University Press, 1971).

Justice is the first virtue of social institutions. ... [L]aws and institutions no matter how efficient and well-arranged must be reformed if they are unjust. *Each person possesses an inviolability founded on justice that even the welfare of society as a whole cannot override.* For this reason justice denies that the loss of freedom for some is made right by a greater good shared by others. The reasoning which balances the gains and losses of different persons as if they were one person is excluded. Therefore in a just society the basic liberties are taken for granted and the rights secured by justice are not subject to political bargaining or to the calculus of social interests.[65]

Rights are best viewed as together comprising a sphere of inviolability in Rawls' sense. This sphere may be represented as follows:

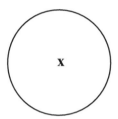

At the centre of the sphere stands the legal and political subject defined by morality equality. We are each of us that undifferentiated — and, therefore, equal — point of concern and respect. As we have seen, equal concern and respect requires minimally that each of us be left alone to live our lives as we see fit. Rights are the measure of equality in that sense. They envelope each of us in a sphere of inviolability which alone provides the liberty we require to make our lives our own. Tyrannies and despotisms are societies different from ours precisely because, in societies of that sort, individuals are not clothed in rights. In those societies, rather, individuals are, to a greater or lesser extent, naked morally and legally.

Rights ensure negative liberty. To say that "B has a right to do X" means that others have a duty not to prevent B from doing X. A right, then, is a legitimate claim that one person can make against others not to interfere. So viewed, *rights are constraints on power*, on the power others may have to interfere with our choices, conduct and projects. But suppose others fail to observe that duty — what then? When others prevent us from doing what we legitimately would, they cause us harm. And viewed from this vantage, the sphere which constrains power's way in our lives consists of those harms against which equality requires that we be saved. Moreover, since others also are enveloped in spheres of rights which impose duties on us towards them, harm not only defines our rights, but sets limits to them. Our rights as individuals end at precisely that point at which our conduct causes harm to others. We have seen that naming, defining and

---

[65] *Ibid.*, at 3-4 (emphasis added).

proving harm is the on-going practice of the legal community. We can now re-phrase this: *it falls to the legal community to maintain the rights of all by deter-mining, case by case, when conduct falls outside of the sphere of protected lib-erty because it has caused harm to someone else.*

G. TOLERATION

Rights constrain power by imposing upon each of us the duty not to prevent others from doing what they legitimately may do. That duty is a duty to be toler-ant, and it is important that we understand precisely what it involves.

Tolerance is not a virtue. Societies such as ours do not require that we nurture in ourselves a generosity of spirit towards others. Nor therefore are we required to approve, let alone to endorse and to encourage, their behaviour or styles of life. Toleration rather is a certain quality of *political conduct* which is required of us in certain circumstances. Those circumstances are these: we disapprove — perhaps even loathe — the behaviour or style of life of some other individual or group, *and* we have the power, individually or collectively, coercively to prevent that behaviour or to punish, if not to extinguish, that way of life. In those circum-stances, toleration consists of our deciding not to deploy our individual or collec-tive power for those purposes. Societies such as ours do require that sort of specifically *negative toleration*. In such societies, individuals and the state are pro-hibited from using their power against forms of life which are thought erroneous.

Toleration in that sense is the burden of moral equality and of personal and political liberty — and therefore of law. Indeed, viewed from the vantage of toleration, *our law is a system of mutual forbearances backed and enforced by rights*. Of course, as with rights more generally, toleration ceases to be manda-tory at the point of harm.

Unhappily, lawyers and judges are not always faithful stewards of political tolerance. Sometimes they choose instead to serve the power of private morality. *Bowers v. Hardwick*[66] is an infamous example. In *Bowers*, an adult male was charged with violating Georgia's sodomy law by committing a sexual act with another adult male in his own bedroom. The law defined sodomy as committing or submitting to "any sexual act involving the sex organs of one person and the mouth or anus of another". After the prosecutor chose not to present the case to a grand jury — a procedure required to obtain an indictment — the accused sued in the U.S. Federal Court to have the statute declared unconstitutional. The trial court rejected the claim, but the Court of Appeals reversed and held that the law "violated the respondent's fundamental rights because his homosexual activity is a private and intimate association that is beyond the reach of state regulation". On further appeal, the United States Supreme Court reversed that judgment.

---

[66] 478 U.S. 186 (U.S.S.C. 1986).

Then Chief Justice Burger's opinion best captures the court's utter abandonment of political toleration:

[T]he proscriptions against sodomy have very "ancient roots". Decisions of individuals relating to homosexual conduct have been subject to state intervention throughout the history of Western Civilization. Condemnation of those practices is firmly rooted in Judeao-Christian [*sic*] moral and ethical standards. [...] To hold that the act of homosexual sodomy is somehow protected as a fundamental right would be to cast aside millennia of moral teaching.[67]

According to this court then, toleration ends not at harm but with infraction of whatever view of private morality the court thinks proper.

H. JUSTICE

Justitia est constans et perpetua voluntas jus suum cuique tribuens — "justice is the constant and perpetual rendering to each his right." Justice is about actions: about "yielding, or allotting, or assigning, or resigning, to each their own".[68] Like liberty, justice is an inter-personal concept. It properly concerns what persons are due — their rights or entitlements — in circumstances where some person or organization (the state especially included) acts with respect to two or more others (persons or organizations). What is due from the just actor — and what is owed as a matter of justice to the objects of the action — is *fairness*.

We can make three sets of distinctions. The first is that between political and social justice. In political justice, the just actor is the state and the recipients of justice are citizens or, as we have been describing them, members of political community. Though it is often used with imprecision, social justice, whatever else might be said of it, is not confined to state actions nor generally is its object the individual.[69] The second is that between formal and concrete justice. Formal justice requires that essentially similar cases be treated the same way and that essentially different cases be treated differently. Concrete justice, on the other hand, concerns what persons are due in particular sorts of cases. The final distinction is between principles of justice and species of justice. We will need to consider each in the context of political justice, the core of which we will find to be legal justice.

In societies such as ours, justice "expresses the respect individuals are owed as ends in themselves, not as means to someone's good, or even to the common

---

67   *Ibid.*, at 196-97.
68   A. Flew, "The Concept, and Conceptions, of Justice" in B. Almond and D. Hill, eds., *Applied Philosophy* (London: Routledge, 1991), at p. 196.
69   See T.W. Simon, "A Theory of Social Justice" in D.S. Caudill and S.J. Gold, eds., *Radical Philosophy of Law* (Atlantic Heights, NJ: Humanities Press, 1995), at p. 34; D. Miller, *Principles of Social Justice* (Cambridge, MA: Harvard University Press, 1999).

good. Justice recognizes the equal standing of the members of the community through an account of the rights and entitlements we can justly claim".[70] Equal treatment is the foundational principle of justice *and* justice does require a regime of rights. But justice is a political virtue independently from rights. And because justice is in this sense free-standing, we can properly inquire what equal care requires of it. Our answer to that question will, in part at least, disclose the principles of justice as such.

Equal concern and respect requires two principles of justice: that like cases be treated in the same way (and unlike cases differently), and that cases be treated in that way according to the requirements of due process. The first principle is, of course, the principle of formal justice. The second principle concerns what is sometimes called natural (or procedural) justice. Natural justice is composed of two principles. The first is that a person should not be a judge in his or her own case (*nemo judex in causa sua*). The second is that a decision affecting the rights or interests of an individual should not be made until he or she has been given an opportunity to be heard (*audi alteram partem*).

All of this should sound familiar. We have already discussed *stare decisis.* And we can now add that *stare decisis* is a doctrine of law because equal application and equal protection are requirements of formal justice. We can also cast the argumentative strategies of lawyers and judges in a new light. Arguments of analogy and difference and arguments of mistake are founded on, and express, principles of justice. Finally, we can claim that whatever else political justice may require, these principles of justice at law are indispensable.

The significance of this claim may become clearer through an examination of the species or kinds of justice which concern not process or procedure, but results. They tell us what individuals are due, how fairness is realized, in the category of cases which they capture and indeed define. There are three kinds of justice in this sense — *distributive, corrective* and *retributive.*

Distributive justice addresses the basic structure by which social and economic goods and resources are distributed in a society. The justice of distributions is a primary concern of all conceptions of justice — and of politicians and legislatures as well — but it is not a concern of legal justice as such. Let's suppose that two car accidents take place on the same day on the same city street. Suppose too that the drivers of the cars who caused the accidents, we'll call them A and B, work for the same employer for exactly the same salary. Also suppose that their victims, X and Y, suffer exactly the same injuries; both are rendered unable ever to work again. Suppose finally that X is a highly paid chief executive and Y is a lowly paid day labourer. Now assuming that fault is proven, the damages which A will be ordered to pay X and B will ordered to pay Y will be dramatically different just because X's and Y's share of material resources are so different. But A will not be able to argue that it is unfair to stick him with the higher award. On the contrary, our law requires A to take his victim as he

---

[70]   *Supra*, note 16, at p. 169.

finds him and if he is unlucky in that regard, then so be it. This requirement is not whimsy. It is compelled as a matter of justice at law. Doers of harm must compensate their victims according to victims' share of resources because legal justice does not contemplate the justice of distributions. Legal justice is individual and particular. It is individual because its objects are the individual parties; and it is particular, rather than systemic, because those individuals must be treated as undifferentiated legal subjects and not as members of some real or imagined extra-legal category. So unfairness would result were a court to aggrandize an award in the spirit of redistribution. Were for instance the court in our example to increase the Y's award because it thought that Y's share of resources was somehow unjust — say, because the judge thought the class system unfair — then it would offend justice at law on two counts. Not only would it have abandoned the rule which governs and thereby violated formal justice, but by identifying Y as a member of a class, it would have violated legal equality as well.

Our example also illustrates the ambit of corrective justice. Justice in this form concerns disturbances to the original distribution of goods and resources and it addresses doers and sufferers of harm in that sense. The aim of corrective justice is to re-establish the conditions of distribution which existed prior to the harm, so far as money can do that. This objective is expressed in a number of ways — as restoring the *status quo ante*, or as putting the victim in the place he or she would have been in but for the harm, or as compensating the victim for his or her loss — but however the matter is put, it concerns the particulars of the issue of harm between two individuals. A great swath of our law — for instance, contracts and torts and, in certain respects, property — concerns corrective justice.

Retributive justice also concerns harm, and its purpose is to inflict a harm, called a punishment, on an individual who has caused harm to another. Some claim that civil damages are punishment in this sense. But that is incorrect because our law distinguishes between, and has very different rules for, compensatory and exemplary or punitive damages. In any event, the primary occupation of retributive justice is the law a crimes which will become our occupation in Chapter 8.

It would perhaps be prudent briefly to recap:

1. Legal justice is political justice.
2. Legal justice is formal and procedural justice.
3. The substantive requirements of justice at law are in the main supplied by the principles of corrective and retributive justice.
4. Those concrete principles of justice are the foundation for the identification of legal harm.
5. Legal harms are articulated by legal rules which express, individually and as a whole, rights to negative liberty.

6. Aside from ensuring that the requirements of formal and procedural justice are met as regards any legislated distributions, distributive justice is not properly a part of legal justice. Unlike legal justice, which is particular and individual, distributive justice is systemic and unavoidably discriminatory.

I.   RESTATEMENT NO. 3

Law is foundational to our way of life. It enshrines our commitment to moral equality, and in that way, establishes the framework for all other aspects of our personal and political lives. Yet its primacy in that sense very much limits law. Because law is about moral equality, it is also necessarily about, and only about, individual rights *and* about the conditions and forms of justice which makes non-arbitrary judgments about those matters possible.

Law's ambitions then are modest. And so need be those of lawyers. Justice at law is critically important to the achievement of civilized life, but a great many human goods cannot be pursued through a life at law. Whatever one thinks it entails, social justice is beyond justice at law. And though distributive justice is properly an object of political justice, that matter falls not to the legal community, but to political authority. Because this is so, legislators have much more complex concerns than do lawyers and judges. They cannot confine themselves to moral equality and formal justice and have instead to venture into the much more treacherous waters of wholesale distributions and discriminations. It is a good that lawyers recognize their own importance and limitations; but it is also a good that they acknowledge the contribution of other actors in the complex drama of our political life.

FURTHER READINGS TO CHAPTER 6

1.   Introductions to Political and Legal Philosophy

Altman, A. *Arguing About Law: An Introduction to Legal Philosophy*. Belmont, CA: Wadsworth, 1996.

Dyzenhaus, D., and A. Ripstein, eds. *Law and Morality: Readings in Legal Philosophy*. Toronto: University of Toronto Press, 1996.

Feinberg, J., and J. Coleman, eds. *Philosophy of Law*. 6th ed. Belmont, CA: Wadsworth, 2000.

Freeman, M.D.A., ed. *Lloyd's Introduction to Jurisprudence*. 6th ed. London: Sweet & Maxwell, 1994.

————. *Legal Theory at the End of the Millennium*. Oxford: Oxford University Press, 2000.

Goodin, R.E., and P. Pettit, eds. *A Companion to Contemporary Political Philosophy*. Oxford: Blackwell, 1993.

Hampton, J. *Political Philosophy*. Boulder, CO: Westview, 1999.

Kuklin, B., and J.W. Stempel. *Foundations of the Law: An Interdisciplinary and Jurisprudential Primer*. St. Paul, MN: West Publishing Co., 1994.

Kymlicka, W. *Contemporary Political Philosophy: An Introduction*. Oxford: Clarendon Press, 1990.

Laski, H.J. *A Grammar of Politics*. 2nd ed. London: Allen & Unwin, 1930.

Lessnoff, M.H. *Political Philosophers of the Twentieth Century*. Malden, MA: Blackwell, 1999.

Lucas, J.R. *The Principles of Politics*. Oxford: Clarendon Press, 1966.

Lyons, D. *Ethics and the Rule of Law*. Cambridge: Cambridge University Press, 1984.

Pincoffs, E.L. *Philosophy of Law: A Brief Introduction*. Belmont, CA: Wadsworth, 1991.

Schauer, F., and W. Sinnott-Armstrong, eds. *The Philosophy of Law*. New York: Harcourt Brace, 1996.

Wolff, J. *An Introduction to Political Philosophy*. New York: Oxford University Press, 1996.

2.   Equality

Beitz, C.R. *Political Equality*. Princeton: Princeton University Press, 1989.

Dworkin, R. "Neutrality, Equality, and Liberalism". In Maclean, D., and C. Mills, eds. *Liberalism Reconsidered*. Totowa, NJ: Rowman & Allanheld, 1983. At p. 1.

_____. *Foundations of Liberal Equality: Tanner Lecture on Human Values XI 1990*. Salt Lake City: University of Utah Press, 1990.

Hill Kay, H. "Models of Equality". [1985] U. Illnois L. Rev. 39.

Johnston, D., ed. *Equality*. Indianapolis: Hackett, 2000.

Lakoff, S.A. *Equality in Political Philosophy*. Boston: Beacon Press, 1964.

Neal, P. "Dworkin on the Foundations of Liberal Equality". (1995), 1 Legal Theory 205.

Pennock, J.R., and J.W. Chapman, eds. *Equality: NOMOS IX*. New York: Atherton Press, 1967.

Temkin, L.S. *Inequality*. New York: Oxford University Press, 1993.

Turner, B.S. *Equality*. New York: Tavistock, 1986.

Williams, B. "The Idea of Equality". In Williams, B. *Problems of the Self*. Cambridge: Cambridge University Press, 1973. At p. 230.

3.   Liberty

Bauman, Z. *Freedom*. Philadelphia: Open University Press, 1988.

Berlin, I. *Four Essays on Liberty*. Oxford: Oxford University Press, 1969.

Cook, M. "A Space of One's Own: Autonomy, Privacy, Liberty". (1999), 25(1) Philosophy & Social Criticism 23.

———. "Authenticity and Autonomy". (1997), 25(2) Political Theory 258.

Denning, A. *Freedom Under The Law*. London: Stevens & Sons, 1949.

Dworkin, R. "We Do Not Have A Right to Liberty". In Cunningham, R.L., ed. *Liberty and the Rule of Law*. College Station, TX: Texas A. & M. University Press, 1979. At p. 167.

———. "Two Concepts of Liberty". In Margalit, E., and Margarlit, A., eds. *Isaiah Berlin: A Celebration*. London: Hogarth Press, 1991. At p. 100.

Feinberg, J. "Legal Paternalism". (1971), 1(1) Can. J. of Philosophy 105.

Friedrich, C.J., ed. *Liberty: NOMOS IV*. New York: Atherton Press, 1966.

Heyman, S.J. "Positive and Negative Liberty". (1992), 68 Chicago-Kent L. Rev. 81.

Kleinig, J. *Paternalism*. Totowa, NJ: Rowman & Allanheld, 1983.

Lindley, R. *Autonomy*. Atlantic Highlands, NJ: Humanities Press, 1986.

Mill, J.S. *On Liberty and Other Essays*. Gray, J., ed. Oxford: Oxford University Press, 1991.

Miller, D., ed. *Liberty*. Oxford University Press, 1991.

Nagel, T. "Freedom". In Nagel, T. *The View From Nowhere*. Oxford: Oxford University Press, 1986. At p. 110.

Patterson, O. *Freedom*. New York: Basic Books, 1991.

Sartorius, R., ed. *Paternalism*. Minneapolis: University of Minnesota Press, 1983.

4. Harm

Digeser, P. *Our Politics, Our Selves? Liberalism, Identity, and Harm*. Princeton: Princeton University Press, 1995.

Epstein, R.A. "The Harm Principle — And How It Grew". (1995), 45 U. Toronto L.J. 369.

Feinberg, J. *The Moral Limits of the Criminal Law, Vol. 1: Harm to Others*. New York: Oxford University Press, 1984.

———. "Legal Moralism and Freefloating Evil". (1980), 61 Pacific Philosophical Q. 122

———. "Harm and Self-Interest". In Hacker, P.M.S., and J. Raz, eds. *Law, Morality, and Society*. Oxford: Clarendon Press, 1977. At p. 285.

Simester, A.P., and A.T.H. Smith, eds. *Harm and Culpability*. Oxford: Clarendon Press, 1996.

Wellman, C., ed. "Symposium on Joel Feinberg's *Harm to Others*". (1986), 5 Criminal Justice Ethics 1ff.

5. Rights

Almond, B. "Rights". In Singer, P., ed. *A Companion to Ethics.* Oxford: Blackwell, 1991. At p. 259.

Feinberg, J. "The Nature and Value of Rights". (1970), 4 J. of Value Inquiry 243.

———. *Rights, Justice, and the Bounds of Liberty.* Princeton: Princeton University Press, 1980.

Freeden, M. *Rights.* Minneapolis: University of Minnesota Press, 1991

Harel, A. "Revisionist Theories of Rights: An Unwelcome Defense". (1998), 11(2) Can. J. of Law & Jurisprudence 227.

McCloskey, H.J. "Human Needs, Rights and Political Values". (1976), 13(1) American Philosophical Q. 1.

Melden, A.I. *Rights in Moral Lives.* Berkeley: University of California Press, 1988.

Penner, J.E. "The Analysis of Rights". (1997), 10(3) Ratio Juris 300.

Raz, J. "Rights and Individual Well-Being". (1992), 5(2) Ratio Juris 127.

———. "Legal Rights". (1984), 4 Oxford J. of Legal Studies 1.

Sarat, A., and T.R. Kearns, eds. *Legal Rights: Historical and Philosophical Perspectives.* Ann Arbor: University of Michigan Press, 1996.

Waldron, J., ed. *Theories of Rights.* Oxford: Oxford University Press, 1984.

———. "Rights in Conflict". (1989), 99 Ethics 503.

———. *Liberal Rights.* Cambridge: Cambridge University Press, 1993.

6. Toleration

Creppell, I. "Locke on Toleration: The Transformation of Constraint". (1996), 24(2) Political Theory 200.

Dees, R.H. "Establishing Toleration". (1999), 27(2) Political Theory 667.

Fletcher, G.P. "The Case for Tolerance". In E.F. Paul, *et al.*, eds. *The Communitarian Challenge to Liberalism.* Cambridge: Cambridge University Press, 1996. At p. 229.

Held, D., ed. *Toleration: An Elusive Virtue.* Princeton: Princeton University Press, 1996.

Horton, J., and S. Mendus, eds. *Toleration, Identity, and Difference.* New York: St. Martin's Press, 1999.

Lazari-Pawlowska, I. "Three Concepts of Tolerance". (1987), 14(1) Dialectics & Humanism 133.

Macedo, S. "Liberal Civic Education and Religious Fundamentalism: The Case of God v. John Rawls?" (1995), 105 Ethics 468.

Mendus, S. *Toleration and the Limits of Liberalism.* Atlantic Highlands, NJ: Humanities Press, 1989.

McClure, K.M. "Difference, Diversity, and The Limits of Toleration". (1990), 18(3) Political Theory 361.

Pattaro, E., ed. "Symposium on Toleration". (1997), 10(1) Ratio Juris 1-123.

Raz, J. "Multiculturalism". (1998), 11(3) Ratio Juris 193.

Richards, D.A.J. "Free Speech as Toleration". In Waluchow, W.J., ed. *Free Expression: Essays in Law and Philosophy*. Oxford: Clarendon Press, 1994. At p. 31.

————. *Toleration and the Constitution*. New York: Oxford University Press, 1986.

Ross, S.L. "A Real Defense of Tolerance". (1988), 22 J. of Value Inquiry 127.

Tinder, G.E. *Tolerance and Community*. Columbia: University of Missouri Press, 1995.

Walzer, M. *On Toleration*. New Haven: Yale University Press, 1997.

7. Justice

Arthur, J., and W.H. Shaw, eds. *Justice and Economic Distribution*. Englewood Cliffs, NJ: Prentice-Hall, 1978.

Barry, B. *Justice as Impartiality*. Oxford: Clarendon Press, 1995.

Bayles, M.D. *Procedural Justice*. Dordrecht: Kluwer, 1990.

Campbell, T. *Justice*. Atlantic Heights, NJ: Humanities Press, 1988.

Chapman, J.W., ed. *Compensatory Justice: NOMOS XXXIII*. New York: New York University Press, 1991.

Fisk, M., ed. *Justice*. Atlantic Heights, NJ: Humanities Press, 1993.

Galston, W.A. *Justice and the Human Good*. Chicago: University of Chicago Press, 1980.

Grant, G. *English-Speaking Justice*. Toronto: Anansi, 1998.

Heller, A. *Beyond Justice*. Oxford: Blackwell, 1987.

Lacey, N. "Theories of Justice and the Welfare State". (1992), 1(3) Social & Legal Studies 323.

Lebacqz, K. *Six Theories of Justice*. Minneapolis: Augsburg, 1986.

Lucas, J.R. *On Justice*. Oxford: Clarendon Press, 1980.

O'Neill, O. "Theories of Justice, Traditions of Virtue". In Gross, H., and R. Harrison. *Jurisprudence: Cambridge Essays*. Oxford: Clarendon Press, 1992. At p. 55.

Perelman, C. *Justice*. New York: Random House, 1967.

Rawls, J. *A Theory of Justice*. Cambridge, MA: Harvard University Press, 1971.

Sandel, M.J. *Liberalism and the Limits of Justice*. Cambridge: Cambridge University Press, 1982.

Sarat. A., and T.R. Kearns, eds. *Justice and Injustice in Law and Legal Theory*. Ann Arbor: University of Michigan Press, 1996.

Shklar, J. "Giving Injustice Its Due". (1989), 98 Yale L.J. 1135.

Sypnowich, C. "Social Justice and Legal Form". (1994), 7(1) Ratio Juris 72.

Weinrib, E.J. "Corrective Justice". (1992), 77 Iowa L. Rev. 403.

Williams, D.L. "Dialogical Theories of Justice". (1999), 11 Telos 109.

Chapter 7

The Rule of Law

[T]he notion of the regulation and reconciliation of conflicts through the rule of law ... seems to me a cultural achievement of universal significance. ... [T]here is a difference between arbitrary power and the rule of law. We ought to expose the shams and inequities which may be concealed beneath this law. But the rule of law itself, the imposing of effective inhibitions upon power and the defence of the citizen from power's all-intrusive claims, seems to me to be an unqualified human good. To deny or belittle this good is, ... a desperate error of intellectual abstraction. More than this, it is a self-fulfilling error, which encourages us to give up the struggle against bad laws and class-bound procedures, and to disarm ourselves before power. It is to throw away a whole inheritance of struggle about law, and within the forms of law, whose continuity can never be fractured without bringing men and women into immediate danger.

E.P. Thompson

A. INTRODUCTION

In Chapter 5, we stipulated that the legal community's authority to construct the public rules which govern all our lives resides on a normative theory of law which identifies both the grounds and conditions of that authority. The Rule of Law is that theory. In this chapter and the next, we shall explore the Rule of Law as the point and justification of legal practice in societies such as ours. In Part III, we shall turn to the conditions of character and conduct which the legal community must satisfy to make good its authority under the Rule of Law.

B. THE CONCEPT OF RULE OF LAW: THE CONSTRAINT OF POWER

The Rule of Law is a political morality. The Rule of Law therefore only concerns the institutions of political community and the nature of the offices and practices defined by those institutions and their limitations. It is best understood in contrast to those other political moralities which, throughout political history, have been its rivals. Tyranny and despotism are political moralities whose ends are the good of the rulers. The end of Rule of Law, on the other hand, is the good of the governed, of the people who are the constituents of political community. In consequence, a Rule of Law state is a moral agent, whose legitimacy depends upon its acting for the good of the people subject to its rule. Unlike despotic and tyrannic regimes, in which the essence of government is the power somehow to compel obedience, government by Rule of Law is government according to those principles of institutional design, practice, and limitation which serve the good of the governed.

That the Rule of Law is a political morality in these senses permits us to frame the two questions which matter most to our task of locating the meaning of Rule of Law. We may ask, first, which values compel political communities to act for the good of the governed? and, second, at the most abstract level, how do political communities so act?

States govern for the good of the governed just because, in such states, the governed are presumed to be persons worthy of equal concern and respect. The Rule of Law is the stable, durable core of the political morality of political communities devoted to moral equality in that sense. Such states are liberal states. To say that the Rule of Law is the core of liberal political morality is to claim: a) that, in societies such as ours, the Rule of Law is the fundament of our "mode of association"[1] in political community and at once therefore a "locus of argumentation"[2] about the terms and conditions of that association; b) that the institutional arrangements of political community, and especially their legitimacy, devolve from that core; and c) that, whatever other principles may govern political community — say equality of material resources or equality of opportunity — they are secondary and derivative and, in the result, contestable in ways that the core principle is not.[3]

Before turning to our second question, we should briefly examine an issue raised by the view that the Rule of Law is the core of liberal political morality. First, that view makes the Rule of Law the minimum moral content of states devoted to the moral equality of their members as individuals. Second, it implies that liberal states may be guided by principles which exceed the requirements of the Rule of Law: the Rule of Law, that is, may not exhaust the political morality, nor the institutional practices, of liberal political communities. And it is this second meaning which raises the issue of the location of those other principles and practices, and of the Rule of Law with respect to them, about which we must be clear.

---

[1] M. Oakeshott, "The Rule of Law" in M. Oakeshott, *On History and Other Essays* (Oxford: Basil Blackwell, 1983), at pp. 119-20.

[2] N. MacCormick, "Rhetoric and the Rule of Law" in D. Dyzenhaus, *Recrafting the Rule of Law: The Limits of Legal Order* (Oxford: Hart Publishing, 1999), at p. 163. See also: G.F. Gaus, "Public Reason and the Rule of Law" in I. Shapiro, ed., *The Rule of Law: NOMOS XXXVI* (New York: New York University Press, 1994), at p. 328.

[3] The status of such secondary principles — and the place of distributive justice particularly — is notoriously difficult. See, for example: N. Lacey, "Theories of Justice and the Welfare State" (1992), 1(3) Social & Legal Studies 323; R. Ashcraft, "Liberalism and the Problem of Poverty" (1993), 6(4) Critical Review 493; R. Ashcroft and B. Scheuerman, "The Rule of Law and the Welfare State: Towards a New Synthesis" (1994), 22(2) Politics & Society 195.

Clearly, there are other institutions, besides the Rule of Law, which are associated with liberal societies — for instance, free markets for the exchange of goods, universities for the cultivation of free inquiry and expression, a free press and representative democracy. Both the liberal state and liberal society have then, in theory and in practice, a configuration which exceeds the institutional form we call the Rule of Law. Detailed exploration (not to mention justification) of these other institutions and principles of modern liberalism is, happily, beyond our purpose. Our sole concern is the proper relationship between principles and institutions of these sorts and the Rule of Law.

In Chapter 6, we found that the requirements of political morality trump the requirements of personal morality in any instance where the two may conflict. We may now add that the requirements of the Rule of Law trump other principles and ends which the liberal state may pursue and the practices of other institutions which characterize liberal society. More particularly, the liberal state and other liberal institutions are subordinate to the principles of governance by the Rule of Law and where the conduct of liberal politics or of liberal institutions violates legal principle, and the principle of legal equality especially, it is the Rule of Law, and not political or institutional practice, which governs.

We come then to our second question: how do liberal political communities institutionalize moral equality? Baldly stated, the answer is this: *at the most fundamental level, liberal political communities make good their commitment to equal care and respect by institutionalizing the state — and the requirements of state — to constrain power, the power of the state itself and, through the state, power more generally.* It is this act which constitutes the liberal state as a Rule of Law state. But bare statement is not enough. What we must understand is the moral calculation which associates constraint of power with moral equality.

That calculation consists of four propositions. First, if individuals are, as persons, equal despite the many differences which obtain between them, then they are due equal care and respect by the institutions of communal life. Second, to treat individuals in that way is to treat them as beings who own and are responsible for their own lives. Third, it falls then to political community to secure for its members, as condition of treating them equally, personal autonomy. Finally, since autonomy is lost when others, collectively or individually, interfere with one's moral independence, treating persons equally requires that the power to interfere be constrained. The fundaments of the Rule of Law — its moral location, its point, and its institutional requirements — follow from this understanding of its moral genesis.

That individuals are *owed*, as a condition of equal treatment, security from power means that the Rule of Law is *a principle of justice*. We have just discovered that liberal political community is guided by principles other than the Rule of Law and that those other principles are, where they are inconsistent with the Rule of Law, subordinate to it. We may now rephrase this understanding. The Rule of Law is a *necessary*, but it is *not* a *sufficient*, condition for a just political community or for a just social order more generally: the requirements of the

Rule of Law do not, and cannot, amount to a complete theory or practice of justice. That this is so has implications with respect to the relationship between the legal and political to which we shall come. It also impacts fundamentally on the point of justice at law.

Ronald Dworkin articulates the point of law in the following fashion:

> [T]he most abstract and fundamental point of legal practice is to guide and constrain the power of government in the following way. Law insists that force not be used or withheld, no matter how useful that would be to ends in view, no matter how beneficial or noble those ends, except as licensed or required by individual rights flowing from past political decisions about when force is justified.[4]

Law, that is, is a practice of *constituting, exercising* and *limiting* power through the state. And justice at law resides in just those practices. In Chapter 3, we discovered that the power of law is confined to, and by, our collective political past and that the doctrine of *stare decisis* expresses this fundamental limitation to law. We shall discover shortly that this past, which at once authorizes and limits law, is a moral past the fabric of which is individual rights. The present point is just this: though law's point, its purpose of constraining power, involves magisterial claims with respect to other facets of individual and communal life, justice at law remains modest in its ambitions.

We come then to the institutional requirements of the Rule of Law which will concern us in the remainder of this chapter and in the next. The Rule of Law requires of states two primary institutional practices — the *separation of powers* and a *regime of rights-bearing rules.* It is through these institutional instruments alone that the liberal state meets its threshold obligation to equality. And it is through them as well that the law's authority over our lives is constituted.

C. THE REQUIREMENTS OF THE RULE OF LAW

These are not mean measures. The authority of the state is thereby made contingent upon its acting through, and in ways which instantiate, these practices. And this puts paid any notion that "the state cannot violate ... the rule of law because it appears as its embodiment."[5] On the contrary, the state is "a bona fide state — and not a mere private force — only if it follow[s] dictates associated with the rule of law"; and it cannot, therefore, "do anything it wish[es] and declare it to be law".[6]

---

4   R. Dworkin, *Law's Empire* (Cambridge, MA: Harvard University Press, 1986), at p. 93.
5   B. Fine, *Democracy and The Rule of Law* (London: Pluto Press, 1984), at p. 174.
6   *Ibid.* This applies as well to state actions which are based on majoritarian mandate through popular elections. Though we cannot pursue the matter here, "the view that the majority have a moral right to dictate how all should live" poses a serious threat both to the liberal state and to any proper understanding or practice of democracy. See: H.L.A. Hart, *Liberty and Morality* (Oxford: Oxford University Press, 1963), at p. 79.

Whatever else a liberal state may properly do, then, its legitimacy begins with and is, in all respects, conditioned by these fundamental institutional requirements.

(i) Separation of Powers

Though it too is a requirement of liberal politics, as here used, separation of powers does not refer to the separation between church (the sacred) and state (the secular).[7] It refers rather to the identity and limitations of the constitutive elements and practices of the secular, Rule of Law state.

Allan observes that "the doctrine of the separation of powers is an implicit requirement of the rule of law".[8] Surely he is right since otherwise any number of features which we associate with the Rule of Law — for instance, an independent judiciary — would have neither foundation nor defence. But the rationale goes much deeper than that. *Separation of powers is the first requirement and criterion of Rule of Law since it alone ensures that the power of the state, which exists to constrain power, is itself constrained. And the separation of powers founds not only the independence of the judiciary, but as well the existence of a free and self-governing legal community from which the judiciary is drawn and of which it is a part.* Assuming that the Rule of Law credentials of the doctrine, we need now to identify and define the powers.

THE POWERS

It was Montesquieu's genius to discover what has rightly been called "a universal principle of political life"[9]: that unaccountable power is arbitrary and abusive power and that political power can only be held to account by the "ballast" of the separation of powers.[10] Montesquieu claimed that "political liberty ... is present only when power is not abused", and that for power not to be abused, "power must check power by the arrangement of things".[11] "In order", he thought, "to form a moderate government, one must combine powers, regulate them, temper them, make them act; one must give one power ballast, so to speak, to put it in a position to resist the other".[12] This understanding led Montesquieu to distinguish between the legislative, executive and judicial powers of the state, and to propose that "liberty is formed by a certain distribution of the

---

[7]   The gist of the division between the sacred and the secular is that religious reasons are private reasons and cannot therefore count as reasons in politics and in law.

[8]   T.R.S. Allan, "The Rule of Law as the Rule of Reason" (1999), 115 Law Q. Rev. 221 at p. 228.

[9]   T. Todorov, *On Human Diversity*, trans. C. Porter (Cambridge, MA: Harvard University Press, 1993), at p. 375.

[10]   A.M. Cohler, *et al.*, eds., *Montesquieu: The Spirit of the Laws* (Cambridge: Cambridge University Press, 1989), at p. 4.

[11]   *Ibid.*, at p. 155.

[12]   *Ibid.*, at p. 63.

three powers".[13] "When legislative power is united with the executive power in a single person or single body of the magistracy, there is no liberty. ... Nor is there liberty if the power of judging is not separate from the legislative power and from the executive power".[14] This is so, he thought, because power will inevitably become despotic or tyrannic, unless one power "is chained to the other by their reciprocal power of vetoing"[15] or unless they are "counter-balanced".[16]

This account of the separation of powers puts us on the right path. Since we now know that the focus is constraint through division, we will not be persuaded by any view which associates the Rule of Law with legislative supremacy or executive privilege. Indeed, we will know that views of that sort cannot represent the Rule of Law since, without more, they constitute violations of it. Yet, despite these rewards, this accounting is neither precise nor expansive enough. It is of course true that the Rule of Law requires that powers of the state take three separate and independent forms, the legislative, the executive and the judicial. But saying this does not tell us why these are the forms nor does it account for the special relationship of the judiciary, in Rule of Law states, to the legal profession and to the legal academy.

There is a prior understanding of separation of powers which accounts for both of these matters, namely, that the separation of powers, which in part defines the Rule of Law state, is a separation between the "political" and the "legal". This view of the matter answers our questions by providing grounds for identifying all of the forms of public practice which characterize Rule of Law states and for differentiating between them. In such states, the political takes two forms, the legislative (rule-making) and the executive (rule execution and enforcement). The legal, on the other hand, takes three forms, the judicial (adjudication), the practising (citizen counselling and representation) and the academic (cultural transmission of the Rule of Law). So viewed, the legal community as a whole, and not just the judiciary, finds its home, and its justification, in the institutional requirements of the liberal state. Moreover, the legal and the political can then be seen as two forms of practice characteristic of the political life of the liberal state.

Law and politics are sometimes thought of as contradictory moments of politics more generally, the one a matter of will and the other of deliberation. But such as view is mistaken and unproductive. In the Rule of Law state, law and politics, though necessarily divided to constrain power, are yet united as practices which constitute *government by law*. And though they differ fundamentally as practices and necessarily so, those differences are much more subtle and intelligent than any difference associated with the distinction between will and deliberation. The legal and the political are each a forum for debate and argument

---

[13] *Ibid.*, at p. 187.
[14] *Ibid.*, at p. 157.
[15] *Ibid.*, at p. 164.
[16] *Ibid.*, at p. 182.

about the terms and conditions of communal and individual life and about the reach of governance by law particularly. The difference between them resides then not in their object, but in the terms in which each frames and carries on that debate. In Chapter 3, we encountered the distinction between principle and policy from which the legal community proceeds. We can now add that this distinction is fundamental to the Rule of Law because it provides the metre for differentiating between the legal and the political and for defining the separation of powers. In each of its forms, the legal is a *forum of principle* because it concerns rights and because it is therefore characterized by an insistence on the priority of the individual. The political, on the other hand, is in both of its forms a *forum of policy* because it concerns what is best overall and because it is therefore characterized by compromises and trade-offs between conflicting purposes and, sometimes, conflicting groups.

THE RELATIONSHIP BETWEEN THE BRANCHES

This identification of the powers, however, tells us nothing about the relations between them nor anything much about the obligations of each. True, we do now know that "each branch of government must be confined to the exercise of its own function and not allowed to encroach upon the functions of the other branches".[17] And we know from our previous explorations that the practices of the branches cannot be distinguished by any metre which expresses the view that the political lays down the rules and the legal follows and applies the rules thus laid down. On the contrary, we know that the political and the legal both make rules and that the difference between them is a matter of context and idiom. We know, that is, that it falls to the political to debate, decide and implement policy and to the legal to debate and protect individual rights on a case-by-case basis. We also know that the judicial branch is in this fashion independent from the political branches *and* they from it. Finally, we know that any proper view of the relation between the branches, and between the political and the legal, more generally, must account both for these fundamental differences of idiom and context and for the mutual constraint of power which is the moral purpose and substance of separation of powers.

We have then to be more precise as regards both the obligations of the branches and the relations between them. So far as the former is concerned, several general comments will have to suffice. First, government by law is a moderate government.[18] It aims to avoid the extremes of self-interest and of passion which typify tyranny and despotism. Accordingly, under the morality of Rule of

---

[17] M.J.C. Vile, *Constitutionalism and the Separation of Powers* (Oxford: Clarendon Press, 1967), at p. 13.

[18] See: Todorov, *supra*, note 9, at pp. 372-77; W. von Humboldt, *The Limits of State Action*, J.W. Burrow, ed. (Indianapolis: Liberty Fund, 1993).

Law, "to tyrannize" in either way "is not to rule".[19] As a general matter, then, we can say that the Rule of Law state, in its political and in its legal manifestations, is obligated to act moderately and, in so doing, to avoid enthusiasms which every so often infect society more generally. Though we cannot canvass the matter of the obligations of the executive and legislative branches in any detail, we can say that, as a practical matter, the Rule of Law "most often contributes to the enactment of good laws".[20] This is so for two related reasons. On the one hand, because the Rule of Law is a rule of justice, it necessarily imports the language of justice into legislative deliberation. And, on the other, because the Rule of Law therefore requires legislatures to enact general laws, it serves formal equality and indeed such rules corporately comprise a morality of equality. Finally, as regards the obligations of the legal and the judiciary particularly, the remainder of this book is very much devoted to just that matter. Indeed, the question of the relation between the legislative and the legal (and the judicial particularly), to which we must now turn, is the beginning.

Our concern is not constitutional review which becomes an issue in liberal states which, like Canada and the United States, happen to have a charter (or bill) of rights. Such constitutional instruments are not a requirement of the Rule of Law and their place in liberal politics, more generally, is a cause of much controversy. Our concern rather is the attitude to positive law, to legislation, which the Rule of Law requires of the legal community generally and of the judicial branch specifically. This is a problem for several reasons. First, there is the matter of the intractable force of interpretation which makes legislation vulnerable to judicial and legal practice. Second, there is the matter of democratic source which confers moral force and dignity on legislation.[21] Third, there is the matter that the legal community and judges particularly have somehow to respect that dignity. Finally, there is matter of the Rule of Law itself which first requires the branches "to resist"[22] and "to counterbalance"[23] one another and then declares the imperative that all institutions comply with legal principle. Now this last matter is the nub. How is the legal at once to respect, to resist and to superintend the political?

This quandary is ancient in our tradition. In 1765, Sir William Blackstone put the matter thus:

> In this distinct and separate existence of the judicial power in a peculiar body of men, nominated indeed, but not removable at pleasure, by the Crown, consists one main preservative of public liberty; which cannot subsist long in any state, unless the administration of common justice be in some degree separated from the legislative and also from the executive power. Were it joined with the legislative, the life, liberty, and property of

---

[19] C.H. McIlwain, *Constitutionalism and the Changing World* (Cambridge: Cambridge University Press, 1939), at p. 43.
[20] Allan, *supra*, note 8, at pp. 97-99.
[21] See: J. Waldron, "The Dignity of Legislation" (1995), 54 Maryland L. Rev. 663.
[22] A.M. Cohler, *supra*, note 10, at p. 63.
[23] *Ibid.*, at p. 187.

the subject would be in the hands of arbitrary judges, whose decisions would then be regulated by their own opinions, and not by the fundamental principles of law; which, though the legislatures may depart from them, yet judges are bound to observe.[24]

But he did not tell us how judges were "to observe" those principles in cases where they have before them unprincipled legislation. In the preceding century, in his judgment in *Doctor Bonham's Case*,[25] Sir Edward Coke was much more candid as regards law's superintendency of the political:

And it appears in our books that in many cases the common law will controul acts of parliament, and sometimes adjudge them to be utterly void: for when an act of parliament is against common right and reason, or repugnant, or impossible to be performed, the common law will controul it, and adjudge such act to be void.[26]

Coke's view has been the focus of debate in the legal community ever since. And little wonder since it both states, and fails to resolve, the complicated requirements of the Rule of Law through the separation of powers.

We cannot solve the riddle of the proper relationship between courts and legislatures here. What we can do is to suggest, and then to illustrate, one solution which sounds in a large swath of legal tradition. The following figure represents the suggestion:

Figure 7.1

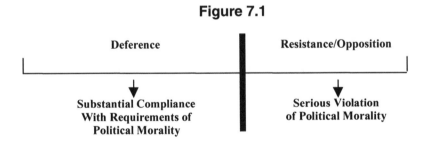

The metre of the continuum of political morality depicted is legal equality, the norms of equal protection and equal application. Under this view, the political morality of equality is operating normally in legislation if legislation substantially accords with equal treatment. In such cases — and, in a healthy political community, they will comprise the vast majority — it falls to the courts, and to the legal community more generally, simply to defer to legislatures.

---

[24] W. Blackstone, *Commentaries on the Laws of England* (1765) Vol. I (New York: Garland, 1978), at p. 269.

[25] 8 Co. Reports 107a.

[26] *Ibid.*, at 117b-118b.

It is the business of legislatures to make distinctions, and an assessment of substantial compliance will require judgment. But judgment needn't mean a tyranny of discretion. Indeed, it is the business of judges (and lawyers) to see that it doesn't. In Chapter 6, we discussed the Supreme Court of Canada's decision in *Andrews*,[27] and found that, according to the Court, legislative distinctions will offend equal treatment only where they express, and depend upon, "irrelevant personal differences" between persons.[28] There is great wisdom in this view. It not only allows legislatures to make the policy decisions and distinctions required by liberal justice, it accords with the whole notion of justice at law by preventing government by whimsy or caprice.

Sometimes, however, the political morality of equality will break down. Legislation will be enacted which counts "irrelevant personal differences" for and against some group or another. When that is the case, it falls to legal community to oppose and to resist legislation and to the judicial branch to declare it violative of fundamental law and as such void.

Unhappily, the morality of deference is often observed in its breach. This is especially the case in jurisdictions, like Canada and the United States, which have a written charter or bill of rights. Unless judges have "the requisite attitudes to law and law-like ways",[29] constitutional instruments of this sort are an enduring occasion for sinning against the commandment of judicial restraint. That commandment is central to responsible judging because, unlike the other branches, the judicial branch is not vulnerable to invasion and is not subject to external control. For those reasons, when the commandment is broken, and to the extent that it is broken, the result is judicial tyranny.

More important for our purposes are cases which concern the obligation of the courts, and of the legal community more generally, to oppose and resist legislation which violates the morality of equal treatment. Of course, our law is full of cases in which courts, especially constitutional courts, have made good that obligation. In Chapter 6, we discussed the Supreme Court of Canada's decision in *Vriend v. Alberta*[30] as an instance of such fidelity. But cases in which courts are without the luxury of a constitutional crutch on which to lean their obligations are more instructive still. We shall therefore conclude our discussion of the separation of powers with two cases of this sort, one which shows the Supreme Court of Canada standing with equality against bad government and the other which reveals the same Court in want of the courage to resist.

In *Roncarelli v. Duplessis*,[31] a Montreal restaurateur sued Maurice Duplessis, then Premier of Quebec, for damages arising out of the cancellation of his licence to sell liquor by the Quebec Liquor Commission. It was not disputed that

---

27 [1989] 56 D.L.R. (4th) 1 (S.C.C.).
28 *Ibid.*, at 11.
29 R.S. Summers, "A Formal Theory of the Rule of Law" (1993), 6(2) Ratio Juris 127 at p. 130.
30 [1998] 1 S.C.R. 493, 156 D.L.R. (4th) 385.
31 [1959] S.C.R. 121, 16 D.L.R. (2d) 689.

Roncarelli's licence was cancelled at the instigation of the defendant whose purpose was to prevent the plaintiff, a Jehovah's Witness, from continuing to furnish bail for other Witnesses charged with various offences. Duplessis's defence was that the Liquor Commission, by statute, had an absolute discretion to cancel any permit and further that he was a public officer fulfilling a public function and had not received the required notice before the action was brought. The Supreme Court found for the plaintiff, despite the law providing untrammelled discretion and the law protecting public officers fulfilling any public function, by holding that there was at law no such thing as absolute discretion and that the law provides no protection to public officers who act unlawfully and outside their duties. In so deciding, the Court held the state of Quebec to standards of the Rule of Law and stood with a plaintiff against a state which would count his religious confession, a patently irrelevant personal characteristic, against him.

In 1912, the Legislature of Saskatchewan made it an offence for any person to "employ in any capacity any white woman or girl or permit any white woman or girl to reside or to lodge in or to work in or, save as a *bona fide* customer in a public apartment thereof only, to frequent any restaurant, laundry or other place of business or amusement owned, kept or managed by any Japanese, Chinaman or other Oriental person".[32] Soon after its coming into force, a prosecution was commenced against one Quong-Wing, a naturalized Canadian citizen, who contested the Act's validity. He lost in Magistrate's Court, in the Saskatchewan Court of Appeal and in the Supreme Court of Canada.[33] At the Supreme Court, the appellant's counsel argued, *inter alia*, that "the aim of the Act is to deprive the defendant and the Chinese generally, whether naturalized or not, of the rights ordinarily enjoyed by the other inhabitants of the Province of Saskatchewan", which is to say, counsel argued equal treatment.[34] Chief Justice of Canada Fitzpatrick made short shrift of this invocation of the Rule of Law:

> Why should [the legislature] not have power to enact that women and girls should not be employed in certain industries or in certain places or by a certain class of people? This legislation may affect the civil rights of Chinamen, but it is primarily directed to the protection of children and girls.
> The Chinaman is not deprived of the right to employ others, but the classes from which he may select his employees are limited. In certain factories women and children under a certain age are not permitted to work at all, and, in others, they may not be employed except subject to certain restrictions in the interest of the employee's bodily and moral welfare. The difference between the restrictions imposed upon all Canadians by such legislation and those resulting from the Act in question is one of degree, not of kind.[35]

---

[32] S.S. 1912, c. 17.
[33] *Quong-Wing v. R.* (1914), 49 S.C.R. 440, affg 4 W.W.R. 1135. Leave to appeal to the Privy Council was refused.
[34] *Ibid.*, at 443 (*per* Fitzpatrick C.J.C.).
[35] *Ibid.*, at 444-45.

Through these analogies, the Court turned equality upside down and inside out, and it did so in order to stand with a racist state against the equality of citizens, and not just the appellant, under law.

So the separation of powers is a wonderfully complex affair. On the one hand, in most cases, restraint and deference alone save judicial independence from licence and tyranny; yet, on the other hand, in some cases, judicial independence can only be saved for principle if judges resist and oppose unjust laws. It is the wisdom and the fragility of our law that it places this burden of principle on the capacity of lawyers to know the difference.

(ii)   A Regime of Rights

The separation of powers is the first institutional arm of government by the Rule of Law. It constrains the power of political community to act in ways which serve ends other than the good of the governed by dividing public power and, through that, by preventing its consolidation. More particularly, the separation of powers is the source institutionally of the legal community and of the judicial branch especially, and it places that community and judges at the very heart of liberal political community. However, the separation of powers is not sufficient to good government nor does it disclose the elemental contribution of the legal community to the constraint of power.

Earlier, we defined the Rule of Law as a "mode of association" in political community and as a "locus of argumentation" about the terms and conditions of that association.[36] Though separation of powers structures liberal government, it provides neither the substance of our association nor the vocabulary of the distinctively public speech we use, we lawyers especially, to argue about what our association requires. Those matters are provided by the second arm of the Rule of Law, *a body of public rules which confers rights which constrain public and private power*. Our exploration of this requirement of government by law will be guided by two questions: first, why rules are necessary? and, second, which rules are necessary? These inquiries will permit us to reach three fundamentally important conclusions: that Rule of Law is the institutional practice of constraining public and private power through a regime of rights entrusted to a free and independent legal community; that the law as a whole consists of rules concerning the nature of harms from which political community will save us safe at law; and that it is the on-going practice of the legal community at the behest of others to discuss — and finally to determine — whether any particular conduct constitutes a harm at law because it constitutes an unacceptable interference with moral independence.

---

[36]   M. Oakeshott, *supra*, note 1, and N. MacCormick, *supra*, note 2 and accompanying text.

WHY RULES?

"Legal rights are conferred by legal rules".[37] This seemingly banal beginning is easily overlooked, especially by those who are new to law. First-year law students encounter the connection between rights and rules in a most haphazard fashion. In property law class, their professor will typically proclaim property to be "a bundle of rights" (though sometimes without explaining the metaphor),[38] and in constitutional law and in criminal law, they will be taught about the rights of citizens against government. But rare is the law student who will connect rights in these contexts with the rest of their courses or, rarer still, with the law as such. So let's be clear at the beginning: *our law as a whole is a "bundle" of rights* which enshrines and protects our negative liberty to be saved safe from harm. But this declaration does not communicate the substance, namely, the reason and fashion in which rules are necessary for Rule of Law. Answering this question will make clear the connection between rules, rights and law.

We can begin by recalling the insight we encountered in Chapter 1, that rules are a means of constraining the discretion of decision-makers. On this ground alone, rules associate themselves with the ethos of the Rule of Law. Rules constrain the legal community from arguing willy-nilly about what the law requires and judges from deciding according to their own lights what in any given case the law is. Lawyers are bound to and by the rules of law, and rules are, for them, jurisdictional, the matter about which they are authorized to speak.

The jurisdictional nature of rules has another aspect. Lawyers and judges are bound to the rules of law, yet we have seen that rules, including legislated rules, are continually remade through analogy and distinguishing and that sometimes they are overruled. From this vantage, rules are a requirement and acknowledgement of the separation of powers. Where power is united, where one decision-maker makes all decisions, rules have "little or no role to play."[39] Where, on the other hand, power is divided, rules become unavoidable because they are a necessary means of constituting, allocating and differentiating decision-making power. Consequently, we might expect that Rule of Law states will have constitutive rules through which the separation of powers is institutionalized.

Rules are the elemental vocabulary of law, not only because they constitute and constrain the power of legal actors to act and to argue, but also because they require decision-makers — legislators, judges, and lawyers — to speak in

---

[37] D.N. MacCormick, "Rights in Legislation" in P.M.S. Hacker and J. Raz, *Law, Morality and Society* (Oxford: Clarendon Press, 1977), p. 189 at 189.

[38] Concerning which, see: J.E. Penner, "The Bundle of Rights' Picture of Property" (1996), 43 U.C.L.A. Rev. 711 (arguing that "property is a bundle of rights" is "little more than a slogan" which has no real "explanatory" force).

[39] F. Schauer, "Rules and The Rule of Law" (1991), 14(3) Harvard J. of Law & Public Policy 645 at 686.

certain ways. These requirements follow from the very notion of regulating conduct by rules, and together they comprise a morality of rule governance.[40]

Rules by their very nature must be *general, clear, publicly accessible, formulated in advance* and *prospective in application*. Each of these dimensions concords with fundamental requirements of the Rule of Law. Generality makes rules apply to classes rather than to particular people or to groups. Generality is a natural vocabulary for political communities governed by the Rule of Law since, in communities of that sort, what counts is our equality beyond difference. Any political community which has as its metre rights rather than roots will speak through rules because rules speak to equality.

That rules must be clear, publicly accessible, and prospective prohibits secret law and promotes *transparency*. Clarity requires that rules be stated in standard form (if a, b, c, then r) and in language which is precise and unambiguous. Public accessibility requires that rules be open, that individuals can find out, at any given moment, what they are. Prospectivity requires that the rules be announced before they apply, and this requirement erects a presumption against rules which aim to apply retroactively. By declaring beforehand and publicly the conditions of their application, rules disclose and make intelligible the nature and limits of governmental power. Unless political institutions are capable of explaining and justifying themselves, not after the fact but through their on-going, rule-governed practices, then the very notions of constraint of power, and of liberty and equal treatment, becomes jest. For absent such rules, rules which are "well-known and available for public apprehension and scrutiny," governmental action must be driven purely by power and must "depend on mythology, mystification, or a 'noble lie'".[41]

To qualify as a rule, under the Rule of Law, a rule must then contain and unambiguously and openly communicate specific, intelligible conditions for its application. Otherwise, it is no rule at all, but a ruse to express and accomplish arbitrary power. In order for rules generally to satisfy these conditions, it is necessary as well that the rules of law be relatively stable over time. This final condition makes sense of our discovery in Chapter 4: though they are often amended to fit new facts, rules are seldom overruled because the Rule of Law requires stability.

Rules and rights have a deeper kinship than even these associations portray. Rules, like rights, constitute relationships. This they do because, when they apply to our affairs, they situate us with respect to others. First there are those others to whom any given rule also applies. The rule creates between us a specifically legal relationship of equality: we each have a claim, as legal subjects, that it apply equally in the sense that each of us will be subject to it and in

---

[40] Lon Fuller's is the seminal account of this morality. See: L.L. Fuller, *The Morality of Law*, rev. ed. (New Haven: Yale University Press, 1969).

[41] J. Waldron, "Theoretical Foundations of Liberalism" in J. Waldron, *Liberal Rights* (Cambridge: Cambridge University Press, 1993), at pp. 35 at 58.

the sense that it will be applied in the same way. As regards those others to whom the rule does not apply, we to whom it does apply have an equality claim against all of them that they be excluded from the rule's application and benefit. Like rights, rules both institute equality and produce claims by the rule-subject against others.

That our law then is committed and confined to rules is not accidental. Rules and rules alone provide the vocabulary appropriate to limited and divided government; and rules are the natural form of expression of government by rights.

WHICH RULES?

The following figure, which illustrates the anatomy of our law, will frame our inquiry:

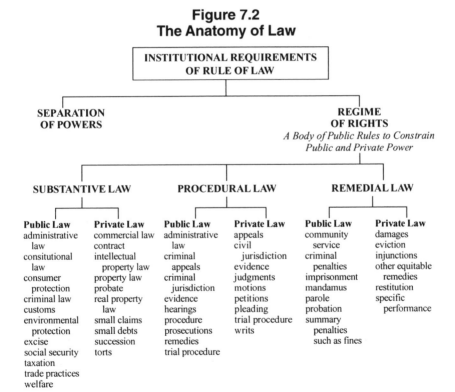

**Figure 7.2
The Anatomy of Law**

INSTITUTIONAL REQUIREMENTS
OF RULE OF LAW

SEPARATION
OF POWERS

REGIME
OF RIGHTS
*A Body of Public Rules to Constrain
Public and Private Power*

SUBSTANTIVE LAW

PROCEDURAL LAW

REMEDIAL LAW

Public Law	**Private Law**	**Public Law**	**Private Law**	**Public Law**	**Private Law**
administrative law	commercial law	administrative law	appeals	community service	damages
consitutional law	contract	criminal	civil jurisdiction	criminal	eviction
consumer protection	intellectual property law	appeals	evidence	penalties	injunctions
criminal law	property law	criminal jurisdiction	judgments	imprisonment	other equitable remedies
customs	probate	evidence	motions	mandamus	restitution
environmental protection	real property law	hearings	petitions	parole	specific performance
excise	small claims	procedure	pleading	probation	
social security	small debts	prosecutions	trial procedure	summary penalties	
taxation	succession	remedies	writs	such as fines	
trade practices	torts	trial procedure			
welfare					

SUBSTANTIVE AND PROCEDURAL LAW

Karl Llewellyn once claimed that an "*accurate* statement of a 'real rule' or of a right includes all procedural limitations on what can be done about the situation".[42] He was right. Our law includes not only those rules which establish and communicate the *substance* of our rights at law, but also rules concerning what steps have to be taken to achieve a legal result with respect to them. Lawyers refer to the former as *substantive law* and to the latter as *procedural* and *remedial law*. Procedural law includes the rules which govern pleading, process, evidence and practice. The law of evidence is particularly important since it consists of rules which govern the proof of the facts which engage the rules of substantive law. Remedial law consists of rules which govern judicial decisions concerning the enforcement of rights, either before or after the fact of their violation. Remedies redress, relieve, or in some other fashion solve a grievance or injury, and they vary according to whether the law involved is substantive or procedural and, if substantive, whether the matter is governed by public or private law. For instance, all other things being equal, remedy in private law generally means damages which consists of monetary compensation for a violation or infringement of a legal right. Remedies in public law range from fine and imprisonment to declarations of various sorts concerning the conduct of a governmental body or official.

It is often said that procedural law is adjectival law inasmuch as the laws of procedure and remedy provide a method of enforcing rights whereas substantive law creates, defines and regulates those rights. But, though illuminating, this is not quite accurate since procedural rules vest real rights in individuals. Lawyers refer to certain of these procedural rights collectively as *rights of natural justice* or *due process*. Among the maxims of natural justice which all lawyers stand ready to invoke are: *nemo judex (debet esse) in sua causa* (the maxim that "no one should judge his own cause" refers to the right to impartiality); *audi alteram partem* (the maxim "hear the other side" refers to the right to a fair and open hearing); *ubi jus, ibi remedium* (the maxim "where there is a right, there is a remedy" refers to the right to a remedy on proper grounds).

PUBLIC AND PRIVATE LAW

If the Rule of Law is the institutionalized morality of constraining power of and through the state, then our law must contain one body of rules to constrain the state's power over our lives and another to constrain the power of private individuals, groups and organizations over our lives. Otherwise, the law's promise of equality through rights would amount to nothing, since then our autonomy would be forever and always vulnerable to the claims and whimsy of the power-

---

[42] K. Llewellyn, *Jurisprudence* (Chicago: University of Chicago Press, 1963), at p. 22 (emphasis in original).

ful. The body of law which constrains the power of the state is called *public law*, and the body which constrains private power, *private law*.

It is sometimes said that the difference between public law and private law resides in the source of the rules of which each is composed. According to this view, public law consists of those bodies of law which are properly dictated by popular will, whereas private law consists of those bodies which should remain independent from politics.[43] This understanding identifies constitutional law and criminal law as public law and remits the law of contract, torts and property to the apolitical custody of the legal community. Any such distinction between lawyer's law and political law is profoundly mistaken and provides an entirely unacceptable conception of the distinction between public and private law. For one thing, many rules of private law are legislated. Think for instance of the rules which govern commercial enterprises such as companies and corporations or the rules governing wills, all of which are legislated. But the problems go much deeper than description.

Public law does differ from private law, but not because the one is political and attaches itself to democratic politics and the other is apolitical and finds its place in the judicial. They differ rather because each has a distinct object. Public law aims to constrain public power; private law aims to constrain private power. So viewed, the distinction between public and private law is no mere "classificatory device that can be used or discarded as seems most convenient",[44] but "an element of a much wider political theory" concerning the public good.[45] We have identified the legal good to be the Rule of Law, and we have said that that good is an expression and requirement of liberal politics. To think otherwise, to propose that private law is a residue of apolitical judicial verities whereas public law is an expression of contingent political will, is to render our law hopelessly divided and bereft of any unifying structure and purpose. Because our law *does* have structural integrity, depicting it in this way is an "ideological distortion" which can serve no purpose beyond professional conceit.[46]

Public law, then, constrains political power and constructs a sphere of rights which defines our place in political society. Private law, on the other hand, constrains social power and constructs a sphere of rights which secures our place in civil society. Certain bodies of law have both public and private law aspects. Family law is an instance. Inasmuch as the rules of marriage and divorce concern the rights of persons as between themselves, family law would appear to be entirely a private law matter. However, when we remember that it is the state itself which constitutes marriage and divorce, naming family law as private law becomes much less certain. Could, for instance, the state properly replace the

---

[43] See for example: A. Altman, *Arguing About Law* (Belmont, CA: Wadsworth, 1996), at pp. 93-96.

[44] N.E. Simmonds, *The Decline of Juridical Reason: Doctrine and Theory in Legal Order* (Manchester: Manchester University Press, 1984), at p. 121.

[45] *Ibid.*, at p. 121.

[46] *Ibid.*, at p. 90.

present definition of marriage, which requires that spouses be of the opposite sex, with one which would permit same sex marriage? If the proper analogy for marriage law is the law of contract, then the answer must be yes since contract leaves the nature of agreements to the parties. On the other hand, if the proper analogy is constitutional law, then the state might not be any more seized of this authority than it has authority to legislate away the division of powers.[47]

D. LAW'S SUBVERSIVENESS

The Rule of Law declares *the priority of justice over power*. Now, neither this declaration nor the practices which it informs is in any fashion utopian. It does not fall to liberal political community to cleanse the world of power, though there are political communities and theories whose aim that is. Rather, by insisting on the primacy of the rights owed to individuals, political communities governed by the Rule of Law seek only to constrain power from having its way unopposed in the world and over our lives. Yet, in inhibiting power, the Rule of Law has an awful and immense influence on power. By dividing the powers of the state, by institutionalizing a free and independent legal community and judiciary, by installing a regime of public and private rights, and by nurturing a sense justice and the vocabulary of rights, liberal political communities become communities in which power is *destabilized*.

That law is subversive of power in this fashion is overwhelmingly important and not least as regards the morality of legal practice. We shall want then to understand the nature of this subversion with some precision. First, the Rule of Law proceeds from a premise which, without more, subverts power. Power expresses itself in abstractions and consolidates in collectivities. Whatever their vocabulary — nation, race, class, gender, ethnicity — abstractions seek, and depend upon, "the leaching away of the person" into some collective.[48] Our law, in contrast, is first and last a commitment to the moral and political primacy of the individual. Legal thought does not leach away the individual in service to power, but instead corrodes the collectives and abstractions in which power takes shape and resides in order to serve and to preserve the individual. This is the source of the narrowness of lawyerly vision which we noted earlier: lawyers care about individual cases and not grand causes because they care about individuals and not abstractions. But there is more to it than that. Our law does not just serve each of us as individuals, in a very important sense, it constitutes our identity as individuals. Law "contribute[s] to the self-identity" of all who are

---

[47] We cannot dwell further on these issues here, except perhaps to note that any acceptable settlement of them would require answer to the question of the state's authority to distribute benefits on what appears to be coerced sexuality.

[48] J. Vining, *From Newton's Sleep* (Princeton: Princeton University Press, 1995), at p. 208.

subject to its rule.[49] The Rule of Law is a rule of rights, and it weaves social relations and identities from a yarn of insistence on the irreducible and universal significance of individuals.

Second, our law requires power to respond in terms other than power itself. Law "introduces a breach in the unity of power".[50] No matter the extra-legal powers of the parties, it falls to the party making a claim to make it out at law and to the party defending against a claim to respond in law. Law is, in this sense, "force available to all" and, as such, it diminishes the force, which beyond the law, is a fellow of social and political power.[51]

Third, rights criticize the distribution of power. This is so, not because rights protect us from power, though they do, but more fundamentally because rights constitute a commitment to side with those who are vulnerable to power. Now, once again, there is nothing starry-eyed about this, nor does it import prejudice into our law. Siding with the vulnerable, rather, inheres in the very notion of rights. Rights approach power with deep suspicion because power tends to deny the sharing of power which rights demand. Rights are, in this sense, a practice of suspicion: *to believe in rights is to believe that power needs always to be justified against the requirements of equality.* We are each of us vulnerable to power. And when power seeks to have its way with us, our rights at law require that power account for itself in the language of rights itself.

That law is for these reasons subversive means everything to legal practice. First of all, it makes the practice of law a practice which unsettles social order. Earlier, we discovered that the past to which law is bound is porous, a past which must always contend with the insistent claims of the present. We can now add that this is not merely an incident of inevitable openness of interpretation and proof, but has to do with the moral purpose of legal practice as such. Because rights are the stuff of legal rules, legal practice is the practice of keeping open and fluid the terms and conditions of public and private life. And in that sense, *law is against order.*

The legal community, we found in Part I, is a community defined by tradition and sustained by the habits of legality. We can now offer a more precise rendering. If legal practice calls power to account, then, from the moral point of view, the legal community is a community institutionalized to oppose power. So viewed, the independence of the legal community expresses the need which characterizes liberal society to have at its centre a tradition whose mission it is to contest power's consolidation generally and the foreclosure of our politics and personal lives particularly. Law proceeds case by case, and is experimental and

---

[49] E.P. Thompson, *The Poverty of Theory or An Orrey of Errors* (London: Merlin, 1978), at p. 288.
[50] T. Todorov, *supra*, note 9, at p. 374.
[51] *Ibid.*

experiential, because its aim is keep open space for innovation in our form of life, space for what Mill called "experiments in living."[52]

Dicey famously, and happily, characterized the Rule of Law as "the predominance of the legal spirit".[53] In Chapter 4, we examined the lawyerly habits which alone make real the spirit of the law. We can now be more exact about them as well. The habits of legality which sustain the Rule of Law are habits which define, and are required by, the place of the legal community in liberal politics. In order to serve individual rights, lawyers must be literate in the traditions which comprise the practices of equality at law. But, as we discovered, literacy is nothing without conscious commitment. And to be committed to law, to its point of constraining power in service to justice, lawyers must be at once impartial and partisan. Impartiality is a requirement and a consequence of the lawyer's commitment to equality, and it informs what Mary Ann Glendon calls "strong toleration" with respect to the circumstances of those who seek the law's protection and solace.[54] This toleration abhors ideological attachment to causes which would lead lawyers to serve the favoured and to deny the rest. Lawyers, rather, must "feel a unity between all citizens — real and not the factitious product of propaganda — which recognizes their common fate and their common aspirations".[55] Yet, neither impartiality nor toleration means neutrality. Just the contrary. *Lawyers are impartial as between different views of what is best overall, and they are tolerant of the lives and foibles of those who come to them, just because they are partisans of liberal political community and deeply devoted to the ideals and practices of the Rule of Law.*

E.   LAW AGAINST ORDER: ILLUSTRATIONS

Government by rights means that harm alone limits our liberty. Consequently, unless and until we cause harm to others, the order of our lives falls to our own devices and discretion. Differently put, absent proof of harm, no order — public or private — can impose its requirements upon us. In Chapter 8, we shall see that the whole of our law is about harm, its nature and its proof, and about when in consequence our self-ordering may properly cease to govern. Our present occupation is illustration. We shall discuss two cases, one prosaic and the other rather more grand, which demonstrate the law's opposition to the claims of order

---

[52] J.S. Mill, "On Liberty" in J. Gray, ed., *On Liberty and Other Essays* (Oxford: Oxford University Press, 1991).

[53] A.V. Dicey, *Introduction to the Study of the Constitution*, 8th ed. (London: Macmillan & Co., 1924), at p. 191.

[54] M.A. Glendon, *A Nation Under Lawyers* (Cambridge, MA: Harvard University Press, 1994), at p. 106.

[55] Learned Hand, "The Contribution of an Independent Judiciary to Civilization" in L. Hand, *The Spirit of Liberty*, 3rd ed. (New York: Knopf, 1960), at pp. 155 at 164, quoted in Glendon, *ibid.*, at pp. 106-107.

against our lives. Incidentally, nothing turns on the fact that the cases involve claims by public authorities. Our law has the same attitude towards private power of all sorts and in various contexts.

In *Pedro v. Diss*,[56] the accused Ya Ya Pedro was charged with assaulting a police officer, one Constable Martin Diss. The facts were these. Late one night in 1979, in London, Diss observed Pedro standing near the door to a house which, it turned out, was his brother's. Diss approached Pedro, identified himself as a police officer, and asked Pedro why he was standing there. Pedro did not answer and walked away. When Diss repeated his question, Pedro told him to "fuck off". Eventually, Pedro did allow himself to be searched. However, when Diss questioned him about a set of keys which he found in his pockets, Pedro walked off again. When Diss grabbed him by the arm and demanded whether Diss lived "here", Pedro answered with another obsenity and swung his arms backwards and stuck Constable Diss in the chest with an elbow. When Diss then grabbed Pedro by his clothing, Pedro responded with a punch. He was eventually subdued with the assistance of two other officers and subsequently charged with assaulting a police officer in the execution of his duty.

At trial, Constable Diss testified that he thought that Pedro was a burglar and claimed that he was authorized by legislation which permitted police to "stop, search, and detain any person who may be reasonably suspected of having or conveying in any manner anything stolen or unlawfully obtained". Pedro was convicted and fined. On subsequent appeal to the High Court, the conviction was overturned. The Court held that when Pedro punched Diss, the constable was not acting in lawful execution of his duty. Consequently, Diss was in no different position than anyone else and, when he laid his hands on Pedro, Pedro was entitled at law to resist.

Now, note, the Court proceeded from the view that police do not have unlimited power to detain people for questioning and that their power to do so is set and limited by law. Where, as here, the police act without authority — because Diss failed to inform Pedro about the source of his authority and about the nature of his suspicions — they act unlawfully and citizens are not obliged to defer to them. This understanding of matters is deliciously legal. It demonstrates our law's defining suspicion of power and its enduring subversion of it.

During the Second World War, the British government enacted legislation which authorized the Secretary of State to detain persons whom the Secretary had "reasonable cause to believe ... of hostile origin or associations". In *Liversidge v. Anderson*,[57] the plaintiff Liversidge was detained under an order made by the Secretary of State, Sir John Anderson. While still in prison, the plaintiff sued for false imprisonment and sought damages and a declaration that his detention was unlawful. Liversidge lost at trial and on first appeal. On subsequent

---

[56] [1981] 2 All E.R. 59. I found this case in J. Waldron, *The Law* (London: Routledge, 1990), at pp. 29-31.
[57] [1942] A.C. 206.

appeal to the House of Lords, the matter turned on whether the Court had authority to assess the reasonableness of the Secretary of State's belief with respect to the plaintiff's "hostile associations" and therefore the authority to demand from him particulars concerning the grounds of his belief.

A majority of the House held that it had no authority to inquire whether the Secretary of State had reasonable grounds nor, in consequence, any authority to compel him to disclose the grounds on which he in fact made the order to detain the plaintiff. What concerns us is Lord Atkin's forceful dissent which, even amid the cause and concern of a world war against tyranny, speaks law to power. After first declaring the issue to be one of "great importance both because the power to make such an order is necessary for the defence of the realm and because the liberty of the subject is so seriously infringed",[58] and then meticulously constructing the governing legislation, his Lordship offers the following statement, at once eloquent and scathing, of the law's meter with respect to power:

> I view with apprehension the attitude of judges who on a mere question of construction when face to face with claims involving the liberty of the subject show themselves more executive minded than the executive. Their function is to give words their natural meaning, not, perhaps, in war time leaning towards liberty, but following the dictum of Pollock C.B. in *Bowditch v. Balchin* [(1850) 3 Ex. 378] ... : 'In a case in which the liberty of the subject is concerned, we cannot go beyond the natural construction of the statute'. In this country, amid the clash of arms, the laws are not silent. They may be changed, but they speak the same language in war as in peace. It has always been one of the pillars of freedom, one of the principles of liberty for which on recent authority we are now fighting, that the judges are no respecters of persons and stand between the subject and any attempted encroachments on his liberty by the executive, alert to see that any coercive action is justified in law. ... I protest, even if I do it alone, against a strained construction put on words with the effect of giving an uncontrolled power of imprisonment to the minister. ... The appellant's right to particulars ... is based ... on a principle which ... is one of the pillars of liberty in that in English law every imprisonment is prima facie unlawful and that it is for the person directing imprisonment to justify his act.[59]

With this display of legal craft and commitment, Lord Atkin stood against power in the name of law. That his courage in so doing honoured the courage of those who were then fighting Nazi tyranny makes his defence of law all the more memorable and instructive to those lawyers whom, in much less perilous times, our law calls to stand against power.

---

[58]   *Ibid.*, at 225.
[59]   *Ibid.*, at 244-45.

F.   RESTATEMENT NO. 4

To speak about law is to speak about power. Law both dispenses and limits power. The Rule of Law is the medium of dispensation and limitation. Through it, the state is at once constituted as the centre of coercive power and dedicated to constraining power, including its own power, for the good of those subject to its rule. This dedication requires government through separated powers and through a regime of public and private rights. Together these institutional practices save all of us safe from unprincipled power.

A free and independent legal community is a necessary dispensation of law's power. The existence of such a community, which includes a free and independent judiciary, is fundamental to limited government which is itself the end of the Rule of Law. Unless government is divided, tyranny is inevitable; and tyranny is inevitable unless there exists an institution whose dedication is the constraint of power. The legal community is thus situated at the centre of government by law and its authority resides in its stewardship of that ideal.

The legal community is a community of discourse, of argument and decision, about the rights of individuals. This makes the practice of law a *moral practice* about the limits of power, and it makes the profession of law a *public vocation.* If the authority of the legal community resides institutionally in divided government, then it resides morally in the legal community's public declaration of and dedication to the political and moral sovereignty of individuals, their rights and their duties.

To speak about law is to speak about justice. Though the laws are our masters, they are yet servants of justice. The legal community is the medium through which mastery becomes service. In identifying, interpreting and applying laws, lawyers proceed from legal commitment, their commitment to lawfulness in human lives and affairs and to the individual rights which alone make lawfulness a possibility. Their practices are saved from whimsy and self-delusion by the traditions of practice and understanding which underpin and express this lawyerly commitment.

Yet, justice at law is different from justice overall. Justice at law requires that individuals be treated equally according to the rules which properly apply to them. Equal treatment in that sense requires lawyers, and judges especially, to proceed from a coherent conception of the Law as a whole. And conceptions of that sort are acceptable only to the extent to which they fit and explain our legal traditions. The Rule of Law *is* the conception of Law which best fits and explains our legal inheritance. But that conception consigns justice at law to the circumstances of particular rules and particular facts and prohibits proceeding on grounds of grander conceptions of what would be best as a matter of justice overall.

Justice at law is justice at all only to the extent that it is bounded in these ways. And though legal "reasoning" in any given case will lack the conclusive force and precision of reasoning in mathematics or geometry, its force and validity can yet be judged according to its legal coherence, which is to say, according to whether it fits and explains the precedential past which, as a matter of law, it must fit and explain.

Justice at law resides in this principled negotiation of our future out of the requirements of our past and the demands of our present. And it is preserved from whimsy and from caprice, not only by legal craft, but by the incremental, case-bound nature of decisions at law. Unlike decisions about Justice overall, which when they are wrong are pervasively wrong, decisions at law are modest in expectation, in influence and in impact. The safety which this modesty provides depends upon lawyers themselves being modest. Lawyers must be committed to the Law and to the bounded justice which it secures; they must not act in service to any Justice which makes of law something unlawful.

FURTHER READINGS TO CHAPTER 7

1.   The Rule of Law

Allan, T.R.S. *Constitutional Justice: A Liberal Theory of the Rule of Law.* Oxford: Oxford University Press, 2001.

————. *Law, Liberty, and Justice: The Legal Foundations of British Constitutionalism.* Oxford: Clarendon Press, 1993.

Barnett, R.E. *The Structure of Liberty: Justice and the Rule of Law.* Oxford: Clarendon Press, 1998.

Blum, J.M. "Critical Legal Studies and the Rule of Law". (1990), 38 Buffalo L. Rev. 59.

Carlson, D.G. "Liberal Philosophy's Troubled Relation to the Rule of Law" (1993), 43 U. Toronto L. J. 257.

Cotterrell, R. "The Rule of Law in Transition: Revisiting Franz Neumann's Sociology of Legality". (1996), 5(4) Social & Legal Studies 451.

Craig, P. "Formal and Substantive Conceptions of the Rule of Law: An Analytical Framework,". [1997] Public Law 467.

Cristi, F.R. "Hayek and Schmitt on the Rule of Law". (1984), 27(3) Can. J. of Pol. Sc. 521.

Dicey, A.V. *Introduction to the Study of the Law of the Constitution.* 8th ed. London: Macmillan & Co., 1924. Especially ch. 6.

Dietze, G. *Two Concepts of the Rule of Law.* Indianapolis: Liberty Fund, 1973.

Dworkin, R. "Political Judges and the Rule of Law". In Dworkin, R. *A Matter of Principle.* Cambridge, MA: Harvard Unversity Press, 1985. At p. 9.

Dyzenhaus, D., ed. *Recrafting the Rule of Law: The Limits of Legal Order.* Oxford: Hart Publishing, 1999.

Endicott, T.A.O. "The Impossibility of the Rule of Law" (1999), 19 Oxford J. of Legal Studies 1.

Fallon, R.H. "The Rule of Law as a Concept in Constitutional Discourse". (1997), 97 Columbia L. Rev. 1.

Fine, B. *Democracy and the Rule of Law.* London: Pluto Press, 1984.

Fletcher, G. "Equality and the Rule of Law". (1990), 10 Tel Aviv U. Studies in Law 71.

Forte, D.F. "The Rule of Law and the Law of Rules". (1990), 38 Cleveland State L. Rev. 97.

Gaus, G.F. "The Rule of Law". In Gaus, G.F. *Justificatory Liberalism*. Oxford: Oxford University Press, 1996. At p. 195.

Harden, I., and N. Lewis, *The Noble Lie: The British Constitution and the Rule of Law*. London: Hutchinson, 1986.

Harding, A.R., ed. *The Rule of Law*. Dallas: Southern Methodist University Press, 1961.

Hayek, F.A. "The Origins of the Rule of Law". In Hayek, F.A. *The Constitution of Liberty*. Chicago: University of Chicago Press, 1960. At p. 162.

Hutchinson, A.C., and P. Monahan, eds. *The Rule of Law: Ideal or Ideology?*. Toronto: Carswell, 1987.

Lucas, J.R. "The Rule of Law". In Lucas, J.R. *The Principles of Politics*. Oxford: Clarendon Press, 1966. At p. 106.

Marsh, N. "The Rule of Law as a Supra-National Concept". In Guest, A.G., ed. *Oxford Essays in Jurisprudence*. Oxford: Oxford University Press, 1961. At p. 223.

Neumann, F. *The Rule of Law*. Warwickshire: Berg Publishers, 1986.

Radin, M.J. "Reconsidering the Rule of Law". (1989), 69 Boston .L. Rev. 781.

Raz, J. "The Rule of Law and Its Virtue". (1977), 93 Law Q. Rev. 195.

————. "The Politics of the Rule of Law". (1990), 3(3) Ratio Juris 331.

Reynolds, N.B. "Grounding the Rule of Law". (1989), 2(1) Ratio Juris 1.

Schauer, F. "Rules and the Rule of Law". (1991), 14 Harvard J. of Law & Public Policy 645.

Scheuerman, W.E., ed. *The Rule of Law Under Siege*. Berkeley: University of California Press, 1996.

————. *Between the Norm and the Exception: The Frankfurt School and the Rule of Law*. Cambridge, MA: Massachusetts Institute of Technology Press, 1994.

————. "Economic Globalization and the Rule of Law". (1999), 6(1) Constellations 3.

Shapiro, I., ed. *The Rule of Law: NOMOS XXXVI*. New York: New York University Press, 1994.

Summers, R.S. "A Formal Theory of the Rule of Law". (1993), 6(2) Ratio Juris 127.

Sypnowich, C. "Freedom and the Rule of Law". In Sypnowich, C. *The Concept of Socialist Law*. Oxford: Clarendon Press, 1990. At p. 59.

Thompson, E.P. "The Rule of Law". In Thompson, E.P. *Whigs and Hunters*. Middlesex: Penguin, 1975. At p. 258.

Tremblay, L.B. *The Rule of Law, Justice and Interpretation*. Montreal and Kingston: McGill-Queen's University Press, 1997.

Waldron, J. "The Rule of Law in Contemporary Liberal Theory". (1989), 2(1) Ratio Juris 79.

Walker, G. deQ. *The Rule of Law: Foundation of Constitutional Democracy.* Carlton: Melbourne University Press, 1988.

Westmoreland, R. "Hayek: The Rule of Law or The Law of Rules". (1998), 17 Law & Philosophy 77.

Whitford, W.C. "The Rule of Law," [2000] Wisconsin L. Rev. 723.

Wolff, R.P., ed. *The Rule of Law.* New York: Simon & Shuster, 1971.

2.   The Separation of Powers

BeVier, L.R. "Judicial Restraint: An Argument from Institutional Design". (1994), 17 Harvard J. of Law & Public Policy 7.

Casper, G. *Separating Power.* Cambridge, MA: Harvard University Press, 1997.

Dawson, R. McG. *The Principle of Official Independence.* London: P.S. King & Son, 1922.

Goldsworthy, J. *The Sovereignty of Parliament: History and Philosophy.* Oxford: Clarendon Press, 1999.

Gwyn, W.B. *The Meaning of the Separation of Powers: An Analysis of the Doctrine From Its Origin to the Adoption of the United States Constitution.* New Orleans: Tulane University Press, 1965.

Montesquieu, C.L. de S. *The Spirit of the Laws.* Cohler, A., *et al.*, ed. Cambridge: Cambridge University Press, 1989.

Neumann, F. "*Rechsstaat*, the Division of Powers and Socialism". In Kirchheimer, O., and F. Neumann. *Social Democracy and the Rule of Law.* Turner, L., and K. Tribe, trans. London: Allen & Unwin, 1987. At p. 66.

Redish, M.H. "Abstention, Separation of Powers, and the Limits of the Judicial Function". (1984), 94 Yale L.J. 71.

Scott, G. *Controlling the State: Constitutionalism from Ancient Athens to Today.* Cambridge, MA: Harvard University Press, 1999.

Sheridan, T. *Discourse on the Rise and Power of Parliaments* (1688). Port Washington, NY: Kennikat, 1970.

Stevens, R. *The Independence of the Judiciary.* Oxford: Clarendon Press, 1993.

———. "Judges, Politics, Politicians and the Confusing Role of the Judiciary". In Hawkins, K., ed. *The Human Face of Law.* Oxford: Clarendon Press, 1997. At p. 245.

———. "A Loss of Innocence? Judicial Independence and the Separation of Powers". (1999), 19 Oxford J. of Legal Studies 365.

Strong, F.R. *Judicial Function in Constitutional Limitation of Governmental Power.* Durham: Caroline Academic Press, 1997.

Talmadge, P.A. "Understanding the Limits of Power: Judicial Restraint in General Jurisdiciton Court Systems". (1999), 22 Seattle U. L. Rev. 695.

Vile, M.J.C. *Constitutionalism and the Separation of Powers.* Oxford: Clarendon Press, 1967.

von Humboldt, W. *The Limits of State Action.* (1791) J.W. Burrow, ed. Indianapolis: Liberty Fund, 1993.

Waldron, J. *The Dignity of Legislation.* Cambridge: Cambridge University Press, 1999.

Whittington, K.E. *Constitutional Construction: Divided Powers and Constitutional Meaning.* Cambridge, MA: Harvard University Press, 1999.

3. Public and Private Law

See Further Readings to Chapter 8.

4. Law and Subversion

Baynes, K. "Rights as Critique and the Critique of Rights". (2000), 28(4) Political Theory 451.

Berman, H. "Towards an Integrative Jurisprudence: Politics, Morality, History". (1988), 76 Calif. L. Rev. 779.

Cain, M., and C.B. Harrinton, eds. *Lawyers in a Postmodern World: Translation and Transgression.* New York: New York University Press, 1994.

Cohen, J. "Critiquing The Legal Order in the Name of 'Critical Morality'". (1995), 16 Cardozo L. Rev. 1599.

Douzinas, C., and R. Warrington. *Justice Miscarried: Ethics and Aesthetics in Law.* New York: Harvester Wheatsheaf, 1994.

Fletcher, C.P. "Comparative Law as a Subversive Discipline". (1998), 46 Am. J. of Comparative Law 683.

Mansbridge, J. "Using Power/Fighting Power". (1994), 1(1) Constellations 53.

Minda, G. *Postmodern Legal Movements: Law and Jurisprudence at Century's End.* New York: New York University Press, 1995.

Pettit, P. "Freedom as Antipower". (1996), 106 Ethics 576.

Selva, H., and R.M. Bohm. "Law and Liberation: Toward an Oppositional Legal Discourse". (1987), 11(3) Legal Studies Forum 243.

Shaffer, T.S. "Jurisprudence in Light of the Hebraic Faith". (1984), 1 Notre Dame J. of Law, Ethics & Public Policy 77.

Shklar, J.N. "The Liberalism of Fear". In Rosenblum, N.L., ed. *Liberalism and the Moral Life.* Cambridge, MA: Harvard University Press, 1989. At p. 21.

Teitel, R. "Transitional Jurisprudence: The Role of Law in Political Transformation". (1997), 106 Yale L.J. 2009.

Vining, J. *From Newton's Sleep.* Princeton: Princeton University Press, 1995.

Chapter 8

The Bodies of the Law

Law is the witness and external deposit of our moral life.

Justice Oliver Wendell Holmes

A. INTRODUCTION

Our rights at law may be illustrated as follows:

Figure 8.1

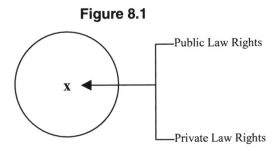

In the last chapter, we segregated rights into these two categories according to the source of the power which each seeks to constrain. Before we proceed to the taxonomy of each body of law, we must characterize more fully public and private law as expressions of the morality of the Rule of Law state.

Public and private law concern, respectively, the quality of the relations between citizens and state and between individuals themselves. These relations do not exist independently from our law. Nor does our law merely structure the datum of pre-existing social and political life in certain ways. Our law rather *constitutes* them. This should not surprise. Our law is an institutionally embedded morality about the place of power in our lives, and as such, its business is both the constitution and limitation of power. So the first thing we can say about the character of public and private law is that each creates the legal relations which are their focus.

We have already discovered that, in so doing, public and private law construct the divide, preeminent in societies such as ours, between the state and civil society. But we must be careful not to lose sight of the law's unity across this divide. Public and private law are both devoted to the constraint of power and each makes good this devotion by institutionalizing the sharing of power which defines the Rule of Law. Moreover, these are the aims and methods of each because both are very political discourses about the requirements of moral equality and moral independence. That "the autonomy of the person, which in the moral domain is all of one piece ... , appears in the legal domain only in the dual form of private and public autonomy ... the liberties of the subject of private law and the political autonomy of citizens" does not mean that the moral unity of our law is fractured.[1] Just the contrary. Public and private law both serve "to restrict the exercise of power" because both aim "to enhance the autonomy, dignity, respect, status and security" of those vulnerable to state and private power.[2]

Unhappily, public and private law are sometimes characterized in fashions which ruin this unity. For instance, it is sometimes claimed that private law comprises a law of obligations whereas public law consists of state-declared prohibitions and entitlements. According to this view, where public law expresses the will of the state with respect to the order of things overall, private law concerns those relationships between persons in civil society which give rise to legally enforceable obligations. But, as a depiction of public and private law, this is wrong.

First, it is impossible to distinguish between public and private law on grounds that public law rules emanate from the state and private law rules from the courts. Our public and private law rights rather each depend on both legislated and judicial rules and our law is in the result more complex, and interesting, than any segregation along these lines can capture. Second, the whole of our law, public and private, is public in the sense that it expresses political morality and is itself expressed in public rules. Third, the rules of both public and private law may easily be cast as either rights or obligations. For instance, the private law tort obligation that "Everyone has a duty to take reasonable care not to harm others" may properly be translated as the right that "All are entitled to be free from harm caused by the careless conduct of others". So also public law: the public law right that "Accused persons are entitled to full disclosure of the case against them" can easily be stated as the obligation "The state has an obligation of full disclosure". This is so because rights imply and require corresponding duties. Finally, because they express rights, the rules of public law and private law without exception have as their concern harm and corporately they communicate our settled moral sentiments regarding what has, and has not, to be forborne in life. For instance, though the law of contract is indeed about obligations, at a more fundamental level, its occupation is the identity of those harms which count in our practices of making promises to one another. The

---

[1]   J. Habermas, "Introduction" (1999), 12(4) Ratio Juris 329 at p. 331.
[2]   D. Oliver, "Common Values in Public and Private Law and the Public/Private Divide", [1997] Public Law 630 at p. 631.

breaking of binding promises becomes a matter of law at all only because our settled convictions about our way of life declare it a wrong that has not to be forborne.

B. PUBLIC LAW: CONSTRAINING STATE POWER

(i) Taxonomy

Figure 7.1 in Chapter 7 attempts to convey the rich complexity of public law. But it fails to impart the order and prominence of the different organs of public law. Judged against the requirements of the Rule of Law, three bodies of substantive public law are fundamental and of those one is primary.

Constitutional law, criminal law and administrative law are fundamental because those bodies of law constitute and identify the state as a Rule of Law state. Each makes a separate and important contribution to the accomplishment of limited government and together they structure the relations between citizens and state which characterize government by law.

CONSTITUTIONAL LAW

Constitutions have three aims: a) to express, formally or by implication, the fundamental values and principles of political community; b) to allocate political power among the legislative, executive, and judicial branches of the state and in federal states (Canada included), to allocate power among the different levels of government and, in so doing, c) to impose limits on the powers of the state in all its forms. Constitutional law concerns therefore the institutionalization of limited, Rule of Law government, and its distinctive contribution consists of rules about the making of rules of law. It is by reason of constitutional rules that the legislative branch is authorized to make law, the executive branch (or as Anglo-Canadian lawyers term it, the "Crown") is authorized to administer and enforce the law, and the judicial branch (and the legal community more generally) is authorized to identify, interpret and apply the law.

It is sometimes said that constitutions may be written or unwritten. For instance, the two great constitutions in the Anglo legal tradition, the American and the English, are sometimes contrasted in this way. But this contrast is not quite accurate. It is true that constitutional rules in the United States (and in Canada) reside in a document called "the constitution" whereas the rules in England do not. Yet, it is also true that the most important rules of any constitution — those concerning the composition and authority of the legislature, the nature and purposes of the executive, and the place of the courts — are in Britain found in certain ancient statutes.[3] It is also true that, unlike Australia, the United States and Canada, the English constitution does not contain a bill or charter of rights which expresses formally the principles and limitations of political community. But when the matter of defining the constitution is addressed more directly, none of these differences counts as much as might otherwise appear.

Take Canada for instance. Its constitution is indeed found written in the *Constitution Act, 1867*,[4] the *Constitution Act, 1982*,[5] and the *Canadian Charter of Rights and Freedoms*,[6] but the constitution of Canada is not exhausted by those documents. Canada's constitution consists as well of other statute law, the principles of the common law and unwritten legal conventions concerning constitutional practice and authority.[7] That this is so makes the written documents more an expression of "the constitution" which in an important sense can then be seen to exist independently from them.

In his commentary on the English constitution, Dicey famously proclaimed that "the general principles of the constitution (as for example the right to personal liberty ...) are with us the result of judicial decisions determining the rights of private persons in particular cases brought before the Courts".[8] There is great wisdom in this view. Though the constitution of the Rule of Law state may be proclaimed in documents, because those documents are but its partial expression, the constitution may be said to reside not in those documents as such, but rather in political and legal practice. Dicey puts the matter thus:

> [W]ith us the law of the constitution, those rules which in foreign countries naturally form part of a constitutional code, are not the source but the consequence of the rights of individuals, as defined and enforced by the Courts; ... thus the constitution is the result of the ordinary law of the land.[9]

So viewed, the constitution depends upon and takes shape in the actions of political actors, and it falls to those actors, and to the legal community especially, to make real the political morality of the Rule of Law in their "ordinary" practices. When "the right to individual freedom is a result deduced from the principles of the [written] constitution, the idea readily occurs that the right is capable of being suspended or taken away".[10] In contrast, when the constitution is considered to exceed any such document and to reside finally in practice, "the

---

[3]   Namely, the *Bill of Rights* (1689), the *Act of Settlement* (1701), and the *Union with Scotland Act* (1707).

[4]   (U.K.), 30 & 31 Vict., c. 3.

[5]   Being Schedule B to the *Canada Act, 1982* (U.K.), 1982, c. 11.

[6]   Part I of the *Constitution Act, 1982*, being Schedule B to the *Canada Act, 1982* (U.K.), 1982, c. 11.

[7]   That this is so in Canada is now a matter of law. See: *Reference Re Secession of Quebec*, [1998] 2 S.C.R. 217.

[8]   A.V. Dicey, *Introduction to the Study of the Law of the Constitution*, 8th ed. (London: Macmillan & Co., 1924), at p. 191.

[9]   *Ibid.*, at p. 199.

[10]   *Ibid.*, at p. 197.

suspension of the constitution, as far as such a thing is conceivable, would mean ... nothing less than a revolution".[11] The importance of conceiving of the constitution in this fashion cannot be overstated. It places the burden of liberty not on some document, but on the commitment of members of political community to make good the values of limited and principled government.

Constitutional law is often said to be the supreme law of political community. This characterization is true in at least two senses. First, the rules of the constitution define political authority, the authority of the courts no less than the authority of the legislative and executive branches. Consequently, the constitution is supreme in the sense that it structures and authorizes all political action. All laws and all exercises of state authority must conform to the requirements of the constitution. When they fail to do so, laws and other state actions have no force and effect to the extent of the inconsistency. The Rule of Law state must act through competent laws and may then only act within the confines of express statutory authority. That state action is accountable in these ways makes the constitution supreme in a second sense. State actions may be rendered a nullity on constitutional grounds, either because the substance of a law offends the constitution or because some governmental agency acted without authority. In a federal state like Canada, the second ground of constitutional contest gives rise to questions concerning constitutional excess, what Canadian lawyers call division of powers cases. The first ground concerns legal equality, both equal protection and equal application, and challenges of that sort are available to citizens in a Rule of Law state whether or not the state happens to have a written bill or charter of rights.

ADMINISTRATIVE LAW

Administrative law has as its concern the administration and implementation of legislation by the executive (the "Crown") and by statutory delegates. It therefore consists of those rules of law which govern and constrain the exercise of the powers and privileges of the executive and the conduct of statutory bodies such as boards, commissions and tribunals. Administrative law is centrally important to the Rule of Law simply because so many aspects of our lives are now subject to regulation by government. Think for instance of the regulation of health and safety, human rights, pay equity and employment, pensions and insurance, environmental protection and land use, communications and transportation, energy, and financial institutions. The bodies which make decisions concerning matters of these sorts, whether they are part of the Crown as such or are instead subordinate statutory actors, may be described comprehensively as "administrative agencies". It is the aim of administrative law to govern the relations between citizens and the state when the state chooses to delegate part of its power to, and to act through, agencies of this sort.

---

[11] *Ibid.*

Though the characteristics and practices of administrative agencies vary greatly, and particularly as regards the character of the decision-makers and the type of decisions made, they are yet united as emanations of the state. The following diagram illustrates this unity:

Figure 8.2
Statutory Delegation

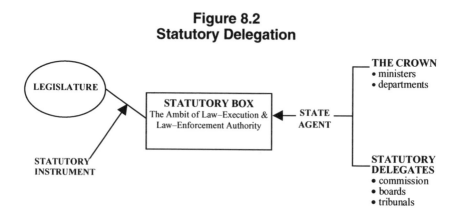

Certain conventions as regards the prerogatives of the Crown aside, the authority of the executive and of statutory bodies to implement and enforce the law resides in legislation. Enabling legislation of this sort defines the agent's ambit of authority, and if a agent acts beyond its authority, outside its statutory box, then its actions are illegal and as such do not constitute a binding implementation or enforcement of the law.

It falls to courts on the petition of citizens to review the conduct of administrative agencies and to determine whether in any given case the executive or a statutory body has acted beyond its authority and, if either has, to remedy the situation. Where an administrative agency is found to have acted within its authority, its acts are said to be *intra vires* (within the powers) and that ends the matter. Where an administrative agency has exceeded its authority, its acts are declared to be *ultra vires* (outside the powers) and the matter of remedy arises. A decision by an administrative agency may be declared *ultra vires* on either of two grounds, namely, that the decision suffers from substantive defects or from procedural error.

The first ground concerns legal authority as such — does the agency have the jurisdiction under its statute to do what it proposes to do? The second ground concerns natural justice — even where the agency had the legal authority to act, did it observe the standards of procedural fairness which are appropriate to it? Substantive defects mean that the agency has lost, failed, or exceeded its jurisdiction and may arise from errors of fact, errors in the interpretation of the enabling legislation, errors of jurisdiction, and errors in exercising a discretion. Procedural errors may arise from bias (including reasonable apprehension of bias) and from failure to meet appropriate standards with respect to notice of hearing, disclosure of relevant information and the hearing itself. But note both inquiries concern jurisdiction. They differ only in the nature of the jurisdiction which is their concern. The second ground asks whether the agency has acted within its jurisdiction by following the rules of procedural fairness; and the first asks whether the agency has acted within the bounds of the jurisdiction conferred upon it by its enabling statute.

Even where they find that an agency has exceeded its jurisdiction, courts are not bound to provide a remedy. The grounds upon which courts will exercise their remedial discretion for and against the petitioner need not concern us. However, we must at least define the remedies available. Traditional remedies include what lawyers call *prerogative writs*, and *injunctions* and *declarations*. We have already encountered the last two which are ubiquitous in law and not unique to public law. When ordered in administrative law matters, the private equitable remedy of injunction prevents an agency from doing whatever it otherwise intended to do; and the private equitable remedy of declaration consists of a judgment, binding as between the petitioner and the agency, as regards the legal rights of the two. The prerogative writs are however public law remedies which are available only against public officials and bodies. They include *prohibition* (an order to prevent an agency's asserting a jurisdiction not granted by its enabling statute); *certiorari* (an order to quash a decision made without legal authority or in violation of procedural fairness); *mandamus* (an order to compel an agency to perform a duty it is required to perform) and *habeas corpus* (an order to secure the release of an individual from unlawful custody).

(ii)   Exploration: The Law of Crimes

The criminal law does not merely prohibit certain conduct. Many laws, other than criminal law, do that. What distinguishes criminal prohibitions is their being declared criminal at all. That declaration has a two-fold effect. First, by defining conduct as criminal, the state is proposing that the conduct involves matters most weighty. Second, the state is also asserting that the gravity of the matter authorizes it to discipline and punish its citizens. Criminal law is about the authority of the state to declare conduct criminal and about its authority to discipline and punish individuals when they act in those proscribed ways.

PRIMACY

Montesquieu claimed that "the citizen's liberty depends principally on the goodness of the criminal laws".[12] That this is so affords the law of crimes primacy among the organs of public law. And it is so for several reasons. First, no body of law, public or private, is more dreadful in its effects. Criminal proceedings

---

[12]   C.L. de S. Montesquieu, *The Spirit of the Laws* (1748) A. Cohler, *et al.*, eds. (Cambridge: Cambridge University Press, 1989), at p. 188.

are seized of a remarkable "status-degrading potency"[13] and, where a citizen is convicted pursuant to those procedures, "the outcome can be loss of liberty without equal in the modern world, and even death".[14] In its process and effect, criminal law makes us vulnerable, in body and in mind, to the coercive power of the state in ways unparalleled in the rest of our law.

The stakes are high in other senses as well. In no other area of the law is the state so often tempted to violate the commandments of liberal political morality, and in no area therefore is the threat to limited government, and the risk of arbitrary law, more severe. Just as important is the consequence of the state's succumbing to these temptations to criminalize the affairs and projects of its citizens. A fundamental object of liberal political community is human flourishing and diversity. When conduct is improperly criminalized and when, as a corollary to that, more and more areas of citizen autonomy become the object of state criminal supervision, the sense of security which individuals require to govern themselves becomes weakened and the "experiments in living" which are the mark of liberal society become threatened or worse extinguished.

In many ways, criminal law also enjoys intellectual primacy. Montesquieu for one claimed that "the knowledge ... concerning the surest rules one can observe in criminal judgments, is of more concern to mankind than anything else in the world".[15] No area of our law illuminates better the relationship between the state and citizens, and none raises with more precision legal and political questions about the reach of individual freedom and state power. Those questions in turn raise a host of issues which illuminate the whole of our law. Included among the latter are our understandings of autonomy, responsibility and causality.

So whether the metre is practice or theory, criminal law is foundational to our law. Though constitutional law makes its contribution in institutionalizing the separation of powers, and administrative law in regulating the regulatory state's drive to regulate our lives, it is through the law of crimes that societies such as ours most display, or fail to display, the character required of them by the Rule of Law. Everything in this respect turns on the goodness of that body of rules which comprise the criminal law.

The law itself testifies to the primacy of criminal law. Lawyers, for instance, think the criminal law so distinct and important that they commonly contrast it with what they term the "civil law", which is to say, with the whole of the rest of the law. More importantly, no other body of our law clothes us with more rights than does the criminal law. Moreover, those rights, both procedural and substantive, are spun from a sturdier yarn than are our "civil law" rights.

---

[13] F.A. Allen, *The Habits of Legality: Criminal Justice and the Rule of Law* (New York: Oxford University Press, 1996), at p. 5.

[14] H. Gross, *A Theory of Criminal Justice* (New York: Oxford University Press, 1979), at p. 7.

[15] Montesquieu, *supra*, note 12, at p. 188.

POINT

It is critical to remember that because criminal law is public law, its overall point is to constrain the power of the state. We have already identified those powers which are criminal law's defining concern. The criminal law serves to constrain the state's *declaratory power* (*i.e.*, its power to declare conduct criminal in the first place) and its *retributive power* (*i.e.*, its power to punish individuals who act in violation of those declarations). We shall investigate the criminal law's practice of constraint with respect to both of these powers in a moment. Our present task is to render more precisely the point of criminal law as public law.

In 1471, Sir John Fortescue, then Chief Justice of King's Bench, opined that he "should, indeed, prefer twenty guilty men to escape death through mercy, than one innocent to be condemned unjustly".[16] In his *Commentaries*, Blackstone reaffirmed this basic moral orientation of criminal law: "It is better that ten guilty persons escape than one innocent suffer".[17] More recently, Deane J., of the High Court of Australia, laid claim once again to this "guiding thesis" of the law of crimes:

> The complementary direct objectives of the administration of criminal law are the conviction and punishment of the guilty and the acquittal of the innocent. The frailty of all human institutions precludes the complete achievement of both. That being so, there is an inevitable tension between them. In the context of such tension, the entrenched and guiding thesis of the criminal law ... is that the second objective is incomparably more important than the first; that the searing injustice and consequential social injury which is involved when the law turns upon itself and convicts an innocent person far outweigh the failure of justice and the consequential social injury involved when the processes of law proclaim the innocence of a guilty man.[18]

But this leaves unexamined the origin of "the precept that the innocent must not be convicted"[19] and our law's characteristic lack of ambivalence about the matter. To say simply, as does the Supreme Court of Canada,[20] that justice requires that it be so is no answer since surely justice requires as well that the guilty be found out and punished. This precept resides at the heart of our criminal law, rather, because our law aims to constrain the power of the state and, in so doing, to prohibit the state from discovering guilt by means which, had our law another point, would be most effective indeed.

---

[16] J. Fortescue, *De Laudibus Legum Angliae* (1468-1471) S.B. Chrimes, ed. (Cambridge: Cambridge University Press, 1949), at p. 65.

[17] W. Blackstone, *Commentaries on the Laws of England* (1765-1769) Vol. 4 (New York: Garland, 1978), at p. 358.

[18] *Van der Meer v. R.* (1988), 82 A.L.R. 10 at 31 (H.C.).

[19] *R. v. Seaboyer*, [1991] 2 S.C.R. 577 at 606.

[20] *Ibid.*

If the transcendent point of our criminal law was to punish the guilty, and not to constrain the state, then our law would have a very different character from what it does. The state could then pursue the truth of guilt by means, such as confinement, forced interrogation and torture, which our law prohibits it. Because the transcendent point is instead constraint, *proof* and not *truth* is the law's metre. Consequently, in our criminal law, the matter of guilt and innocence is assessed not against truth but against proof. That this is so makes good the precept which itself makes good the point of our law.

That truth is in this fashion subordinate to proof does not make our law unconcerned with truth. The result rather is that it is concerned with a different and greater truth. *Truth in our criminal law is at its most abstract level a political truth about the terms and conditions and limits of state power.* At a more practical level, it is about legal truth, namely, those conditions, which are the stuff of every criminal trial, required for the legal conclusion that this accused is guilty. Truth overall is not the business of criminal law. Its business rather is political and legal truth. Those truths make it proper to declare accused persons "guilty" or "not guilty", but never to declare them "innocent". Innocence in this fuller sense is a stranger to our law because it depends upon a quality of truth which is beyond the point and purpose of our law.

STRUCTURE

Our criminal law is structured around the two powers which it expresses and constrains, the declaratory power and the retributive power. The part which concerns the latter is termed the "general part" of criminal law, and it consists of those general principles of criminal liability that apply, or ought to apply, to all crimes. The part which concerns the former is called the "special part", and it provides the details of particular crimes and arranges them into families of offences. We will explore the general part in the next section. Our present concern is the special part. We will start with the definition of crime as such. This definition will allow us to deal with the matter of the law's constraint of the state's declaratory power.

Blackstone's identification of crimes as "public wrongs" is the beginning.[21] That a crime is a crime because it somehow harms the "public" means that certain other definitions are unacceptable. First of all, this view of the matter constructs a foundational distinction between sin and crime. That an act may be immoral by some religious standard does not, without much more, make it a crime. But if this is so, then personal morality is excluded as the foundation of crime, and everything must turn on the nature and meaning of "public wrong". Some claim that "public" here refers to conventional social morality. According to this view, the state should declare as criminal acts which society regards as

---

[21]   Book 4 of the *Commentaries*, "Of Public Wrongs", is devoted to the criminal law. See: *supra*, note 17.

wrong. But in that case, "public" must mean nothing more than the transient views of the majority. Such an understanding is unacceptable on two grounds. It would render individuals vulnerable to punishment on account alone of their dissenting from the majority's view of what is right or proper and that is without more an affront to the law's commitment to moral independence. It would also subject them to arbitrary law to the extent that social morality is both poorly articulated and subject itself to uncontainable change and variation over time. Still others would reduce "public wrong" to whatever the state says it is. But such a view concedes unlimited and unqualified power to the state and is therefore unacceptable as an account of criminal law in a Rule of Law state.

There is another view which associates "public wrongs", not with the right of the public to punish, but with rights, which are held by individuals and violated by the criminal, who in appropriating those rights has taken an "unfair advantage" of others.[22] According to this understanding, the public is harmed when, and only when, any of the individuals who comprise it are harmed. Now, though this view misses an important matter to which we'll refer in a moment, it does associate the notion of crime with the political morality of the Rule of Law state. And it is in that association that any acceptable definition of crime as a public wrong must reside.

The proper metre for crime is then not morality as such, but political morality specifically. Many crimes, of course, are grave moral wrongs. But not all crimes are grave moral wrongs, and not all grave moral wrongs are crimes. Yet, all crimes *ought* to be grave violations of political morality and all grave violations of political morality *should* be crimes. According to liberal political morality, a harm consists of other-regarding conduct which seriously infringes the moral autonomy of others. The rights of others are violated in this way when the conduct at issue invades the security persons must have as regards their persons and their property. For instance, culpable homicide is a crime because it invades the victim's right to bodily security; and first degree murder is the most heinous crime because the murderer has then not only violated the victim's right to security, but has intentionally extinguished the victim as a holder of rights.

Liberal political morality requires then that the law of crimes contain two major categories or families of offences, "crimes against the person" and "crimes against property". But there is a third category, namely, "crimes against the state". This category consists primarily of the offences of treason and sedition which aim to protect the state, not as a source of power, but as the custodian and agent of the morality of political community. Indeed, as an emanation of power, the state neither deserves nor can it command loyalty or protection. However, where the state owes its existence and legitimacy, not to force, but to moral consensus and moral action, it is proper that the law of crimes prohibit acts intended to destroy that agreement and action.

---

[22] H. Morris, "Persons and Punishment" (1968), 52 Monist 475.

First-year law students very soon discover that our criminal law very much lacks the structural integrity which our political morality requires of it. Indeed, so much so is this the case, that some have been moved to declare "the criminal law ... a lost cause, from the point of view of principle".[23] In Canada, for instance, though it is structured in part around "offences against the person" (Part VIII) and "offences against rights of property" (Part IX), the *Criminal Code*[24] consists in these and other parts of a veritable hodgepodge of offences. Included among these are offences which criminalize self-regarding conduct and offences which criminalize activities which are victimless. Such "crimes" are not "crimes" at all, unless the measure of crime is state power to declare *anything* it wishes to be criminal. And in that event, the criminal law stops being an expression of Rule of Law, and becomes instead an instrument, pure and simple, of despotic power. Of course, not any conduct should be declared criminal. And we will want briefly to examine the principles which should both guide and limit the state's criminal law declaratory power.

Our law has traditionally drawn a distinction between acts which are wrong by their very nature (for instance, murder and larceny) and acts which are "wrong" on grounds alone that they happen to be prohibited by some statute (for instance, driving on the wrong side of the road or driving without a licence). Lawyers use the Latin words *malum in se* to refer to the first category and *malum prohibitum* to refer to the second. There is great wisdom in this distinction. First, it allows us to make judgments with respect to the relative importance of each of the many prohibitions which comprise our law. Second, it demands that we identify and justify the measure on which, in our view, the importance of laws ought to be appraised. We have already concluded that the measure proper to the whole of our law is liberal political morality. So viewed, the difference between real wrongs and "wrongs" defined by administrative policy and convenience is that the one and not the other sounds substantially in the requirements of political morality. In this way, the distinction guides us to the conclusion that wrongs *malum prohibitum* are not properly the objects of criminal law and find their home instead in regulatory regimes to which the risks of criminality do not attach.

That said, a bare summary of the principles of liberal political morality as regards criminality will have to suffice. These principles, which alone constitute "the principled core of criminal law", are as follows:[25] a) "the criminal law should be used, and only used, to censure persons for substantial wrongdoing"

---

[23] A. Ashworth, "Is the Criminal Law a Lost Cause?" (2000), 116 Law Q. Rev. 225 at p. 253.

[24] R.S.C. 1985, c. C-46.

[25] I take these words and the statement of principles which follows from Ashworth, *supra*, note 23, at pp. 253-56. For a more detailed view, see: J. Gardner, "On the General Part of the Criminal Law" in A. Duff, ed., *Philosophy and the Criminal Law: Principle and Critique* (Cambridge: Cambridge University Press, 1998), pp. 205 at 229-32. And for what is presently the *locus classicus* on the matter, see: J. Feinberg, *The Moral Limits of the Criminal Law*, 4 Vols. (New York: Oxford University Press, 1984-1988).

(that is, for other-regarding conduct that causes substantial harm to others or to the state as the custodian of moral equality); b) "criminal laws should be enforced with respect for equal treatment and proportionality" (that is, offences should be defined in terms which incorporate equal protection and they should be enforced and administered in a manner proportionate to the nature of the wrongdoing); c) "persons accused of substantial wrongdoing ought to be afforded the protections appropriate to those charged with criminal offences" (that is, there should be no offences to which the whole of the general principles of criminal law do not apply); and d) "maximum sentences and effective sentence levels should be proportionate to the seriousness of the wrongdoing" (that is, the quality of punishment must be a consequence of the gravity of the wrongdoing and therefore neither arbitrary nor a matter of political climate). Together these principles would place fundamental limitations on the state's declaratory power. The first prohibits criminalizing conduct which does not substantially offend the morality of equality; and, even where that threshold is satisfied, the remainder articulate conditions which must also be met as regards application, enforcement, proof and punishment.

RIGHTS OF THE ACCUSED

We have already discovered that criminal law is about proof and not truth. This is so because the general part of the criminal law has as its purpose the protection of individuals from the power of the state to discipline and punish. These protections exist, of course, as rights. So when we say that the law is about proof and not truth, we mean to say that it is about rights and not revelation. This puts the accused in a special place in our law. Because the criminal law seeks to afford us all protection from the state's retributive power, the person who stands accused stands as our representative against the state. Our rights are no greater than are his, and if he is punished in ways that derogate from political morality, then our rights too are diminished and we too are made vulnerable. The accused, then, is everyman: our undifferentiated equal who, unlike us, has had the state's power direct towards him and who, like us, depends on the law's integrity to save him safe from unjust harm.

Our concern is the nature of those rights which stand between us and the state's retributive power. We know that rights come in two sizes, substantive and procedural. We shall here consider only the former, and will not attempt even to summarize the laws of criminal evidence, procedure and process. Nor as regards substantive rights shall we attempt to deal with the specifics of doctrine which, in any event, tend to vary by jurisdiction. Our focus rather are those general principles expressed in rights which characterize criminal law in Rule of Law states.

We noted earlier that nowhere in our law is the cloth of rights so hardy and multi-layered than in the law of crimes. The following diagram illustrates the depth of this protection:

Figure 8.3
Rights of Accused Persons

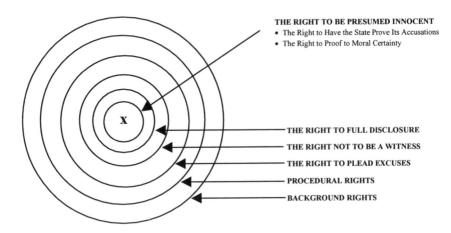

The background rights of the accused reside in certain principles about criminal liability which guide the creation, interpretation and application of criminal laws and which the other, more specific rights presume. There are at least three such principles. The *nullum crimen sine lege* principle declares the right that none of us can be subject to the state's retributive power unless there is first a law. This "no crime without law" principle protects us from the *in terrorem* threat of sanctions imposed after the fact (as lawyers say *ex post facto*) and in that way, empowers each of us to explore and exercise our autonomy without fear of unforeseeable penal consequences. The connection to autonomy is unmistakable:

> If ... persons are punished under laws they could not have known when acting, this not only undermines the preconditions of informed choice and lanning, it also disregards the limits of human responsibility and is therefore both unfair and an affront to human dignity.[26]

The prevention of social fear and paralysis is the principle's most general blessing, but it also serves autonomy in more direct ways. For one thing, since all laws have to be general, the principle has the effect of banning "bills of attainder", or laws which single out particular people for punishment. It also informs lawyerly and judicial practice with respect to the interpretation of criminal laws. The so-called rule of strict construction (or as it is sometimes put, the "rule of lenity") requires that penal legislation be interpreted narrowly so as to limit

---

[26] R. Summers, "The Ideal Socio-Legal Order: Its 'Rule of Law' Dimension" (1988), 1 Ratio Juris 154 at p. 160.

the scope of criminal liability and to benefit the accused. The Supreme Court of Canada has put the matter thus:

> It is unnecessary to emphasize the importance of clarity and certainty when freedom is at stake. ... [I]f real ambiguities are found, or doubts of substance arise, in the construction and application of a statute affecting the liberty of a subject, then the statute should be applied in such a manner as to favour the person against whom it is sought to be enforced. If one is to be incarcerated, one should at least know that some Act of Parliament requires it in express terms, and not, at most, by implication.[27]

There are two corollaries to this. First, because they favour liberty, defences are given a wide and liberal construction. Second, strict construction confines interpretation to the plain meaning of the statutory words and prohibits teleological or purposive interpretation. Unhappily, courts sometimes violate this prohibition and, when they do, they resolve ambiguities in favour of the state and against the accused.

The second principle, *nulla poena sine crimine*, declares our right not to be punished unless we have committed a crime. This "no punishment without a crime" principle also limits punishment to that which is provided for by the law.

The third principle goes to the moral structure of crime, *actus non facit reum, nisi mens sit rea*: "an act does not make [the doer of it] guilty, unless the mind be guilty". This principle makes guilt personal. One is guilty by reason of one's conduct rather than one's status, and by reason of one's moral agency rather than one's conduct alone. That moral responsibility is a condition of criminal liability has at least two elemental implications. First, it excludes from the ambit of criminal law those who are mentally unfit to take responsibility. Accordingly, children and some mentally ill persons are excused even when they do commit criminal wrongs. Second, so far as the rest of us are concerned, punishment is permitted only where we have committed a criminal act for which we are morally responsible. This condition leads to the definition of crime with which all first-year law students become familiar. Under our law, a crime consists of the commission of a prohibited act (the *actus reus*) with the required degree of moral fault (the *mens rea*). The *actus reus* may consist of an act, an omission or sometimes even a state of being (for example, being in possession of some prohibited matter, such as a weapon). The *mens rea* is the so-called subjective element of the crime because it concerns the accused's state of mind at the time of the commission of the alleged offence. The state of mind required is defined by the criminal law at issue (and in Canada, by the various offence provisions of the *Criminal Code*), and varies from intent, recklessness, and wilful blindness to negligence and mistake.

We shall now turn briefly to the more specific rights.

---

[27] *Marcotte v. Canada (Deputy Attorney General)* (1976), 19 C.C.C. (2d) 257 at 262 (S.C.C.).

The Right to Disclosure: Our law prohibits trial by ambush. Because criminal law seeks to constrain the state's retributive power, the state is obligated to disclose to the accused the whole of the evidence, inculpatory and exculpatory, in its possession. The disclosure obligation is *not* reciprocal, that is, the accused is under no obligation to disclose evidence to the state. The Supreme Court of Canada's redaction of the right leaves no mistake about the political morality of disclosure:

> [T]he fruits of the investigation which are in the possession of counsel for the Crown are not the property of the Crown for use in securing a conviction but the property of the public to be used to ensure that justice is done. In contrast, the defence has no obligation to assist the prosecution and is entitled to assume a purely adversarial role toward the prosecution.[28]

Evidence is public in the crucial sense that the public, each and every one of us, has an interest in the state's power to punish and in the accused's opportunity to make full answer and defence to the state's accusations against him or her.

The Right to Be Presumed Innocent: This right is so central to our criminal law that it has been called the "one golden thread" running "throughout the web of the English Criminal Law".[29] We shall want to appreciate why it enjoys this special status and to get some sense of what it requires. We have already discussed the *ei qui affirmat* principle which places the burden of proof on the party who affirms a case and not on the party who denies it. In one sense, the presumption of innocence is simply an expression of that principle in the context of the criminal law. But that sense of the matter does not disclose, at least not fully, the presumption's pride of place in our law of crimes. About 150 years ago, the Massachusetts Supreme Court caught the gist of the matter more fully:

> The burden of proof is upon the prosecutor. All the presumptions of law independent of evidence are in favour of innocence; and every person is presumed innocent until he is proved guilty. If upon such proof there is a reasonable doubt remaining, the accused is entitled to the benefit of it by an acquittal. For it is not sufficient to establish a probability, though a strong one arising from the doctrine of chances, that the fact charged is more likely to be true than the contrary; but the evidence must establish the truth of the fact to a reasonable and moral certainty; a certainty that convinces and directs the understanding, and satisfies the reason and judgment, of those who are bound to act conscientiously upon it.[30]

The right to be presumed innocent contemplates then both the state's having the burden of proof and the nature of that burden. In order to punish anyone of us for allegedly committing a criminal act, the state must prove, not only that we indeed committed the act (*actus reus*), but also that we did so with the required

---

[28]   *R. v. Stinchcombe* (1991), 68 C.C.C. (3d) 1 at 7 (S.C.C.).
[29]   *Woolmington v. D.P.P.*, [1935] A.C. 462 at 481 (H.L.).
[30]   *Commonwealth v. Webster*, 59 Mass. 259 at 320 (1850).

moral fault (*mens rea*); and to do that, it must proffer evidence with respect to both matters which convinces to a moral certainty. The presumption of innocence is indeed the "golden thread" of criminal law because it is the central barrier between us and the state and the chief constraint on the state's retributive power.

The Right Not to Be a Witness: The accused is not required to testify in his or her own defence nor may he or she be called by the state to assist its case. Though in many ways these rights against compellability are part and parcel of the presumption of innocence, they are so fundamental that they deserve to be viewed as establishing the free-standing right to remain silent. From this right devolves a host of evidentiary rules which protect accused persons against self-incrimination.

The Right to Plead Excuses: Even where the state proves that the accused committed the prohibited act and was at fault in so doing, our law requires that the accused be given the opportunity to plead excuses which, if made out by the accused, forbid or limit the state's authority to punish the accused. A range of the excuses or "defences" are established in our law. For instance, accused persons may plead self-defence even where they have intentionally killed or harmed an attacker. Or they may plead duress when their commission of an offence was coerced by others. The rationale once again is to limit retributive power, in the case of defences by allowing accused persons to justify their otherwise criminal acts.

RETRIBUTIVE JUSTICE

Criminal law is often conceived as having a number of socially beneficial purposes. It is sometimes said that its aim is the prevention of criminal conduct by threatening punishment on the commission of offences. Others claim that it is about educating the community in proper standards of conduct required for mutually advantageous social life. Still others claim that criminal law finds its purpose in the rehabilitation of those who act in seriously anti-social ways. However, though criminal law may in fact sometimes have these purposes, policies of that kind can justify neither the rules of criminal law nor the punishment which follows upon successful prosecution.

Criminal law, rather, is *the practice of vindicating and restoring the political morality of equality.* Kant put the matter thus:

> What kind and what degree of punishment does public legal justice adopt as its principle and standard? None other than the principle of equality ... that is, the principle of not treating one side more favourably than the other. Accordingly, any undeserved evil that you inflict on someone else among the people is one that you do to yourself. If you vilify him, you

vilify yourself; if you steal from him, you steal from yourself; if you kill him, you kill yourself.[31]

Criminal law achieves justice in this sense in two ways. It affords accused persons due respect of their autonomy by limiting the state's declaratory and retributive powers. And, where within those limitations, accused persons are found guilty, it affords them due respect by acknowledging and making good their right to be punished.[32] Simply, then, retributive justice is the practice of respecting the rights to autonomy of all and of respecting the right of those who culpably do harm to be made to suffer harm in return.

That this is so precludes any view which would associate criminal law with revenge on behalf of the victim. Indeed, the vindication and restoration of political morality which is the aim of criminal law does not, and cannot, contemplate the hurt suffered by the victim as an individual. Criminal harm is communal harm; and criminal law can be anchored in "victim rights" only at the cost of losing its integrity.[33] Criminal law as retributive justice also precludes justifying decisions on prudential or utilitarian grounds. Oldenquist puts this nicely: "The pursuit of Adolf Eichmann, Josef Mengele, and other Nazis in their dotage, tending their rose gardens in South America, makes no utilitarian sense. They will not do their crimes again, nor would their punishment deter others".[34] We pursue criminals of this sort, as we do others who commit serious wrongdoing, rather, because "a moral community exacts retribution for its own good and not primarily to inform, connect, cure, use, or send any kind of message to the criminal" or for that matter, to others.[35]

C. PRIVATE LAW: CONSTRAINING SOCIAL POWER

The rules of private law express rights which serve equality and autonomy by protecting us from legal harms which arise, not from state conduct, but from the conduct of private persons. Though the distinction between public and private law resides in this difference, we must remember that, when it acts as a private person, the state too is subject to private law rules. For instance, were an officer of the state, in the conduct of his or her duties, to cause anyone of us harm through the negligent operation of a motor vehicle, then, on proof of the matter, the state would be liable for the harm in the tort of negligence. Likewise when

---

[31] I. Kant, *The Metaphysical Elements of Justice*, trans. J. Ladd (Indianapolis: Bobbs-Merrill), at p. 99. See also: J.-F. Lyotard, "The Other's Rights" in S. Shute and S. Hurley, eds., *On Human Rights* (New York: Basic Books, 1993), at p. 135.
[32] For the "right to punishment", see Morris, *supra*, note 22.
[33] About which, see: A.A. White, "Victims' Rights, Rule of Law, and the Threat to Liberal Jurisprudence" (1998-1999), 87 Kentucky L.J. 357.
[34] A. Oldenquist, "An Explanation of Retribution" (1988), 85 Journal of Philosophy 464.
[35] *Ibid.*

the state acts as a party to contracts or when it takes or invades our property: it no less than anyone of us is subject to the law of contract and property. State liability points to another matter that we should also recall. The category "person" is not confined to human beings and includes other entities, such as the state and private organizations such as corporations, on which our law confers legal personality. Lastly, private law too has special rules as regards children and the mentally ill and incompetent.

(i) Taxonomy

That said, our present concern is substantive private law. We shall briefly explore the law of property and the law of contract to disclose the contribution of each to the constraint of power. Then we shall pause at some length on the law of torts.

PROPERTY LAW

We tend to think of property as "things" we own — a house, a car, a book, some tract of land, and so on. But this is a mistaken view, at least for lawyers. As are the rest of our private law rules, the rules of property law are concerned with the relations between legal persons, and property law, as a body of rules, is distinct from the other rules which govern our relationships because its concern is our relationships as regards things. Property at law may therefore be defined as:

> the network of legal relationships prevailing between individuals in respect of things. ... "[P]roperty" comprises bundles of mutual rights and obligations between "subjects" in respect of certain "objects", and the study of property [is] an inquiry into a variety of socially defined relationships and morally conditioned obligations.[36]

So viewed, property is an institution, some say the basic institution, which constitutes our relations with respect to the resources which beings such as we need to survive and to flourish. In the absence of "property" in the legal sense, our survival and our advancement would depend upon our strength or stealth in obtaining and retaining the goods we need. With the institution of property, the acquisition and use of goods is not merely regulated, but those rules express the political morality on which our relations more generally are predicated. Property in consequence becomes a matter both of the acquisition of rights and of their limitation.

The objects of property relationships also defy our common understanding. The "things" involved are indeed often tangible, like automobiles, furniture and land, but just as often they are intangible. Think, for instance, of bank accounts,

---

[36] K.J. Gray and P.D. Symes, *Real Property and Real People* (London: Butterworths, 1981), at pp. 8-9.

shares in companies or in mutual funds, and the like. Each of these intangibles is a "thing" in respect to which the law of property governs our relations. Indeed, it could be safely said that intangibles of this sort are increasingly the "objects" that matter most to property. Think for instance property in artwork, in music and in literary works, in genetically engineered drugs, plants and animals, and of inventions of all sorts. Property with respect to intangibles like these is constituted by copyright, trademark or patent rights, which together comprise the ever-more-important body of rules called "intellectual property".

The rules of property govern the acquisition and disposition of rights in things and the use of those things by persons, both those who do and those do not have rights with respect to them. Rights in things may be acquired, or disposed, by inheritance, by gift, or by purchase. The most important right which attaches to property in a "thing" is the right at law to exclude others from it. Indeed, that a "thing" is capable of being exclusive in this sense is what makes it possibly an object of property at all. Consequently, there are many things, for example air, that cannot be property and must be shared. Things of this sort are often referred to as *res communes*.

But we have to be careful not to conflate property rights with ownership since not all property rights attach to ownership. Our law rather makes a foundational distinction between possession and ownership, and it accords rights both to those in possession of a thing and those who own it. Possession is roughly control over a thing, whereas ownership is aptly caught by the notion of title, *i.e.*, the best right with respect to control of the thing in the long run. For example, if Bob buys a house from Bill, he becomes its owner, provided the house belongs to Bill. Bob may decide to rent the house for a year to Bruce upon Bruce promising to pay $800 a month in rent. When the house is handed over to Bruce, he gets legal possession of it, and if anyone interferes with his quiet enjoyment of the house, he may initiate legal proceedings against them. Indeed, during the term of the rental, even Bob, the owner, generally may not interfere with Bruce's use of the house. The main difference between the rights afforded at law to Bruce and Bob is that Bob as owner can completely dispose of the house, that is, he can make another legal person the owner. It is true that, in some cases, a possessor like Bruce can transfer his possession to another person (through a sublet), but, except in a few rare instances, he cannot make another the owner. Possessors of land, however, may sometimes displace the owner. This is called at law "adverse possession" and is a consequence of the *Statutes of Limitations* which prescribe that where one party has openly occupied land without the owner's permission for a certain period of time, the party in adverse possession may resist an action by the owner to recover the land on grounds that he has become its owner through the possession.

There are two other twists which we should briefly canvass before turning our attention to the structure of property law and then to the limitation of property rights. Both owners and possessors can generally raise money or obtain credit on the security of their property. Security arrangements are governed by a device called a "mortgage", whereby an owner, who is borrowing money, agrees that the lender shall own and be able to dispose of the property should the borrower not repay the loan on the terms agreed. Most people are familiar with the mortgage in respect to the loan agreements they enter to purchase houses and automobiles, but security arrangements of this sort are normal practice in the conduct of commercial relations. The "pawn" is a similar arrangement with respect to articles of property: an owner leaves the article with a lender, the pawn broker, which serves as security for the amount loaned; the owner may redeem the article upon payment of the loan with interest.

The equitable doctrine of trust also affects property rights. Under a trust, one party becomes legal owner of a thing on condition that he holds it to the use and benefit of someone else, the beneficiary. The rights of the beneficiary with respect the thing are called equitable ownership. Distinct from legal ownership, equitable ownership gives the beneficiary protection against breaches of the trust by the legal owner, the trustee, and against others who may interfere with the beneficiary's use and enjoyment of the thing.

Our law recognizes a distinction between *real property* and *personal property*. Generally, realty has as its object land, whereas personalty has as its object things other than land, called *chattels*.[37] The law of property is structured around this distinction. Consequently, in first-year property class, law students study both the law of personal property and the law of real property. Among the issues typically canvassed in the former are the rights of finders and the rules of bailment. Real property is a much more exhaustive (and exhausting) study. Among the matters studied are the concept and variety of "tenure" and the creation of various interests, called "estates", in land.

Though ownership is absolute as regards the disposition of things, property rights, including the rights of owners, are not absolute with respect to the use of things. On the contrary, both the law of property itself and other bodies of law limit the rights of property. We cannot here delve deeply into the matter. A few examples will have to suffice to show that the law property no less than the rest of our law is about constraining power, both of others as against us and we as against them. The law of torts includes the action of nuisance which both protects our property rights against other property rights and limits our property rights with respect to them. Suppose, for instance, that your next door neighbour uses his backyard late into every evening to practise with his heavy metal band. The law of nuisance provides you protection from such unreasonable interferences with your enjoyment of your property and, in so doing, limits both your use and your neighbour's use of property. In the past 40 or so years, the proper use and enjoyment of property, particularly of land, by owners and possessors has become a matter of much social and political concern. The result has been a

---

[37] "Chattel" is a medieval English word for "cattle". Most likely, "chattel" was used to classify all things other than land because in medieval England cattle were, next to land, the most important objects of property.

spate of legislation which aims to limit property rights in service to land use planning generally and environmental protection in particular.

In sum, the law of property is about the acquisition and use of resources which beings such as we need to survive and flourish in a civilized manner. As it is elsewhere in our law, the measure of civility in property is equality, and the rules of property ensure that our holdings are secure despite the differences of power, political and personal, which obtain between us.

CONTRACT LAW

The law of contracts consists of legal rules about agreements. By making binding agreements with one another, we clothe ourselves with rights and our interests in the matter then become backed by the coercive authority of the state. "Freedom of contract" has long pedigree in Western politics and philosophy and indeed has sometimes served as a slogan for political protest and reform. We should do well then to begin our discussion with the place of contracts in our way of life.

It is often claimed that the law of contract is important for practical or instrumental reasons. Clearly, no economy but the most primitive could survive in the absence of the possibility of enforcement of agreements which the law of contracts provides us. And, of course, our economic lives, and in many respects the whole of our lives, are guided by agreements on whose performance we rely. Economic and social life would be very different from what they are if contracts of sale, rent, loan, employment, insurance, and so on were not enforceable at law. So, it is indeed true that the law of contracts produces an environment for our affairs on which we very much depend. But, though contract law is instrumental in creating that environment, its justification concerns matters much deeper and significant.

An example will serve to reveal that something else is afoot in our law. Suppose Bob promises Bill that he will provide him with $10,000 to start the e-business about which Bill has been talking for months. Suppose too that in reliance on this promise, Bill buys computer equipment and hires an assistant. Suppose finally that Bob changes his mind and refuses to advance Bob the money promised. Under our law, Bob will be able to resist any claim by Bill against him for breach of his promise on grounds that there was between them no binding agreement. Now, were our law purely instrumental, it would make no sense to deny a person like Bill who has relied to his detriment, and quite possibly to the economy's detriment, on a freely made promise.

That our law sides with people like Bob by allowing them not to stand by their promises has to do with the political morality which our law expresses. Though keeping promises is a cardinal principle of personal morality, the political morality of law will enforce only certain promises. It therefore makes no difference at law that people like Bob offend moral dogma more generally. His breaking his promise only has legal significance if he has caused Bill a legal harm. And the legal harm against which our law protects arises in contract only if the agreement was binding legally and if in consequence disappointed parties like Bill have suffered by relying legally. Our law of contracts then is about saving us safe from the harm caused by our reasonable reliance upon binding agreements.[38]

This is to say that not all agreements are contracts, that only legally binding agreements give rise to rights, and that we rely on the rest at our peril. It is also to make everything turn on which agreements are legally binding. Our contract rules erect two conditions in the absence of either of which disappointed reliance will be classified as an offence rather than as a harm. First, there must in fact have been an agreement. Our law uses the language of "offer and acceptance" to determine whether an agreement exists. The rules of offer and acceptance serve to determine whether the parties knew whom each other was; whether they concerned themselves with the same subject matter; and whether they came to a mind — lawyers say *ad idem* — with respect to the matter. On these grounds, an agreement may fail because the parties were mistaken about one another's identities (I thought you were the landlord but you were in fact a tenant); because they were talking at cross purposes (I thought we were talking about the purchase of a computer while you thought I was buying a stereo); or because, though they properly identified both each other and the subject matter, they never finally came to terms and no definite commitment was in consequence undertaken by either party (you and I were just too vague about the terms of sale and delivery).

The second condition is this: to be legally binding, agreements must not only be clear and definite, they must by their terms be reciprocal as regards benefits and burdens. Each party, that is, must have something to gain, and to lose, from the agreement. Lawyers generally refer to this as the "consideration requirement" which quite properly is said to exclude from the law's protection one-sided agreements and agreements whose consideration is now past or which consists of agreeing to do what has previously been agreed upon. Consideration makes abundant sense in terms of the reliance harm which is the object of contract law. Indeed, it is only because the parties can gain mutually from an agreement[39] that either, in the case of breach, could be said to have had something on which they relied to their detriment. So the consideration requirement is

---

[38] For two early, and now classic, essays on the reliance interest, see: L.L. Fuller and W.R. Purdue, Jr., "The Reliance Interest in Contract Damages: 1" (1936), 46 Yale L.J. 52; and L.L. Fuller and W.R. Purdue, Jr., "The Reliance Interest in Contract Damages: 2" (1937), 46 Yale L.J. 373.

[39] Incidentally, contracts formed by a mutual exchange of promises to do something in the future are termed "executory" contracts, in contrast to contracts which have been executed or performed. Where the future performance of an executory contract depends upon some other contingency, the contract is called a "conditional" contract which, in the absence of the condition coming to pass, has no legal significance.

the stuff of legal harm and without it no legal harm can have been suffered by either party.[40]

There is a caveat to the consideration requirement. Suppose Bob made his promise of money to support Bill's business ambitions in a written document which was, as lawyers say, "signed, sealed and delivered". Documents of this sort are called "deeds" or "covenants under seal", and where they govern the relations between the parties, a one-sided agreement, like Bob's promise to make a gift of the money to Bill, will under our law yet be declared binding. This too makes sense in terms of reliance harm. Where a party making a promise of a gift or a favour undertakes to reduce the promise to writing and to affix his or her signature to such a document in the presence of witnesses, then it makes sense to say that the party to whom the promise was made reasonably relied on the promise. Of course, contracts need not be written, nor if they are, need the written document comprise the whole of the contract. Contracts which are either not in writing at all or only partially in writing are called "parol contracts". Moreover, both parol and written contracts may, in their entirety or in part, be implied or inferred from the conduct of the parties. Of course, written contracts tend to be express contracts, but even then, a court may find that certain terms are implied.

Reference is sometimes made to an intention to create legal relations either as a third condition or as an independent requirement of offer and acceptance. Under this view, undertakings of a private nature (I promise that I will take you to dinner next Friday evening) are thought to be excluded from the law's countenance notwithstanding that we undertake them seriously and are clear about them just because they are private. The better view of this requirement is that, though there was agreement, it fails as a contract because it concerns offence (personal morality) and not harm (political morality).

We should say something about remedies for "breach of contract". A breach occurs when one of the parties to a contract fails to perform the agreed upon promise. In that event, our law corrects the reliance harm suffered by "innocent" party by making good the reliance. This means putting that party in the position it would have been in had the other party performed its part of the bargain. Generally, this is done through the award of damages which compensates the innocent party to the extent of its reliance. Where, however, an award of damages would not correct the harm (as for instance where the subject matter of a contract of sale is a one of a kind object like a work of art), courts may order specific performance which requires the party in breach to do exactly as it promised. Our law also allows an innocent party to withdraw from an agreement which the other party clearly intends not to perform. Lawyers call this remedy "rescission".

---

[40] By and large, our law pays no mind to the adequacy of free exchanges nor does it attempt after the fact to judge the fairness of bargains.

Like property law, contract law both creates and limits rights. It is part and parcel of a binding agreement that the parties have reciprocal benefits and burdens, and, in that sense, limitations on contractual rights are inherent. But they are limited in a more robust way as well. A valid agreement will yet not be binding if it was produced by fraud or deceit, or resulted from mistake (Bill pays Bob a sum of money for a debt he in fact owes to Bruce) or from coercion (Bill agrees to pay Bob a sum of money because Bob threatens to beat him up unless he does), or has as its subject matter something which is otherwise against the law (Bill agrees to pay Bob a certain sum of money if Bob will kill Bruce). In 1760, Lord Mansfield identified the substance of these sorts of cases: "The gist of this kind of action is, that the defendant, upon the circumstances of the case, is obliged by the ties of natural justice and equity to refund the money".[41] Relief will be had from the terms of a contract, then, when it unjustly enriches one of the parties. Whether there is a wider swath of principle concerning unfairness and inequality on which to obtain relief from the burdens of unfair contracts is a matter of some controversy. As mentioned previously, it is very much the attitude of our law that we are simply stuck with the unhappy consequences of contracts freely made. "[T]he Chancery mends no man's bargain", as Lord Nottingham long ago declared.[42] If grounds for relief beyond restitution do exist, they will then consist of exceptions to that governing rule.

(ii) Exploration: The Law of Civil Wrongs

Tort law is preeminently lawyers' law. The word "tort" — which is French for "wrong" — and its cognates "tortfeasor" (the person who commits a tort) and "tortious" (pertaining to torts) have no currency beyond the language of lawyers. But this historical oddity, which we owe to the Norman conquest of England, cannot disclose or explain tort law's central place in our private law.

Initial Characterization

As we have seen, the public law of crimes secures our persons and our property against serious wrongdoing, but it does not serve us directly as victims.[43] Rather, because the criminal law views harms to persons and property as public harms, the victim, the private person who was in fact harmed, is in a very real (and necessary) sense lost from view. The law of torts is often described as the law of civil wrongs. And when this is understood properly, there is wisdom here. For

---

[41] *Moses v. Macferlan* (1760), 2 Burr. 1005 at 1012.

[42] *Maynard v. Moseley* (1676), 3 Swans 651 at 655, 36 E.R. 1009.

[43] The *Criminal Code* of Canada does contain provisions which afford courts the authority to require offenders to make restitution to their victims, but these provisions are rarely used and are in any event very much subsidiary to the retributive point of criminal law. In addition, some provinces have criminal compensation statutes which allow victims of crime to seek compensation from public funds.

the law of torts protects us against harms to our interests in a fashion not provided by any other body of law. First, as regards crimes which are committed against us, tort law allows us as victims to pursue the criminal for compensation. Consequently, a single act may constitute both a crime and a tort; for the former, the wrongdoer will be punished and for the latter, he may be required, as a private individual, to compensate his victim. Second, though the law of torts protects our persons, our property and even our contractual relations, it does so in ways and under circumstances different from the law of property, contracts and crime and to which those bodies of law do not properly apply. For instance, while obligations in contract and property are in an important sense voluntary, tort obligations are imposed and entirely involuntary. Moreover, though tort law is like property law in protecting property, and like criminal law in protecting persons, and like contract law in protecting contracts, it also protects against harms — for instance, harms to our reputations and to our mental well being — that those other bodies of law do not. Finally, though torts, like the whole of the law, has as its concern our rights, it assesses their violation on grounds sometimes very different from the rest of our law.

We may then initially characterize the law of torts along the following dimensions:

Figure 8.4
Characterizing the Law of Torts

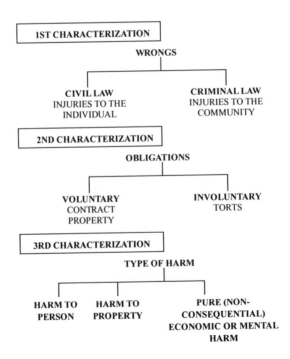

Of course, tort law shares with the law of contract and property the remedies of reparation (compensatory damages) and restraint (injunctive relief) and in torts too, the former is the normal remedy.

WHAT IS TORT ABOUT?

Though helpful in establishing the lay of the land, this characterization is not specific enough. The following figure illustrates one way of looking at torts which can serve as a guide:

Figure 8.5

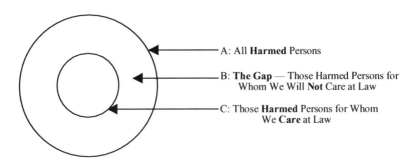

A: All **Harmed** Persons

B: **The Gap** — Those Harmed Persons for Whom We Will **Not** Care at Law

C: Those **Harmed** Persons for Whom We **Care** at Law

So viewed, tort law is about: a) justifying the distinction between B's and C's; b) deciding, on that basis, whether any individual harmed person is a B or C; and, in consequence, c) negotiating the size of the gap. Tort law, therefore, is part of our general political practice of dealing with the harms people suffer in life — of deciding which harms are permissible at law and which are not.

Justification: Save for certain historic exceptions, which lawyers group together under the rubric of strict liability, fault is the threshold to rights and obligations in tort. Two consequences follow. First, a harmed person cannot possibly be a "rights-violated B" unless he or she was harmed by another who was at fault in so doing. Second, we may cause harm with immunity provided only that we are not at fault. Exceptions aside, then, fault is the whole of tort law. It defines what a tort is; and it structures the rules of tort into recognizable bodies of law.

Definition: A tort exists where: a) one party, through its actions[44] or inactions,[45] harms another in a legally recognized way (harms to that person's person or property generally, though *sometimes* harm purely to the person's economic

---

[44] Lawyers call actions that harm "misfeasance".

[45] Lawyers call inactions that harm "nonfeasance".

or mental well-being); and b) the relationship between the doer of the harm and the sufferer of harm is one of fault and therefore of right and obligation.

Structure: Certain categories of cases excepted, tort law is structured around the bases of fault at law. Those bases are intent and negligence. *Intent*: A relationship of right and obligation exists between a doer and sufferer of harm if the doer intended the harm. This basis of fault constructs the body of intentional torts, namely: battery, assault, intentional infliction of mental suffering, false imprisonment, trespass to land and chattels and intentional economic harm. *Negligence*: A relationship of right and obligation exists between a doer and sufferer of harm where the doer was negligent in causing the harm. This basis of fault constructs the tort of negligence which encompasses not only bodily injuries and property injury, but sometimes pure mental suffering and pure economic harm. *Exceptions*: These are torts which developed separately in the common law, namely: defamation, nuisance, strict liability and occupiers liability. In some, fault is intent based; in others, it is based on negligence; and in still others, right and obligation may exist without fault.

INTENTIONAL HARM

Liability: To prove fault, the sufferer of harm must discharge both a general and particular onus. That is, the plaintiff must prove that the defendant acted volitionally and with intention to cause the consequences which followed; and he or she must prove that that volitional act and those intended consequences qualify under the definition of the tort about which he or she complains. The definitional requirements comprise the law's view of when our interests in personal security and personal dignity have been invaded and, as such, provide a vocabulary for argument about rights violations. Through this vocabulary, lawyers and courts finally negotiate how much personal insecurity and personal indignity individuals have to forebear in conducting their lives and affairs.

Vocabulary: Our purposes prevent our exploring at any length the law's vocabulary for arguments about rights and forbearance. We will have to be satisfied with thumbnail sketches of the major intentional torts. Hopefully, this will impart some of the tone and tenor. *Battery* is harmful or offensive contact, direct or indirect, caused by another's positive act. *Assault* is the only tort that protects mental disturbance in the absence of physical manifestation or injury, and it is in consequence strictly construed. An assault sounds where the plaintiff had a present apprehension of imminent harmful or offensive contact. The defendant need intend to scare the plaintiff only, though he or she must have had the apparent ability to carry through with the threat. Unlike battery, mere obstruction will suffice as will words alone. *Intentional infliction of mental suffering* sounds where the defendant knew or ought to have known that his conduct would cause mental harm; the harm is somehow or another physically manifested; and the defendant's conduct is such that it would cause mental suffering in a reasonable person, except where the defendant has knowledge of the plaintiff's special vulnerability. *False imprisonment* is a total deprivation of physical movement, and it therefore falls to the plaintiff to have searched for and taken advantage of reasonable routes of escape. *Trespass* exists with every intentional invasion of private property by whatever means. No injury beyond the trespass itself is required. We shall no more than name the *intentional torts to economic interest* which together comprise a common law morality for market relations. The so-called *business torts* are: deceit; interference with contractual relations; intimidation; conspiracy; and interference with economic interests by unlawful means.

Defences: The issue as regards defences is which of the plaintiff's or defendant's actions may excuse liability for proven fault. Since the intentional torts aim to preserve our autonomy, by securing our bodies and our dignity, and since their effect is to determine how much personal insecurity and indignity we have to forebear, the defences unsurprisingly have everything themselves to do with autonomy. A defendant's invasion of a plaintiff's autonomy will be excused where the actions of either constitutes what, in our law's view, is a legally significant exercise of autonomy. What, therefore, is being negotiated in the defences is the legal significance of autonomous acts between individuals, one of whom has intentionally harmed another. Briefly stated, the defences of autonomy recognized at law are: *consent* (the defendant's invasion of the plaintiff's right is excused where the plaintiff consented to the invasion in a legally significant manner); *self-defence* (the defendant's invasion is excused where it constitutes a legally significant defence of his own right and autonomy); *defence of third person* (the defendant's invasion is excused where it constitutes a legally significant defence of a third party's right and autonomy); *defence of property* (the defendant's invasion is excused where it constitutes a legally significant defence of its property right); *necessity* (the defendant's invasion may be excused where the defendant's actions were undertaken to avoid an imminent threat or peril to human life); and *legal authority* (the defendant's invasion is excused where it was undertaken pursuant to legal authority).

INADVERTENT HARM

Liability: A defendant is liable for inadvertent harm if, and only if, he or she is at fault for a legally recognized injury. Fault of this kind is called negligence at law, and it resides on three foundations, all of which must obtain. Simply stated, we are liable for the harms we unintentionally cause others if: a) our conduct was unreasonable; b) in the circumstances, we had a duty at law to avoid unreasonable conduct; *and* c) our unreasonable, duty-owing conduct in fact caused the other person's legally recognized injury. As was the case with the intentional torts, what is at issue in negligence is whose autonomy will prevail and whose liberty will therefore be constrained, the doer of the harm or the sufferer of harm. Again, we can here offer only an overview.

The first argument of principle concerning whose autonomy ought properly to prevail is *standard of care*. If the doer's conduct was not faulty in this sense, then its autonomy must prevail. On the other hand, even if the defendant did not act reasonably, it might yet prevail if it was not under a duty to avoid acting unreasonably or if that unreasonable conduct did not cause the harm. The law holds us to the standard of reasonable care in conducting our affairs, and it assesses reasonableness objectively in terms of what a reasonable and prudent person would have done in the same circumstances.

We may, however, act as unreasonably as we wish unless we are under a *duty at law* to act reasonably. That this is so makes the question of duty the essential foundation of the tort of negligence. Moreover, it is with the principle of duty that our law most directly discloses the metre of our rights and obligations with respect to the harm that living our lives inevitably causes. In *Donoghue v. Stevenson*,[46] the House of Lords articulated the principle of liability for the harms we cause through conduct which fails to conform to the standard of reasonableness:

> The liability for negligence ... is no doubt based upon a general public sentiment of moral wrong doing for which the offender must pay. But acts or omissions which any moral code would censure cannot in a practical world be treated so as to give a right to every person injured by them to demand relief. ... The rule that you are to love your neighbour becomes, in law, you must not injure your neighbour; and the lawyer's question, who is my neighbour? receives a restricted reply. You must take reasonable care to avoid acts and omissions which you can reasonably foresee would be likely to injure your neighbour. Who, then, in law, is my neighbour? The answer seems to be: persons who are so closely and directly affected by my act that I ought reasonably to have them in contemplation as being so affected when I am directing my mind to the acts and omissions which are called in question.[47]

In this beautifully rendered passage, the House not only segregates personal and political morality, but in articulating the latter's requirements with respect to inadvertent harm, it also proffers a principle which both preserves and limits our rights to live our lives as we see fit. Political community cannot require us to love one another, lest there be neither love nor freedom left in the world. But it can require us to conform to communal standards of reasonable conduct in those circumstances where harm to others is reasonably foreseeable. Indeed, that our liberties are constrained in those circumstance serves our liberty to conduct our affairs without the burden of careless interferences from others.

The third arm of liability, *factual causation*, requires the plaintiff to prove that "but for" the conduct complained of no harm would have been sustained. This likewise preserves and secures our liberties. Only if the harm would not have occurred without us, will our liberty be constrained; and if we ourselves are harmed in that way, the invasion of our liberty will find solace at law.

---

[46] [1932] A.C. 562.
[47] *Ibid.*, at 580 (*per* Lord Atkin).

Extent of liability: Our ability to lead our lives in Lord Atkin's "practical world" is preserved and limited as well by the second inquiry of principle which our law of negligence mandates. A negligent, duty-owing defendant is not *necessarily* liable for all of the harm it causes. On the contrary, we are liable only for those harms which are our fault and only to those others for whom we are responsible. Our law here again uses the moral vocabulary of reasonable foreseeability. Since our unreasonable conduct may have endless ramifications in the world, the very possibility of making our lives our own requires that we be liable only to reasonably foreseeable types of plaintiffs who are injured in reasonably foreseeable types of accidents, and in reasonably foreseeable kinds of ways. Everything turns, as it properly must, on the moral location of the injured person to our acts. Otherwise there would, at least under modern conditions, be no place for liberty in the day-to-day conduct of our lives, or at least no liberty that could not later be subject to judicial surveillance.

Defences: Three defences are available to defendants found liable under these inquiries of principle and if a defendant cannot avail itself of one of them, it will be accountable for full compensation to the plaintiff. The first two defences arise from the injured person's exercise of autonomy with respect to the circumstances of the injury. Where it is made out by the defendant, the defence of *contributory negligence* by the plaintiff reduces the defendant's liability on the ground that the plaintiff was partially responsible for the injury it suffered. The defence of *voluntary assumption of risk* — lawyers refer to it as *volenti non fit injuria* — goes not to causation, but to the moral significance of consent. Where *volenti* is made out, the defendant will be fully exonerated. In consequence, the defence is strictly construed. The last defence is *illegality*, or as lawyers put it, *ex turpi causa non oritur actio* ("out of a base consideration, an action does not arise"). However, it now seems that, in Canada at least, *ex turpi* is no longer available as a defence to personal injury claims in negligence.

D.   RESTATEMENT NO. 5

Liberal political community is a moral community. Its purpose is to subject power and ambition, public and private, to the reason of moral constraint. The Rule of Law is the institutional medium of that constraint. Through the separation of powers and the institution of a regime of public and private rights, the Rule of Law constitutes limited power and secretes the moral reality of government under law.

Our law is an institutionally embedded morality about individual and collective life. Law values equality, our equal worth, above all else, and the laws which are its expression together require that we live together under conditions of equal care and respect. Law is at once an invitation and an order. It invites us to share our diverse fates as equals, and if we decline, it stands ready to coerce our courtesy.

The Rule of Law is an ongoing institutional practice. It provides a public language for deliberation and contest concerning the requirements of equality, and it assumes that the door is ever open to the revision of our political commitments and practices. Law, in this way, creates a cleavage between authority and liberty which it never intends, and never can, reconcile. Law rather is the practice of producing liberty, in the name and cause of equality, through this never certain equilibrium.

FURTHER READINGS TO CHAPTER 8

1.   Public and Private Law

Allan, T.R.S. "The Limits of Public Law". In Allan, T.R.S. *Law, Liberty, and Justice: The Legal Foundations of British Constitutionalism.* Oxford: Clarendon Press, 1993. At p. 211.

Birks, P., ed. *English Private Law.* 2 Vol. Oxford: Oxford University Press, 2000.

Brudner, A. *The Unity of the Common Law.* Berkeley: University of California Press, 1995.

Craig, P.P. *Public Law and Democracy in the United Kingdom and the United States of America.* Oxford: Clarendon Press, 1990.

————. "Dicey: Unitary, Self-Correcting Democracy and Public Law". (1990), 106 Law Q. Rev. 105.

Elliot, D.W., and R.E. Warskett, eds. *Introduction to Public Law*, 4th ed. North York, ON: Captus Press, 1999.

Goodall, K. "'Public and Private' in Legal Debate". (1990), 18 Internat'l J. of the Sociology of Law 445.

Howard, C. "Public Law and Common Law". In D.J. Galligan. ed. *Essays in Legal Theory.* Melbourne: Melbourne University Press, 1984. At p. 1.

Loughlin, M. *Public Law and Political Theory.* Oxford: Clarendon Press, 1992.

Lucy, W. *Understanding and Explaining Adjudication.* Oxford: Oxford University Press, 1999.

MacNeil, M. *et al.*, eds. *Introduction to Private Law Relationships.* 2nd ed. North York, ON: Captus Press, 1995.

Oliver, D. "Common Values in Public and Private Law and the Public/Private Divide". [1997] Public Law 630.

Radbruch, G. "Public and Private Law". In K. Wilk., ed./trans. *The Legal Philosophies of Lask, Radbruch and Dabin.* Cambridge, MA: Harvard University Press, 1950. At p. 152.

Simmonds, N.E. "The Changing Face of Private Law: Doctrinal Categories and the Welfare State". (1982), 2 Legal Studies 257.

Stone, M. "On the Idea of Private Law". (1996), 9 Canadian J. of L. & Jurisprudence 235.

Teubner, G. "Contracting Worlds: The Many Autonomies of Private Law". (2000), 9(3) Social & Legal Studies 399.

van Caenegem, R.C. *An Historical Introduction to Private Law.* Cambridge: Cambridge University Press, 1992.

Weinrib, E. *The Idea of Private Law.* Cambridge, MA: Harvard University Press, 1995.

Weinrib, J., and K. Kumar, eds. *Public and Private in Thought and Practice.* Chicago: University of Chicago Press, 1997.

2.   Criminal Law

Allen, F.A. *The Habits of Legality: Criminal Justice and the Rule of Law.* New York: Oxford University Press, 1996.

Ashworth, A. *Principles of Criminal Law.* 3rd ed. Oxford: Clarendon Press, 1999.

Beccaria, C. *On Crimes and Punishments and Other Writings.* (1764) Cambridge: Cambridge University Press, 1995.

Duff, A., ed. *Philosophy and the Criminal Law.* Cambridge: Cambridge University Press, 1998.

Farmer, L. *Criminal Law, Tradition and Legal Order.* Cambridge: Cambridge University Press, 1997.

Feinberg, J. *The Moral Limits of the Criminal Law.* 4 Vol. New York: Oxford University Press, 1984.

Fletcher, G.P. *Basic Concepts of Criminal Law.* New York: Oxford University Press, 1998.

Hall, J. *General Principles of Criminal Law.* 2nd ed. New York: Bobbs-Merrill, 1960.

Mattravers, M., ed. *Sentencing and Political Theory.* Oxford: Hart Publishing, 1998.

Morawetz, T., ed. *Criminal Law.* New York: New York University Press, 1991.

Morris, H. "Persons and Punishment". (1968), 52 Monist 475.

Pauley, M.A. "The Jurisprudence of Crime and Punishment From Plato to Hegel". (1994), 39 Am. J. of Jurisprudence 97.

Pennock, J.R., and J.W. Chapman, eds. *Criminal Justice: NOMOS XXVII.* New York: New York University Press, 1985.

Robinson, P.H. *Structure and Function in Criminal Law.* Oxford: Clarendon Press, 1997.

Stuart, D. *Canadian Criminal Law: A Treatise.* 3rd ed. Toronto: Carswell, 1995.

White, A.A. "Victims' Rights, Rule of Law, and the Threat to Liberal Jurisprudence". (1998-99), 87 Kentucky L.J. 357.

Williams, G.L. *Criminal Law: The General Part.* 2nd ed. London: Stevens, 1961.

3.   Tort Law

Atiyah, P.S. *The Damages Lottery.* Oxford: Hart Publishing, 1997.

Cane, P., and J. Stapleton, eds. *The Law of Obligations: Essays in Celebration of John Fleming.* Oxford: Clarendon Press, 1998.

Crane, P. *The Anatomy of Tort Law.* Oxford: Hart Publishing, 1997.

Englard, I. *The Philosophy of Tort Law.* Aldershot: Dartmouth, 1993.

Fleming, J.G. *The Law of Torts.* 8th ed. Sydney: The Law Book Co., 1992.

Klar, L.N. *Tort Law.* 2nd ed. Toronto: Carswell, 1996.

Levmore, S., ed. *Foundations of Tort Law.* New York: Oxford University Press, 1994.

Markesinis, B.S. *Tort Law.* 4th ed. Oxford: Clarendon Press, 1999.

Owen, D.G., ed. *Philosophical Foundations of Tort Law.* Oxford: Clarendon Press, 1995.

Weinrib, E., ed. *Tort Law.* New York: New York University Press, 1991.

———. "Two Conceptions of Tort Law". In R.F. Devlin, ed. *Canadian Perspectives on Legal Theory.* Toronto: Emond Montgomery, 1991. At p. 29.

PART III

LIVING THE LAW

Chapter 9

The Lawyer's Honourable Office

We love law, not because reason requires it, but because our commitment to our discipline serves the needs of the public to whom, and for whom, we are responsible.

Paul Carrington

[M]embership in the bar is a privilege burdened with conditions.

Cardozo, J.

A. INTRODUCTION

Our story about lawyers and the normative construction of society is so far incomplete. That the legal community is a requirement of the Rule of Law does not without more tell us much of anything about the kind of legal community the Rule of Law requires. This second matter raises the conditions on which the authority of the legal community resides, which is our concern in this Chapter.

The Rule of Law makes "students of law, professional academics, legal practitioners and judges ... the *special* clientele of the rule of law",[1] and it places on them "a special responsibility"[2] for our way of life. Our purpose is to disclose the nature of that "special role".[3] We shall find that the authority of the legal community is an authority born of public service and that authority of that kind comes with a high price tag indeed.

B. PROFESSIONAL VOCATION/PUBLIC OFFICE

Law students attend "professional" law schools. Lawyers are members of a "profession" and have therefore uniquely "professional" obligations. We use the word "professional" all the time, but seldom do we use it with any precision.

---

[1] R.S. Summers, "A Formal Theory of the Rule of Law" (1993), 6(2) Ratio Juris 127 at p. 128.

[2] R. Dahrendorf, *Law and Order* (Boulder, CO: Westview, 1985), at p. 150. See also: J. Raz, "The Rule of Law and Its Virtue" (1977), 93 Law Q. Rev. 195 at p. 208 ("the rule of law ... [is] the special responsibility of the courts and the legal profession").

[3] Summers, *supra*, note 1.

224 On Coming to Law

(i) Jobs, Careers and Vocations

The concept of profession is available in a distinction we commonly make with respect different forms of labour. Bellah puts the matter thus:

> In the sense of a "job," work is a way of making money and making a living. It supports a self defined by economic success, security, and all that money can buy. In the sense of "career," works traces one's progress through life by achievement and advancement in an occupation. It yields a self defined by a broader sort of success, which takes in social standing and prestige, and by a sense of expanding power and competency that renders work itself a source of self-esteem. In the strongest sense of "calling," work constitutes a practical ideal of activity and character that makes a person's work morally inseparable from his or her life. It subsumes the self into a community of disciplined practice and sound judgment whose activity has meaning and value in itself, not just in the output or profit that results from it. But the calling not only links a person to his or her fellow workers. A calling links a person to a larger community, a whole in which the calling of each is a contribution to the good of all. [...] The calling is a crucial link between the individual and the public world. Work in the sense of the calling can never be merely private.[4]

This understanding of vocation is not at all foreign to our law. We say, for instance, that lawyers are "called" to the bar, and that they are "admitted" into the legal community. But there is more here than facial similarity. Our using phrases like these is proper precisely because law is a profession and because professions are vocations.

Roscoe Pound defined a "profession" as "a group ... pursuing a learned art as a common calling in the spirit of public service".[5] That law is "a learned art" signals that it is a heritage from the past and not something that any single generation of practitioners creates anew. That law is pursued "in the spirit of public service" means that it justifies itself in terms other than self interest. That law is "a common calling" captures Bellah's notion of vocation. Professions, law included, qualify as such for just these reasons: *they are traditions which create offices and have purposes other than self interest.*

(ii) The Meaning of Office

Justice Robert Jackson of the U.S. Supreme Court once defended his Court's authority in the following terms: "[W]e act in these matters not by authority of our competence but by force of our commissions".[6] In this, he was invoking the authority of his office. *An office is a position of trust and a warrant of authority*

---

[4] R.N. Bellah, *et al., Habits of the Heart* (Berkeley: University of California Press, 1985), at p. 66.
[5] R. Pound, *The Lawyer from Antiquity to Modern Times* (St. Paul: West Publishing, 1953), at p. 5. For an analysis of difficulties presently associated with the word, see: S.F. Barker, "What is a Profession?" (1992), 1 Professional Ethics 73.
[6] *West Virginia State Board of Education v. Barnette*, 319 U.S. 624 at 640 (1943).

under constituted authority which has as its purpose service to others.[7] The meter of office does not reside in, though it may involve, knowledge or proficiency or expertise. It resides rather in the office holder's fidelity to the trust of which it is composed and to the service which it demands. All offices are public in the sense that they are defined by a concern with others and not by self interest. But not all offices are public in the sense that they concern the affairs of others in political community. The office of lawyer is a public office in that sense, while the offices of doctors and priests are not.

That the lawyer's office is public does not at all mean that the lawyer is a governmental actor. The office of lawyer is public rather by virtue of the character of the others who are the object of its service, namely, all members of political community, and by the nature of the lawyer's service to them. That service to all others is mandated by the political morality of the Rule of Law, and it consists of protecting the rights of individuals as equal members of political community.

That offices may not be reduced to some function associated with expertise or competence means that holding an office is a privilege, and not a right, which must depend on qualifications of some other sort. Those conditions contemplate the notion of fitness: conferral and continuance of lawyerly office properly depends upon the supplicant's character and conduct. More generally, *the authority of legal community is contingent on its members, individually and corporately, displaying the traits of character and forms of conduct which the Rule of Law requires of them.* Therein is the grist of authority with which we must now contend.

First, however, there is another matter which deserves brief attention. The office of the lawyer has often been described instead by the phrase "officer of the court". Though it includes the idea of "office", this is nonetheless an unhappy turn of phrase which "confuses lawyers and misleads the public".[8] Not only does it not have a standard meaning, it fails to offer any real instruction with respect to either lawyer character or lawyer conduct. Most importantly, it is often conceived in a way that associates lawyerly obligations exclusively with the judicial system. Views of that sort are unacceptable for three reasons. First, though academic and practising lawyers do indeed have obligations to the courts, those obligations have more to do with holding the judiciary to account than, as is often thought, with lawyers serving as subordinate defenders of the judicial *status quo*. Second, any acceptable view of the moral obligations of lawyers must account for the distinct obligations of the different branches of the legal community. The "officer of the court" view tends instead simply to ignore the obligations of judges and academic lawyers. Finally, to meet at all the requirements of rationality and completeness, views of lawyerly obligation must both identify their grounds and structure their advice in a way that accounts for all of

---

[7]   See: M. Walzer, *Spheres of Justice* (New York: Basic Books, 1983), ch. 5, "Office".

[8]   E.R. Gaetke, "Lawyers as Officers of the Court" (1989), 42 Vanderbilt L. Rev. 39 at p. 39.

the parties to whom obligations are owed. The "officer of the court" account does neither. It associates it prescriptions with no moral foundation, stated or implied; it offers no system which relates different obligations to one another; and it misses entirely the matter of obligations to the public. This last defect is especially troubling since the morality of lawyering descends from the obligations which lawyers owe to civil society.

C. BEING A LAWYER: CONDITIONS OF SERVICE

Neither space nor purpose allows us to offer a detailed account of the obligations of service of the legal community. We can however provide an overview of the moral and ethical demands which attach to, and together comprise, the office of lawyer as such. We can also briefly sketch the special obligations owed by each of the practising, judicial and academic branches.

What follows proceeds from two premises, namely, that the Rule of Law is the animating principle of the lawyer's office, and that the Rule of Law places both moral and ethical demands on lawyers. The second premise relies on a distinction between ethics and morality about which we must be clear. A great many law schools offer courses in legal ethics and virtually every law society now has a code of ethics. But, according to the view taken here, those courses and codes are misnamed because their concern most often is morality and not ethics. Morality and ethics may be distinguished in the following fashion.[9] Ethics has to do with *character*; it asks and attempts to answer a question which all of us at some point ask ourselves, "What kind of person should I *be*?" Morality, on the other hand, has to do with *conduct*; it asks and attempts to answer a question quite different from the first, namely, "What in any given circumstance (or even overall) should I *do*?".

Offices raise both questions. This should not surprise since offices by their very nature concern fitness and fitness requires of office holders, not only that they act in certain ways, but also that they exhibit certain inclinations with respect their office. Indeed, it is not too much to say that, as regards offices at least, morality and ethics, conduct and character, are interdependent. Offices presume that officers will act as their offices require them to act because they are persons of the sort who wish to act that way. Take for instance the office of priest or rabbi: priests and rabbis are presumed to want to act in priestly and rabbinic ways because, in some important sense, they "are" priests and rabbis. Certainly, no office, including lawyerly office, can proceed on the view that character does not count or that the absence of moral transgression is alone

---

[9]   For more on the distinction, see: J. Habermas, "Morality and Ethical Life" (1988), 83 Northwestern U.L. Rev.; and M. Cooke, "Authenticity and Autonomy: Taylor, Habermas, and the Politics of Recognition" (1997), 25 Political Theory 258.

enough. To conceive of matters in either fashion would reduce the office to empty observance which would sap its animating concern of service to others.

(i)   The Requirements of Office

What character and conduct are required of lawyers by virtue alone of their status as lawyers and independently from their location in the judicial, academic or practising branches? We shall offer a three-part reply.

THRESHOLD: CRAFT COMPETENCE

Craft competence is a threshold condition: whatever else is required of lawyers morally and ethically, those things are required of them because they are first lawyers at all. Charles Fried put this rather wonderfully: "So what is it that lawyers and judges know that philosophers and economists do not? The answer is simple, The Law".[10] Which is to say, a person is a lawyer at all because he or she is competent in those things which lawyers do, and what lawyers do is practice their craft. In consequence, "no lawyer can fulfil his or her vocation without first achieving a high degree of [craft] competence".[11] Legal craft requires lawyers to have a sophisticated sense of the overall point of their practice. We earlier dubbed this requirement "legal consciousness". But whatever it is called, it imports into lawyerly craft, not just the need for intelligence, but the need as well for a cultivated appreciation of and for law's enterprise. Indeed, it is this second sense of the matter which informs the ethical requirements to which we shall now turn.

CHARACTER

No less than the interpretive communities devoted to Shakespeare or to the Bible, lawyers too must believe that their texts and their community's traditions with respect to those texts are somehow fundamentally important. Earlier we said that interpretive communities require of their members an act of faith as regards the value of the community's on-going enterprise. But faith is never blind. One commits oneself to an interpretive enterprise because one understands and appreciates its point. The point of the legal enterprise is the Rule of Law. Lawyers read and interpret and apply legal texts in order to serve the rights of individuals, to save them safe from arbitrary and hurtful power. To commit

---

[10]   C. Fried, "The Artificial Reason of the Law or: What Lawyers Know" (1981), 60 Texas L. Rev. 35 at p. 57.

[11]   C.F. Mooney, "Law: A Vocation to Justice and Love" in F.A. Eigo, ed., *The Professions in Ethical Context: Vocations to Love and Justice* (Philadelphia: Villanova University Press, 1986), 59 at p. 83.

oneself to law's enterprise means therefore committing oneself to the priority of justice over power and all that we have found that to entail.

That law constrains power through an institutionalized practice of opposition and subversion means that lawyers, who to avoid bad faith must commit themselves to law, must be persons of a certain sort. Simply, they must be persons for whom the law's pledge of saving lives safe from illegitimate power is central to their self-understanding and motivation, they must be lawyers to their very roots, lawyers for whom law is a vocation which guides and informs the whole of their lives. Lawyers of this authentic kind are seized of what has been aptly termed a "protestant" character.[12] They are persons for whom the way of power in the world is, without more, a matter of much moral moment and of abiding political suspicion. Agnostic of power's right, the lawyer is "the man of justice, the man of law, he who opposes to power, despotism, the abuses and arrogance of wealth, the universality of justice and the equity of an ideal law".[13] *The habits of legality depend finally upon certain habits of the heart.*

It is those habits of character which alone permit lawyers to make good their primary obligation of serving as the faithful and partisan stewards of the Rule of Law. But doing so is yet a complicated affair not least because the Rule of Law is at once a creature of and a containment to political community. "It stands in the dual relationship of suspicion towards and dependency on [political authority]".[14] This relationship of opposition and dependence is of course a problem for all lawyers but for none more so than public lawyers.

The political and executive branches of the state are sources of power which it falls to the legal community to help constrain. But, unlike judges and academic and private lawyers, government lawyers are employed directly by government, and this fact raises serious questions concerning whether those lawyers can ever exhibit and act on the trait of character required of lawyers. Moreover, government lawyers do not have clients (as do private practitioners) nor charges like parties (as do judges) or law students (as do academic lawyers) on which to hang their independence and accountability. Rather, they report to, and receive their briefs from, the executive.

The Anglo-American model of government dealt with the overall unseemliness of this situation by institutionalizing the Offices of the Attorney General and the Solicitor General. These Offices were supposed to stand apart from the executive and to owe duties not to the political but to the legal. That most

---

[12] R. Dworkin, *Law's Empire* (Cambridge, MA: Harvard University Press, 1986), at pp. 190, 252, & 413.

[13] M. Foucault, *Power, Truth, Strategy*, eds. M. Morris and P. Patton (Sydney: Feral, 1979), at p. 43, quoted in C. Douzinas and R. Warrington, *Justice Miscarried: Ethics, Aethetics and the Law* (Hertfordshire: Harvester Wheatsheaf, 1994), at p. 15. Foucault's use of the masculine arises from historical context: he was describing the traits of character of "the great civil lawyers of the eighteenth century" who were all men.

[14] F.A. Allen, *The Habits of Legality: Criminal Justice and the Rule of Law* (New York: Oxford University Press, 1996), at p. 6.

jurisdictions continue to differentiate between these offices, and between the offices of the Minister of Justice and the Attorney General especially, speaks to this origin. However, the fact that the offices of Minister of Justice and Attorney General are now always occupied by the same member of the Executive and that the office of Solicitor General particularly is everywhere thought as just another cabinet position speaks to the total collapse of these traditions. If ever they did, then, these offices can provide no solace for government lawyers. We cannot solve this riddle here. A caution will have to suffice: government lawyers are at the very least a special case because they seem not to fit the requirements of lawyerly office.

CONDUCT

To be a lawyer is to be subject to one obligation above and before all others: *judges and academic and private lawyers are obliged to act as the good faith stewards of the Rule of Law.* All other obligations which attach to lawyers in any of these practices depend upon, and devolve from, this primary obligation.

This seminal obligation imposes exact, and exacting, duties. It requires first that lawyers understand and commit themselves to the law. Recall the distinction we encountered in Chapter 1 between the internal and external points of view. One can faithfully discharge any office, public or private, only if one adopts an internal point of view with respect to it. For instance, faithful discharge of a clerical office depends upon priests and rabbis viewing their office as something which is good in itself and not as something which is an instrument for some good external to the office. Were a priest or rabbi to take the latter point of view, say by viewing their offices as the best career options in terms of work load, compensation and prestige otherwise available to them, then members of their congregations would be right to charge them with bad faith and inauthenticity. Likewise lawyers: on the pain otherwise of bad faith, they too must view their office as a practice which is a good and an end in itself.

To profess the law in this way requires lawyers to commit themselves to serving others. Karl Llewellyn once described law as "a service institution: in service lies its soul — service to client or cause or class, or for some dream which embraces all classes or even a world".[15] So viewed, the ideal of law which lawyers profess requires of them *confession to others*, to their needs, to their rights. Service to others resides at the very heart of the Rule of Law. The Rule of Law requires that laws be accessible in open, clear, and published rules. But "the accessibility of law ... must mean more than publication of statutes and judicial opinions and their availability in law libraries".[16] It requires as well, indeed especially, that lawyers be accessible and available to others. This is the one matter

---

[15] K.N. Llewellyn, "The Study of Law as a Liberal Art" in K.N. Llewellyn, *Jurisprudence: Realism in Theory and Practice* (Chicago: University of Chicago Press, 1962), at pp. 375 at 391.

[16] Allen, *supra*, note 14, at p. 17.

of distributive justice which properly falls to lawyers: the Rule of Law commands lawyers to serve others, fairly and without distinction and for the other's
sake.

Private lawyers especially now very often fail this test of their office. Access
to justice has been not just impeded, but fundamentally corroded, by what one
justice of the Supreme Court of Canada has declared to be the "astronomical"
fees of the private bar.[17] However, it is just not the bar which is pledged to serve,
and to be accessible to, needful others. We shall now turn to an overview of the
service obligations of each of the branches of the legal community.

(ii) Obligations of the Branches

Lawyerly office has a general and a special part. The general part consists of
those matters of character and of conduct, which we have just canvassed, which
pertain to all who occupy the office. The special part consists of those virtues
and obligations which attach separately to the offices of judge, private lawyer
and academic lawyer. We shall attempt to provide nothing more than an overview of judicial, practising and academic obligations. But not only will we not
then deal with the virtues characteristic of the different branches, as regards obligations, our intention will be to identify the structure and then simply to state
the core as regards the others to whom each branch is responsible. This discipline is necessary, not only because of the demands of this book, but more importantly because the devils which hide in the details of obligation are best left
to sustained and serious study.

ACADEMIC LAWYERS

The academic branch exists both to transmit the tradition of the Rule of Law
and, in its scholarship especially, "to criticize not only rule departures, but also
any anti-rule attitudes of officials and judges in particular".[18] The others to and
for whom academic lawyers are responsible are then law students and the members of the other branches of the legal community.

It falls to law professors to inculcate in their students two things: *belief* in the
Rule of Law as a universal human good and in the lawyer's office as an obligation of service, and *competence* in the lawyerly craft of governance by law. In
order to achieve these purposes, law professors must minimally transmit to students knowledge and vision. Llewellyn claims that law professors must "preach"
the law.[19] "Sermons", he says, are the "kindling [that] starts the fire".[20] In order

---

[17] See: J. Tibbetts, "Lawyer Fees 'Astronomical' Supreme Court Judge says" *National Post*, October 22, 1999, at p. A4 (reporting Justice Binnie's commentary on lawyer fees as a detriment to
access to justice).

[18] Summers, *supra*, note 1, at p. 130.

[19] Llewellyn, *supra*, note 15, at p. 393.

[20] *Ibid.*

to preach the law, law professors must themselves be faithful stewards of the Rule of Law. In that sense, they owe it to their students to love the law and to stand ready to disclose that fidelity through their teaching. There is hard lesson here: *no one who does not believe in the goodness of our law should pose as a teacher of it.*[21]

Of course, "kindling is not enough".[22] Law professors have as well to transmit, through their knowledge of the law, lawyerly craft. Yet the two are not unrelated. Llewellyn makes the following observation:

> It is almost amusing to see the eagerness with which [some] law teachers who shun all mention of high ideals roll up their sleeves to inculcate low ideals (which still are true ideals) known as better doctrine or the wiser rule or the true principle in some particular aspect of some particular "field." [...] [Yet], any teaching which goes to skill in any of the crafts, if accompanied by inquiry into what the craft is for, ... brings out of a class a fighting discussion which induces not only a sense of craft-responsibility, but a sense informed.[23]

According to Llewellyn, then, vision and craft are interdependent, and law professors owe both to their students. This should not surprise. Time and again, we have found that in law, the universal and the particular are incurably twinned and that legal craft depends upon the discovery of the general in the particular and the particular in the general.

This interdependence is on display every time a law professor reconstructs the law for students. Dicey put this matter in a way which would repay the attention of all law professors and students:

> It is for the law professors to set forth the law as a coherent whole — to analyse and define legal conceptions — to reduce the mass of legal rules to an orderly series of principles and to aid, stimulate and guide the reform and renovation of legal literature.[24]

This should not surprise either. Each of the bodies of our law consists of a tissue of rules and principles which devolve from, and instantiate and inform, final principles which we have been calling their "point." In large measure, the craft of lawyering itself consists of doing those things which law professors do with bodies of rules. And, when law professors do those things in the company of students, they are making good their obligation to transmit to them the crafts of law.

---

[21] About which see: P. Carrington, "Of Law and the River" (1984), 34 J. of Legal Education 222.

[22] Llewellyn, *supra*, note 15, at p. 393.

[23] *Ibid.*

[24] A.V. Dicey, *Can English Law Be Taught At The Universities?* (1883), quoted in D. Sugarman, "Legal Theory, the Common Law Mind and the Making of the Textbook Tradition" in W. Twining, ed., *Legal Theory and the Common Law* (Oxford: Oxford University Press, 1986), at pp. 26 at 30.

As regards the responsibilities of academic lawyers to the judicial and practising branches, a few notes will have to suffice. It falls to academic lawyers to
hold judges and lawyers to account at the bar of the Rule of Law. This accounting is criticism, and criticism requires distance. Academic lawyers must therefore neither practice nor plead the law. Pleading cases before courts
compromises the academic lawyer entirely. Indeed, "where academic lawyers
frequently appear as advocates before courts, there is often a deficiency of
healthy academic criticism of any departures from the rule of law ...".[25] Engaging in other forms of private practice are equally as corrosive of the academic
lawyer's obligation to guide and renovate the law. Simply, lawyers who owe
partisan obligations to clients have neither the freedom nor the luxury to view
the law as a principled whole. On the other hand, it is absolutely essential for
academic lawyers to think themselves as part of, and as obliged to, the legal
community. Academic lawyers should therefore be called members of a society
of lawyers. And they should also view the judicial and practising branches, as
well as other academic lawyers, as the normal and natural audience for their
scholarly works.

PRIVATE LAWYERS

The bar exists to counsel citizens about the claims of power, public and private,
over their lives and, sometimes, "to advocate before courts the causes of citizens
adversely affected by departures from the rule of law".[26] But, though it forms a
part of the whole, this redaction does not sufficiently capture the complex of
obligations with which the practising branch, more so than either of the other
branches, finds itself burdened.

We noted previously that the bar's obligation to the public is primary. We
noted as well that this obligation contemplates lawyers being available to people, to their serving as conduits to justice. Now, this obligation may be stated in
more general terms: *the practising branch corporately is obligated to serve the
public by making good in people's lives the fact and force of law.* It is for this
reason that the failure of lawyers to be available to people may properly be said
to effect their "alienation from the law": people are alienated only because access to the law is rightfully theirs.[27] The whole of the bar's other obligations
arise from this core. To be more precise: it is only because the bar is responsible
for law's forceful presence in society that individual members have obligations
to clients, to other lawyers and to the courts. We shall dwell briefly on each of
these derivative duties.

Lawyers have obligations to clients because clients are first members of political community to whom lawyers owe fidelity to law. Whether they are acting

---

[25] Summers, *supra*, note 1 at p. 130 (note 4).
[26] *Ibid.*
[27] J. Raz, "The Politics of the Rule of Law" (1990), 3(3) Ratio Juris 331 at p. 339.

as advocates or advisors, lawyers owe their clients *a duty of zealous representation*. Honouring this obligation means something very different from serving as the client's obedient lapdog. Indeed, "about half of the practice of a decent lawyer consists of telling would-be clients that they are damned fools and should stop".[28] Their duty, that is, resides in enforcing the law in their clients' lives.

Lawyers are equal as members of the society of lawyers; and they signal this collegiality through expressions which connote friendship and equality. But the obligations of lawyers between themselves neither begin nor conclude in any of this. Lawyers are equal in two senses. They are each of them members of a professional society which owes its existence, not to the merits of its members, but to the requirements of civilized political community; and, on that account, they have all of them a core obligation to serve the equality of others. The obligations lawyers owe to one another are a consequence of this professional equality which defines them as lawyers. Above all else, *lawyers owe one another a duty to preserve the independence and integrity of their society*. This duty contemplates a host of subordinate duties, all of which are perhaps captured by the duty to save their society safe as a site in which the habits of legality, on which others so very much depend, are nurtured and enforced.

Lawyers, finally, owe obligations to the courts. Lawyers and judges are equal as members of the legal community. They therefore owe one another the same respect and courtesy, born of equality, which lawyers more generally owe one another. Yet, in another sense, judges and lawyers are not equal. Judges have, and lawyers do not, the authority to declare the law and determine facts. Judges owe their law declaration and fact finding authority to the state which appoints them, former lawyers one and all, as judges. The obligations which lawyers owe to judges as judges arises from the menace which authority gained in this way presents to the Rule of Law.

When we discussed the problem of government lawyers earlier, we noted that government lawyers suffer from an aggravated case of an infliction which affects the entire legal community, namely, "the dual relationship of suspicion toward and dependence upon [political authority]".[29] Judges are like government lawyers inasmuch as they owe their appointments, not to political authority writ small, but to governmental power writ large. This along with fact that their appointments are tenured for life and largely not subject to review makes of the judiciary a threat to governance by law. Sir Matthew Hale, Lord Chief Justice under Charles II, famously declared that "The twelve red coats in Westminster Hall are able to do more mischief to the nation, than as many thousands in the

---

[28] M.A. Glendon, *A Nation Under Lawyers* (Cambridge, MA: Harvard University Press, 1994), at p. 75 (the dictum is Elihu Root's).

[29] Allen, *supra*, note 14.

field".[30] Some Americans, as early as the founding of the republic, were even more direct:

> Independent in the fullest sense of the word. There is no power above them, to control any of their decisions. There is no authority that can remove them, and they cannot be controlled by the laws of the legislature. In short, they are independent of the people, of the legislature, and of every power under heaven. Men placed in this position will generally soon feel themselves independent of heaven itself.[31]

Practising lawyers, with academic lawyers, owe to judges a duty of supervision and control. Indeed, lawyers alone are so placed to ensure that judges remain faithful to the Rule of Law. By themselves faithfully discharging that responsibility, lawyers serve both the judges and the people who depend upon them for justice in their affairs.

JUDGES

Lawyers and judges are partners in the creation of law. This was put well by Justice Holmes: "Shall I ask what a court would be, unaided? The law is made by the Bar, even more than by the Bench".[32] Judges therefore have a duty to recognize and respect lawyers as their colleagues in law's enterprise. They also owe duties of restraint and respect to the legislative and executive branches which we have canvassed previously. What remains for us here is their duty as custodians of the Rule of Law. They owe this duty to the public generally and to the parties who appear before them.

We may begin with John Stuart Mill's splendid statement regarding the proper place and practice of courts in societies such as ours:

> [A] Court of Justice acting as such ... does not declare the law *eo nomine* and in the abstract, but waits until a case between man and man is brought before it judicially involving the point in dispute: from which arises the happy effect that its declarations are not made at a very early stage in the controversy; ... that the Court decides after hearing the point fully argued on both sides by lawyers of reputation; decides only as much of the question at a time as is required by the case before it, and its decision ... is drawn from it by the duty which it cannot refuse to fulfil, of dispensing justice impartially between adverse litigants.[33]

---

[30] J. Dalrymple, *Memoirs of Great Britain and Ireland*, Vol. 1, 2nd ed. (London: Strahan & Cadell, 1771), at p. 153, quoted in A. Havighorst, "James II and the Twelve Men in Scarlet" (1953), 69 Law Q. Rev. 522 at p. 522.

[31] Brutus (Robert Yates) March 20, 1788 reprinted in the *Anti-Federalist.* See: M. Dry, ed., *Complete Anti-Federalist: Selections* (Chicago: University of Chicago Press, 1985).

[32] Justice O.W. Holmes, Jr., "The Law", Suffolk Bar Association Dinner, February 5, 1885 in *Speeches* (1913) at pp. 16-18.

[33] J.S. Mill, *Considerations on Representative Government* (1861), reprinted in J.S. Mill, *Utilitarianism, Liberty, and Representative Government*, H.B. Acton, ed. (London: Dent, 1972), at p. 403.

Judges govern in a fashion more direct and more substantial than do other lawyers. Where lawyers argue about law and fact, judges declare the law and determine the facts. They are in consequence especially bound by "the concern for [their] subjects which is the most basic requirement which political morality imposes on those who govern".[34] As Mill so eloquently understood, *this requires judges to take ever so seriously the parties who appear before them.*

The parties are for judges the beginning and the end of matters. Judges care about, and only can care about, individual cases. This is so because they are bound to the parties in fact and in duty. There is no judgment without the parties, nor is any judgment proper beyond the parties. Judges fail to do justice when they *use* the parties as a occasion to declare law. And the sign of their doing so is always abstraction, a reaching for law beyond the needs of the parties to whom they owe allegiance. There is something very deep and moving at play when judges do justice by honouring the limits and practice of their office. Justice is revealed as that which "always addresses itself to singularity, to the singularity of the other, despite or even because it pretends to universality".[35] We have found evidence of this beauty at several points. Law is for judges (and lawyers) never an abstraction. It resides rather in the particulars of the lives of those others who seek the law's solace. And it is in that realm which law's generality alone properly speaks.

In making justice for the parties, judges also serve political community more widely. Lord Devlin once claimed that "the social service which the judge renders to the community is the removal of a sense of injustice".[36] There is wisdom in this. Though judges are confined to the parties, to their arguments and their issues, by respecting those limitations, and by resisting the temptation to govern more widely, judges make secure the community's sense that justice is possible under government by law. When they determine, on the particular facts of individual lives, whether and when public or private power has exceeded the limits prescribed by the rules of law, they vindicate the Rule of Law. In this way, through the good faith discharge of the office, the practice of judges at the "molecular" level of the individual case has purchase at the "molar" level of society: each and every case justly decided reaffirms our way of life overall.[37]

---

[34] R. Dworkin, *A Matter of Principle* (Cambridge, MA: Harvard University Press, 1985), at p. 370.
[35] J. Derrida, "The Force of Law: The 'Mystical Foundations of Authority'" (1990), 11 Cardozo L. Rev. 919 at p. 955.
[36] Lord Devlin, "Judges and Lawmakers" (1976), 39 Modern L. Rev. 1.
[37] I take this analogy from Justice Holmes:
> I recognize without hesitation that judges do and must legislate, but they can do so only interstitially; they are confined from molar to molecular motions.
See: *Southern Pacific Co. v. Jensen* 244 U.S. 205 (1917) at 221.

D.   BEING A LAW STUDENT: CONDITIONS OF PREPARATION

From one point of view, law students are simply university students. As do their fellows in other university faculties and departments, law students attend classes, take notes, study, write exams and term papers, and hope for the best. They just happen, unlike other students, to do those things in the law school. Understood this way, being a law student is an entirely private affair, the proper measure of which is self-interest and self-satisfaction, not obligation. But this view of the matter fails to take law students at all seriously.

By coming to the law, law students must be taken to be declaring two intentions, the intention to pursue a profession *and* the intention to pursue the law's profession in particular. Together, these intentions make the law student's life a decidedly public life. That they have chosen a profession at all means that law students are more "concerned with a life [than] with a living".[38] As we have seen, professional life, unlike a career or a job, consists of a devotion to the needs of others and is, unlike a career or a job, necessarily public in that sense. That law students have chosen the legal profession means however that they have committed themselves to public life in an even more robust fashion.

The public nature of legal office confers upon law students a very special public status. Though they are not admitted members of the society of lawyers, their intention to take up the lawyer's office affords them the privilege to stand as a student of law in the company of lawyers. In Canada, and in many other countries, after students graduate law school, this privilege is formalized in articles of clerkship. But that formality does not initiate their membership in the legal community. *Law students rather become members of the legal community when they commence law school and by virtue alone of declaring themselves ready to serve the Law.* Law students are in this sense in a position very much like novitiates in a religious community. Though holy office has yet to be conferred upon them, novitiates are nonetheless considered members of the order on grounds of their declared faith in the office to which they have presented themselves.

With status comes obligation. *Law students serve the Rule of Law by preparing themselves to serve as its faithful stewards during their life at the Law.* This is their sole service and their exclusive obligation during the period of their professional preparation. And, though law professors and even their fellow students may assist, in the final analysis, tendering this service and observing this obligation falls to the good faith, intelligence and industriousness of individual law students.

Professional preparation is too complex a matter for brief summation. What we must do here is identify the obligations which our law imposes on law students directly and on pain of bad faith or dereliction of duty. Two are primary.

---

[38]   F. Frankfurter, *Of Law and Life* (Cambridge, MA: Harvard University Press, 1965), at p. 70.

Law students have first to come to an informed view of the point of professional preparation. Absent such an understanding, law school becomes a jumble of courses strung together by no more meaningful a thread than the three years required to complete the required number. There are a number of ways in which law students can meet this obligation. Some law schools require students to take introductory courses which aim to impart the fundamentals of our law. Properly conceived and executed, courses of this sort are a great help. However, they are not always successful, nor are they always available. In any event, good law students will not depend upon them and will instead undertake independent action. For instance, they will avail themselves of the wisdom residing in their community's rich and often ancient literature on the study of law; they will locate and study contemporary articulations of legal education and professional preparation; and, perhaps especially, they will seek out fellow students and law professors with whom to share the burden and excitement of a life newly started.

The point of law school is to transmit to each generation of lawyers the habits of legality. We will not parse here again the elements of that craft on which the conferral and execution of lawyerly office entirely depends. Our concern is the law student's part in the process. And, in that regard, three things stand out. *Law students must read the law.* Before anything else, lawyers are readers of legal texts. Like other communities devoted to texts, the legal community reads its texts in a way disciplined by its own traditions. It falls to students of the law to acquire competence as legal readers. Law professors of course stand ready to help in this, but their assistance will be useless unless law students shoulder for themselves the burden of reading law.

Law students must read about the law. The lawyer's library contains texts other than case reports and volumes of statutes. Chief among these are *treatises, articulations* and *biographies.* Treatises provide reconstructions of entire bodies of law, say, torts or trusts or the law of crimes. The legal community is blessed with a long line of scholarly works of this kind, which construct doctrine in light of the overall point of a body of rules. Good law students read this literate, and in each of their courses, they study along with the primary texts a leading treatise. Their industry pays dividends, not only immediately in terms of scholarly achievement, but subsequently over the length of their lives at the law.

Articulations are more ambitious than treatises. Where treatises focus on a single body of the law, articulations take as their subject the law as whole in all of its parts. Lawyers generally refer to work of this kind as jurisprudential. Virtually every law school offers at least one in jurisprudence, and where remarkably jurisprudence is not a required subject, good law students enlist voluntarily. They do so because they understand that our law depends upon, and expresses, ultimate principles which jurisprudence has as its purpose to expose and articulate. Lawyers have authored jurisprudential works from the beginning of our law, and many of these are counted among the great works of western civilization.

Felix Frankfurter once counselled that "the potentialities of a lawyer's life is to be gathered from the biographies of those who have lived such a life and have revealed the relation of the legal profession to a life of deep satisfaction".[39] There is nothing surprising in this. If one wants to discover what it means to live a life of a certain sort, one looks to others who have led such a life with some distinction. Sometimes these lives are available to us in person. Such is happily the case in law when an accomplished senior lawyer or judge chooses to act as mentor to a junior lawyer. More often though, lives well lived in any form of life are available to us only indirectly and after the fact through biographies. There is an astoundingly rich body of legal biography. Good law students will turn to these works, not only to seek guidance on many of the concerns canvassed in this chapter, but also to enrich and deepen their commitment to the law.

Law students must care to read law. We have so far addressed certain discrete obligations which good law students will discharge. We have not however discussed what makes a law student a good law student. Recall the distinction between ethics and morality drawn earlier in this chapter. According to that distinction, ethics concerns "whom one should be" whereas morality concerns "what one should do". We noted too that, though these concerns are conceptually distinct, as a matter of practice, character and conduct are interdependent. With this in mind, let us say that good law students are law students *who care about law*. It is this trait of character, this caring, which motivates them to perform those acts on which their fitness to serve others will later depend. But, alas, as in most other things, there is in law seldom an epiphany. Law students take responsibility for their lives at law simply by taking responsibility. And it is through acting morally in that fashion that they form the character which our law requires of them.

E.   RESTATEMENT NO. 6

The authority of the legal community is an authority born of service to others. Lawyers serve others through their faith in the ideal of law and through their performance of those practices which that ideal requires and defines. Lawyers are bound together in community by that faith and those practices.

The legal community is a community of character. Faith and performance do not appear unaided. Commitment and conduct depend rather on the character of the men and women who at any point in time compose law's community. They must be persons for whom the law's promise is a calling to a life of loyal service.

The legal community is a covenantal community constituted by its pledge to others. Law's pledge resides in continuity, not of precepts and doctrines, but of

---

[39]   *Ibid.*, at p. 73.

vision and practice concerning the right ordering of human affairs. For this reason, the legal community does not promise certainty in human life, but constancy with respect to its terms and conditions. *Covenants can be broken.* They can betrayed, and they can be neglected. Lawyers break their covenant with political community when they break their faith with the law or pervert their practices to serve their own interests. When lawyers, individually or corporately, do either of these things, they dishonour their office and forfeit their authority and their community.

FURTHER READINGS TO CHAPTER 9

1.   The Vocation, Ethics and Responsibility of Lawyers

Barker, S.F. "What is a Profession?". (1992), 1 Professional Ethics 73.

Bresler, K. "Pretty Phrases: The Prosecutor as Minister of Justice and Administrator of Justice". (1996), 9 Georgetown J. of Legal Ethics 1301.

Bingham, T. "Judicial Ethics". In R. Cranston, ed. *Legal Ethics and Professional Responsibility.* Oxford: Oxford University Press, 1995. At p. 35.

Brooks, R.O. "Ethical Identity and Professional Responsibility". (1990), 4 Georgetown J. of Legal Ethics 317.

Burns, R.P. "The Purpose of Legal Ethics and the Primacy of Practice". (1998), 39 Wm. & Mary L. Rev. 327.

Calamandrei, P. *Eulogy of Judges.* Philadelphia: American Bar Assoc., 1992.

Coquillette, D.R. *Lawyers and Fundamental Moral Responsibility.* Cincinnati: Anderson Publishing, 1995.

Devins, N., special ed. "Government Lawyering". (1998), 61 Law & Contemporary Problems 1-222.

Ferren, J.M. "The Corporate Lawyer's Obligation to the Public Interest". (1978), 33 Business Lawyer 1253.

Forsyth, W. *Hortensius: An Historical Essay on the Office and Duties of an Advocate.* 3rd ed. London: Murray, 1879.

Gaetke, E.R. "Lawyers as Officers of the Court". (1989), 42 Vanderbilt L. Rev. 39.

Gavison, R. "Holmes's Heritage: Living Greatly in the Law". (1998), 78 Boston U. L. Rev. 843.

Gerber, L.E. "Can Lawyers Be Saved? The Theological Legal Ethics of Thomas Shaffer". (1993-94), 10 J. of Law & Religion 347.

Gordon, R. "Corporate Law Practice as a Public Calling". (1990), 49 Maryland L. Rev. 255.

Green, B.A. "Why Should Prosecutors 'Seek Justice'?". (1999), 26 Fordham Urban L. J. *607.*

Gutmann, A. "Can Virtue Be Taught To Lawyers?". (1993), 45 Stanford L. Rev. 1759.

Hamilton, J.W., and M. Wylie, eds. "Special Issue: The Legal Profession and Ethics". (1995), 38 Alberta L. Rev. 719-943.

Kennedy, A.M. "Judicial Ethics and the Rule of Law". (1996), 40 St. Louis U. L. J. 1967.

Kronman, A.T. "The Fault in Legal Ethics". (1996), 100 Dickinson L. Rev. 489.

———. "Living in the Law". (1987), 54 U. Chicago L. Rev. 835.

———. "Practical Wisdom and Professional Character". In Coleman J., and E.F. Paul, eds. *Philosophy and the Law*. Oxford: Basil Blackwell, 1987. At p. 203.

Lawry, R.P. "The Central Moral Tradition of Lawyering". (1990), 19 Hofstra L. Rev. 311.

Luban, D. *Lawyers and Justice: An Ethical Study*. Princeton: Princeton University Press, 1988.

———. ed. *The Good Lawyer: Lawyers' Roles and Lawyers' Ethics*. Totowa: Rowman & Allanheld, 1984.

MacKenzie, G. *Lawyers and Ethics*. 2nd ed. Toronto: Carswell, 1999.

Nelson, D.L., D.M. Trubek, and R.L. Soloman, eds. *Lawyers' Ideals/Lawyers' Practices*. Ithaca, N.Y.: Cornell University Press, 1992.

Noonan, J.T. Jr., and R.W. Painter, *Professional and Personal Responsibilities of the Lawyer*. Westbury: Foundation, 1997.

Payant, V.R. "Ethical Training in the Profession: The Special Challenge of the Judiciary". (1995), 58(3/4) Law & Contemporary Problems 313.

Pearce, R.G. "Recovering the Republican Origins of the Legal Ethics Codes". (1992), 6 Georgetown J. of Legal Ethics 241.

Posner, R.A. "Professionalisms". (1998), 40 Arizona L. Rev. 51.

Postema, G. "Moral Responsibility in Professional Ethics". (1980), 55 New York U. L. Rev. 63.

Riley, J.G. "Ethical Obligations of Judges". (1993), 23 Memphis State U. L. Rev. 507.

Rhode, D.L. "The Professionalism Problem". (1998), 39 Wm. & Mary L. Rev. 283.

———. "Too Much Law, Too Little Justice: Too Much Rhetoric, Too Little Reform". (1998), 11 Georgetown J. of Legal Ethics 989.

———. "Moral Character as a Professional Credential". (1985), 94 Yale L. J. 491.

———. "Ethical Perspectives on Legal Practice". (1985), 37 Stanford L. Rev. 589.

Sandalow, T. "The Moral Responsibility of Law Schools". (1984), 34 J. of Legal Education 163.

Seymour, W.H. *The Obligations of the Lawyer to His Profession*. New York: New York City Bar Assn., 1968.

Sharswood, G. *An Essay on Professional Ethics*. 5th ed. Philadelphia: T. & J.W. Johnson, 1984.

Simon, W.H. "'Thinking Like A Lawyer' About Ethical Questions". (1998), 27 Hofstra L. Rev. 1.

———. *The Practice of Justice: A Theory of Legal Ethics.* Cambridge, MA: Harvard University Press, 1998.

———. "Visions of Practice in Legal Thought". (1984), 36 Stanford L. Rev. 469.

Sullivan, B. "Professions of Law". (1996), 9 Georgetown J. of Legal Ethics 1235.

Terrell, T.P. "A Tour of Whine Country: The Challenge of Extending the Tenets of Lawyer Professionalism to Law Professors and Law Students". (1994), 34 Washburn L. Rev. 1.

Warren, S. *The Moral, Social and Professional Duties of Attornies and Solicitors.* London: Blackwood, 1848.

Wasserstrom, R. "Lawyers as Professionals: Some Moral Issues". (1975), 5 Human Rights 1.

Winston, K.I. "A Civic Vocation". (1989), 6 Harvard Public Policy Rev. 1.

Conclusion

Taking It Personally

[T]he purpose of the community of lawyers within the community is that the ordinary citizens shall always have at their disposal the man who can protect them, who can defend them, who can stand up before arbitrary power from whatever quarter it may come and assert the inalienable rights of the individual to the eternal freedoms. That is the centre of all the lawyer's work and the lawyer's ambition.

Lord Birkett

Each generation of lawyers makes its own contribution to the architecture of the law.

Anthony T. Kronman

Law means so pitifully little to life. Life is so terrifyingly dependent on law.

Karl N. Llewellyn

Lawyers speak truth to power. This book has been about the nature, sources, context and conditions of that speech. Its conclusion does not intend, in any systematic way, to summarize what we have discovered about these matters. We shall conclude instead with a brief meditation on the importance of lawyering to human affairs.

The law's truth is equality. Whatever our differences, and despite our differences, it is the goodness of our law to make each of us the authors of our lives. Our law wraps each of us in a *cloth of rights* which saves us safe from harm and which secures our bodies and minds and our spirits and property for ourselves, to do with as we will. Our law works this goodness through its faithful stewards, the judges and lawyers who are its practitioners. For we have found that "the protection of the individual ... can only be achieved in a country with a democratic culture, and a culture of legality with a tradition of independence for the courts [and] the legal profession".[1] We have found too that this grant of lawyer autonomy presumes and is conditional upon lawyerly craft and virtue.

Lawyers make good the goodness of the law by immersing themselves in the traditions which communicate its point and practices:

---

[1] J. Raz, "The Politics of the Rule of Law" in J. Raz, *Ethics in the Public Domain* (Oxford: Clarendon Press, 1994), pp. 354 at 362.

To the student of the law there come down from all the glorious history of the profession of advocacy, great traditions and ethical ideals and lofty conceptions of the honor and dignity of the profession, of courage and loyalty for the maintenance of the law and the liberty that it guards. It is to a Bar inspired by those traditions, imbued with this spirit ... — a Bar jealous of the honor of the profession and proud of its high calling for the maintenance of justice — that we must look for the effective administration of justice.[2]

The legal tradition is, in this way, a moral and ethical confrontation for each generation of lawyers. It demands that each generation of practitioners devote itself to the law and to shoulder the burden of equality. When lawyers rise to the challenge of their tradition, they pledge themselves to contribute to its betterment. This indeed is the *primary obligation* of each generation: each is obliged *not* to leave the tradition worse off on account of its participation. This obligation charges lawyers with *maintaining the cloth of rights*. And their success in this lies in the protection they provide others, protection not only against *legal nudity*, which in human affairs is an always present possibility, but also against any *tattering of the dress of equality and liberty*.

These are perilous times for the legal tradition. It is said that ours is a time whose "embarrassment and scandal" is that "we must confess to having no cosmic backups for our condemnation of Auschwitz".[3] This general moral and ethical malaise has seeped into the community of lawyers. For the past 30 or so years, the legal community has been experiencing an ever more urgent crisis of faith. This crisis is signalled by a large scale failure of the internal point of view. Many lawyers think their tradition a mask which hides law's real motor and purpose. It is no matter that some take this instruction as cause for progressive social engineering and others as an occasion for satisfying their lust for material gain. The result is the same in either case: the legal community has become *fragmented*. The issue of fragmentation is the moral and ethical confusion which presently infects both the legal community as an institution and its officers as individuals. Simply, too many lawyers are now at sea: individually and corporately, too many know not what they are *to do* or whom they are suppose *to be*.

The legal community is the sole custodian of the law's goodness. If the legal community is fragmented so too then is law's tradition of equality and liberty through rights. To the extent that lawyers fail their tradition's test of faith, the liberty of those others whom lawyers are pledged to protect and serve is imperilled. Rights of course are not lost all at once. One of the many lessons of the murderous 20th century is that rights are lost by increment. First, the legal subject is differentiated and then rights are differentiated and diminished. But tatters

---

2   Elihu Root, Address to American Bar Association, 1916, as quoted in Canadian Bar Association
     Report on Legal Education and Ethics (1918), 4 *Report of the Canadian Bar Association, 1919*,
     pp. 129 at 130-31. Quoted in W.W. Pue, "Lawyering for a Fragmented World: Professionalism
     after God" (1998), 5(2/3) Internat'l J. of the Legal Profession 125.
3   J.D. Caputo, *Against Ethics* (Bloomington: Indiana University Press, 1993), at p. 236.

can over time consume the whole cloth, and with legal nudity comes, *every time,* murder.

Our law alone prevents barbarity. Our law alone preserves politics from turning against the individual with enmity. Our law alone permits civilized life to flourish. And in all of this, in preserving our "nomos" of freedom and equality,[4] our law depends upon the goodness of lawyers. That so many lawyers are not shouldering this dependence, that they are infidels in law's tradition, is threatening our way of life. We should then conclude our journey through the pathways of our law by exploring briefly the nature of this lawyerly goodness on which our law and life so very much depend.

Ronald Dworkin claims that "the liberal principle of equality is a principle of political organization that is required by justice, not a way of life for individuals".[5] And he is right *except* for lawyers. Others are free through law to dissent from equality and, provided that they hurt no one, to conduct their affairs on any basis and towards any ends which they wish. Indeed, this is the very purchase and point of limited government under Rule of Law. Lawyers however are another matter since they are *officers of limited government.*

Their office prevents lawyers from being "players of roles".[6] They must instead be "actors who merge with their parts": they must "regard the normative structure of society as *home*".[7] For lawyers, *our law's very public political morality must be personal.* It must inform the whole of their lives and form the core of their selves, their sense of self, their identity. On this, and on nothing less, does the authority and goodness of law depend.

That lawyers must in this fashion take the law's political morality personally is a burden and a blessing. The burden resides not only in what it prevents them from doing, but also in what it consigns them to doing. There are no solomonic solutions to living a life of law. Lawyers rather are condemned to the insecurity of forming themselves, their identities as lawyers *and* as persons, through their day-to-day practices over the wealth of their time at the law. Knowing that "by engaging in the activity of law one makes oneself into a certain kind of person" does not relieve this anxiety, though for good lawyers it provides the solace of direction.[8]

The blessings of the lawyer's life are many. These blessings, *all bred of service,* should be clear from the course of our journey, so we shall conclude not

---

[4] R. Cover, "Nomos and Narrative" (1983), 97 Harvard L. Rev. 4. Cover's excellent essay should be read by every first-year law student.

[5] R. Dworkin, *A Matter of Principle* (Cambridge, MA: Harvard University Press, 1985), at p. 203. But see his *Law's Empire* (Cambridge, MA: Harvard University Press, 1986), at p. 189 (law as integrity "fuses citizens' moral and political lives").

[6] R. Dahrendorf, *Law and Order* (Boulder, CO: Westview Press, 1985), at p. 152.

[7] *Ibid.* (emphasis added)

[8] M.A. Glendon, *A Nation Under Lawyers* (Cambridge, MA: Harvard University Press, 1994), at p. 240.

with rehearsing those possibilities, but with the words of a very great lawyer on
the lawyer's life:

> I say — and I say no longer with any doubt — that a man may live greatly
> in the law as well as elsewhere; that there as well as elsewhere his thought
> may find its unity in an infinite perspective; that there as well as elsewhere
> he may wreak himself upon life, may drink the bitter cup of heroism, may
> wear his heart out after the unattainable.[9]

---

[9]   Oliver Wendell Holmes, Jr., "The Profession of the Law" in *The Occasional Speeches of Justice
Oliver Wendell Holmes* (Cambridge, MA: Harvard University Press, 1962, M.D. Howe com-
piler), pp. 28 at 29.

APPENDIX

The Lawyer's Library: A Beginning

Lawyers are *perforce* readers of texts. Good lawyers, however, are something more. They are bibliophiles. They *love* the books of law, and they surround themselves with them. Good lawyers are literate. They know the great works of their tradition and, over the length of their life at law, they immerse themselves in them. They also are alert to the leading works of their time, and they read those articulations of the law, not just to nourish their practice, but also to deepen their understanding and commitment to the law.

Good lawyers also read legal biography. They know, as Ludwig Wittgenstein once put it, that "not only rules, but also examples are needed for establishing a practice". So they read about lives lived greatly in the law, sometimes to emulate them, but always to seek instruction from them.

The bibliography which follows tracks the reading habits of good lawyers, and is therefore structured around the great works of the legal tradition, leading contemporary works and legal biography. The bibliography is *not* exhaustive, nor could it be, and it is admittedly very selective (a few exceptions aside, the works are either by or about lawyers) and somewhat personal (if not perhaps idiosyncratic). Its sole intention is to give newcomers a sense of the literary fundamentals of law. And if they later elect a life in the law, maybe this bibliography can serve as a guide and a foundation for the law library which, if they come to love the law, they will be led to collect.

1. Great Works (and works about their period)

Austin, John (1790-1859). *The Province of Jurisprudence Determined.* Cambridge: Cambridge University Press, 1995.

Beccaria, Cesare (1738-1794). *On Crimes and Punishments.* Indianapolis: Bobbs-Merrill, 1963.

Blackstone, Sir William (1723-1780). *Commentaries on the Laws of England*, 4 Vol. New York: Garland, 1978.

de Bracton, Henry (d. 1268). *Bracton on the Laws and Customs of England.* Cambridge, MA: Harvard University Press, 1968.

Burke, Edmund (1729-1797). *Reflections on the Revolution in France.* Indianapolis: Bobbs-Merrill, 1955.

Coke, Sir Edward (1552-1634). *An Abridgement of the Lord Coke's Commentary on Littleton.* New York: Garland, 1979.

Fortescue, Sir John (1394-1476). *De Laudibus Legum Anglie*, ed./trans. S.B. Chrimes. Cambridge: Cambridge University Press, 1949. Recent edition: *Sir*

John Fortescue: On the Laws and Governance of England. Cambridge: Cambridge University Press, 1997.

de Glanvill, Randulf (1130-1190). *The Treatise on the Laws and Customs of the Realm of England Commonly Called Glanvill*, ed. G.D.G. Hall. London: Nelson, 1965.

Hale, Sir Matthew (1609-1676). *The Analysis of the Law.* New York: Garland, 1978.

———. *The History of the Common Law of England.* Chicago: University of Chicago Press, 1971.

———. *Pleas of the Crown.* London: Professional Books, 1972.

———. *The Prerogatives of the King.* London: Selden Society, 1976.

Hawkins, William (1673-1746). *A Treatise of the Pleas of the Crown*, 7th ed. London: Butterworths, 1795.

Holt, Sir John. *Court of King's Bench. A report of cases argued, debated, and adjudged in B.R. in the time of the late Queen Anne ... during which time Lord Chief Justice Holt presided in that court.* London: E. & R. Nutt & R. Gosling, 1737.

Littleton, Sir Thomas (1402-1481). *Littleton's Tenures in English.* Littleton, CO: Rothman, 1985.

Lord Mansfield (1705-1793). *Court of King's Bench. Reports of cases argued and adjudged in the Court of King's Bench during the time of Lord Mansfield's presiding in that court ....* By Sir James Burrow, 5 Vol., 5th ed. London: Butterworth, 1812.

———. *A Treatise on the Study of The Law*, Classics in Legal History, Vol. 26. New York: W.S. Hein, 1974.

Mill, John Stuart (1806-1873). *On Liberty and Other Essays*, ed. J. Gray. Oxford: Oxford University Press, 1991.

Montesquieu, Charles Louis de Secondat. *The Spirit of the Laws*, eds./trans. A. Cohler, B. Miller, and H. Stone. Cambridge: Cambridge University Press, 1989.

Saint German, Christopher (1460-1540). *St. German's Doctor and Student.* London: Selden Society, 1974.

Selden, John (1584-1654). *Ad Fletam dissertatio.* Cambridge: Cambridge University Press, 1925.

———. *A Brief Discourse Touching the Office of Lord Chancellor of England.* London: Thomas Lee, 1677.

———. *Of the Dominion; or, Ownership of the Sea.* New York: Aron, 1972.

———. *Table Talk of John Selden.* London: Quaritch, 1927.

Smith, Sir Thomas (1513-1577). *De Republica Anglorum.* Cambridge: Cambridge University Press, 1982.

Spelman, Sir John (1480-1546). *The Reports of Sir John Spelman.* London: Selden Society, 1977-78.

*****

Baker, J.H. *The Legal Profession and the Common Law.* London: Hambledon, 1986.

———. *The Third University: The Inns of Court and the Common Law Tradition.* London: Selden Society, 1990.

———. *An Introduction to English Legal History*, 3rd ed. London: Butterworths, 1990.

Beattie, J.M. *Crime and Courts in England, 1660-1800.* Princeton: Princeton University Press, 1986.

Berman, H.J. *Law and Revolution.* Cambridge, MA: Harvard University Press, 1983.

———. "Religious Foundations of Law in the West: An Historical Perspective". (1983), 1 J. of Law & Religion 3.

———. "Introductory Remarks: Why the History of Western Law is not Written". [1984] U. of Illinois L. Rev. 511.

———. "Towards an Integrative Jurisprudence: Politics, Morality, History". (1988), 76 Calif. L. Rev. 779.

———. "The Origins of Historical Jurisprudence: Coke, Selden, Hale". (1994), 103 Yale L. J. 1651.

———. (with C.J. Reid). "The Transformation of English Legal Science: From Hale to Blackstone". (1996), 45 Emory L. J. 437.

———. "The Western Legal Tradition in a Millennial Perspective: Past and Future". (2000), 60 Louisiana L. Rev. 739.

Birks, P., ed. *The Life of the Law.* London: Hambledon, 1993.

Brand, P. *The Making of the Common Law.* London: Hambledon Press, 1992.

Brewer, J. and J. Styles, eds. *An Ungovernable People: The English and their Law in the Seventeenth and Eighteenth Centuries.* New Brunswick, NJ: Rutgers University Press, 1980.

Coquillette, D.R. *The Anglo-American Legal Heritage: Introductory Materials.* Durham: Carolina Academic Press, 1999.

Hay, D. *et al.*, eds. *Albion's Fatal Tree: Crime and Society in Eighteenth Century England.* New York: Pantheon, 1975.

Holdsworth, Sir W.S. *A History of English Law*, 16 Vol. London: Methuen, 1903f.

Maine, Sir H.S. *Ancient Law.* London: Murray, 1906.

Maitland, F.W. *Doomesday Book and Beyond: Three Essays in the Early History of England.* Buffalo: W.S. Hein, 1970.

———. *The Forms of Action at Common Law.* Cambridge: Cambridge University Press, 1936).

———. *A Sketch of English Legal History.* New York: Putnam, 1915.

Oldham, J. *The Mansfield Manuscripts and the Growth of English Law in the Eighteenth Century.* Chapel Hill: University of North Carolina Press, 1992.

Plucknett, T.F.T. *Early English Legal Literature.* Cambridge: Cambridge University Press, 1958.

Pocock, J.G.A. *The Ancient Constitution and the Feudal Law.* Cambridge: Cambridge University Press, 1957.

Pollock, Sir F. *Essays in the Law.* Holmes Beach, Fla.: Wm. W. Gaunt, 1994.

Prest, W.R. *The Rise of the Barristers: A Social History of the English Bar, 1590-1640.* Oxford: Clarendon, 1986.

Sainty, Sir J. *A List of English Law Officers, King's Counsel, and Holders of Patents of Precedence.* London: Selden Society, 1987.

Simpson, A.W.B. *Leading Cases in the Common Law.* Oxford: Clarendon Press, 1995.

———. *A History of the Common Law of Contract: The Rise of the Action of Assumpsit.* Oxford: Clarendon, 1975.

Thompson, E.P. *Whigs and Hunters: The Origin of the Black Act.* London: Allen Lane, 1975.

Van Caenegem, R.C. *Royal Writs in England from the Conquest to Glanvill.* London: Selden Society, 1958.

Walker, D.M. *The Oxford Companion to Law.* Oxford: Clarendon Press, 1980.

Wigmore, J.H. *Evidence in Trials at Common Law,* 10 Vol. Boston: Little Brown, 1923.

2.   Leading "Contemporary" Works

The following works concern both public and private law and legal theory. All have been influential and have become part of their particular canon. Whether any of these works will be counted among the great works of the legal tradition must be left to the future, though each has already met the threshold of influence. Of course, were space and convenience no objection, a great many other works could have properly been added to this list. Moreover, several of the works listed in the previous section — those by Baker, Berman, Pocock and Thompson come immediately to mind — are contemporary classics which also are candidates for greatness.

Ackerman, B.A. *Social Justice in the Liberal State.* New Haven: Yale University Press, 1980.

———. *We the People,* 2 Vol. Cambridge, MA: Harvard University Press, 1991.

Ashworth, A. *Principles of Criminal Law,* 3rd ed. Oxford: Clarendon Press, 1999.

Atiyah, P.S. *An Introduction to the Law of Contract,* 5th ed. Oxford: Clarendon Press, 1995.

———. *Law and Modern Society,* 2nd ed. Oxford: Oxford University Press, 1995);

———. *The Sale of Goods,* 9th ed. London: Pitman, 1990.

Berlin, I. *Four Essays on Liberty.* Oxford: Oxford University Press, 1969.

Birks, P. *Introduction to the Law of Restitution.* Oxford: Clarendon Press, 1985.

———. *English Private Law,* 2 Vol. Oxford: Oxford University Press, 2000.

Bridge, M.G. *Sale of Goods*. Toronto: Butterworths, 1988.

Clark, R. *Corporate Law*. Boston: Little Brown, 1986.

Cross, R. *Precedent in English Law*. Oxford: Clarendon Press, 1961.

———. *The Golden Thread of the English Criminal Law: The Burden of Truth*. Cambridge: Cambridge University Press, 1976.

———. *Statutory Interpretation*, 3rd ed. London: Butterworths, 1995.

de Smith, S.A. *Judicial Review of Administrative Action*, 5th ed. London: Sweet & Maxwell, 1995.

Dworkin, R. *Sovereign Virtue: The Theory and Practice of Equality*. Cambridge, MA: Harvard University Press, 2000.

———. *Law's Empire*. Cambridge, MA: Harvard University Press, 1986.

———. *Taking Rights Seriously*. Cambridge, MA: Harvard University Press, 1977.

Ely, J.H. *Democracy and Distrust: A Theory of Judicial Review*. Cambridge, MA: Harvard University Press, 1980.

Finnis, J.G. *Natural Law and Natural Rights*. Oxford: Clarendon Press, 1979.

Fleming, J.G. *An Introduction to the Law of Torts*, 2nd ed. Oxford: Clarendon Press, 1985.

———. *The Law of Torts*, 9th ed. Sydney: LBC Information Services, 1998.

Frank, J. *Law and the Modern Mind*. New York: Coward-McCann, 1949.

Fuller, L.L. *The Morality of Law*, rev. ed. New Haven: Yale University Press, 1964.

Gilmore, G. *Security Interests in Personal Property*. Boston: Little Brown, 1965.

———. *The Death of Contract*. Columbus: Ohio State University Press, 1974.

Goode, R.M. *Commercial Law*, 2nd ed. London: Penguin, 1995.

Griffith, J.A.G. *The Politics of the Judiciary*, 4th ed. London: Fontana Press, 1991.

Habermas, J. *Between Fact and Norm: Contributions to a Discourse Theory of Law and Democracy*, trans. W. Rehg. Cambridge, MA: Massachusetts Institute of Technology Press, 1996.

Hart, H.L.A. *The Concept of Law*, 2nd ed. Oxford: Clarendon Press, 1994.

Horwitz, M.J. *The Transformation of American Law, 1780-1860*. Cambridge, MA: Harvard University Press, 1977.

———. *The Transformation of American Law, 1870-1960: The Crisis of Legal Orthodoxy*. New York: Oxford University Press, 1992.

Llewellyn, K.N. *The Bramble Bush*. New York: Oceana, 1951.

———. *The Common Law Tradition: Deciding Appeals*. Boston: Little Brown, 1960.

———. *Jurisprudence: Realism in Theory and Practice*. Chicago: University of Chicago Press, 1962.

Luban, D. *Lawyers and Justice: An Ethical Study*. Princeton: Princeton University Press, 1988.

MacCormick, N. *Legal Reasoning and Legal Theory*. Oxford: Clarendon Press, 1978.

Nicholas, B. *An Introduction to Roman Law*. Oxford: Clarendon, 1962.

Penner, J.E. *The Idea of Property in Law*. Oxford: Clarendon Press, 1997.

Pound, R. *Interpretations of Legal History*. New York: Macmillan, 1923.

———. *The Spirit of the Common Law*. Boston: Jones, 1921.

Rawls, J. *A Theory of Justice*. Cambridge, MA: Harvard University Press, 1971.

———. *Political Liberalism*. New York: Columbia University Press, 1993.

———. *The Law of Peoples*. Cambridge, MA: Harvard University Press, 1999.

Raz, J. *The Concept of a Legal System*, 2nd ed. Oxford: Clarendon Press, 1980.

———. *The Authority of Law*. Oxford: Oxford University Press, 1979.

———. *The Morality of Freedom*. Oxford: Clarendon Press, 1986.

Smith, L.D. *The Law of Tracing*. Oxford: Clarendon Press, 1997.

Stevens, R.B. *Law School: Legal Education in America from the 1850s to the 1980s*. Chapel Hill: University of North Carolina Press, 1983.

Tetley, W. *Maritime Liens and Claims*, 2nd ed. Montreal: Yvon Blais, 1998.

von Hayek, F.A. *The Constitution of Liberty*. Chicago: University of Chicago Press, 1960.

———. *The Mirage of Social Justice*. Chicago: University of Chicago Press, 1976.

———. *The Political Order of a Free People*. London: Routledge & Keegan Paul, 1979.

Waldron, J. *The Right to Private Property*. Oxford: Clarendon Press, 1988.

———. *The Dignity of Legislation*. Cambridge: Cambridge University Press, 1999.

Weinrib, E.J. *The Idea of Private Law*. Cambridge, MA: Harvard University Press, 1995.

3.   Legal Biography

Following is a bibliography of biographies of famous legal lives. Legal biography is an incredibly rich literature. Though this bibliography attempts to list important American, English and Canadian works, it is nonetheless very selective. Any number of great lives, and any number of important biographies, are excluded. Moreover, it excludes biographical essays and works of autobiography by lawyers, of which in both cases there are a great many.

Ackroyd, P. *The Life of Sir Thomas Moore*. New York: Doubleday, 1998.

Arnup, J.D. *Middleton: The Beloved Judge*. Toronto: McClelland & Stewart, 1988.

Baker, L. *Brandeis and Frankfurter: A Dual Biography*. New York: Harper & Row, 1984.

———. *John Marshall: A Life in Law*. New York: Macmillan, 1974.

Bale, G. *Chief Justice William Johnstone Ritchie: Responsible Government and Judicial Review*. Ottawa: Carleton University Press, 1991.

Appendix 253

Batten, J. *Robinette: The Dean of Canadian Lawyers*. Toronto: Macmillan, 1984.

Beveridge, A.J. *The Life of John Marshall*, 2 Vol. Boston: Houghton Mifflin, 1916-1919.

Bowen, C.D. *The Lion and the Throne: The Life and Times of Sir Edward Coke (1552-1634)*, 1st ed. Boston: Little Brown, 1957.

Boyer, P. *A Passion for Justice: The Legacy of James Chalmers McRuer*. Toronto: University of Toronto Press, 1994.

Burnet, G. *The Life and Death of Sir Matthew Hale*. London: Wm. Shrowsbery, 1682.

Cosgrove, R.A. *The Rule of Law: Albert Venn Dicey, Victorian Jurist*. Chapel Hill: University of North Carolina Press, 1980.

Cray, E. *Chief Justice: A Biography of Earl Warren*. New York: Simon & Schuster, 1997.

Djwa, S. *The Politics of the Imagination: A Life of F.R. Scott*. Toronto: Douglas & McIntyre, 1987.

Fifoot, C.H.S. *Lord Mansfield*. Oxford: Clarendon Press, 1936.

———. *Frederic William Maitland: A Life*. Cambridge, MA: Harvard University Press, 1971.

Freeman, I. *Lord Denning: A Life*. London: Hutchinson, 1993.

Gerhart, E.C. *America's Advocate: Robert H. Jackson*. New York: Bobbs-Merrill, 1958.

Goodhart, A.L. *Five Jewish Lawyers of the Common Law*. London: Oxford University Press, 1949.

Gunther, G. *Learned Hand: The Man and the Judge*. New York: Knopf, 1994.

Guth, D.J., ed. *Brian Dickson at the Supreme Court of Canada, 1973-1990*. Winnipeg: Canadian Legal History Project, 1998.

Heward, E. *Lord Mansfield*. Chichester: B. Rose, 1979.

———. *Lord Denning: A Biography*, 2nd ed. Chichester: B. Rose, 1997.

Hill, F.T. *Lincoln the Lawyer*. Littleton, CO: Rothman, 1986; New York: Century, 1906.

Hull, N.E.H. *Roscoe Pound and Karl Llewellyn: Searching for an American Jurisprudence*. Chicago: University of Chicago Press, 1997.

Johnson, H.A. *The Chief Justiceship of John Marshall, 1801-1835*. Columbia: University of South Carolina Press, 1997.

Kaufman, A.L. *Cardozo*. Cambridge, MA: Harvard University Press, 1998.

Kenyon, G.T. *The Life of Lloyd, First Lord Kenyon, Lord Chief Justice of England*. Littleton, CO: Rothman, 1990; London: Longmans Green, 1873.

Klumpenhouwer, L. and L. Knafla. *Lords of the Western Bench: A Bibliographical Dictionary of the Supreme and District Court Justices of Alberta, 1876-1990*. Edmonton: Legal Archives Society of Alberta, 1997.

Lockmiller, D.A. *Sir William Blackstone*. Gloucester: Smith, 1970.

Lyon, H. and H. Block, *Edward Coke: Oracle of the Law*. Littleton, CO: Rothman, 1992; Boston: Houghton Mifflin, 1929.

Marjoribanks, E. *For the Defence: The Life of Sir Edward Marshall Hall.* New York: Macmillan, 1930.

Mason, A.T. *Harlan Fiske Stone: Pillar of the Law.* New York: Archon, 1968.

McConnell, W.H. *William R. McIntyre: Paladin of the Common Law.* Montreal and Kingston: McGill-Queens University Press, 2000.

Parrish, M.E. *Felix Frankfurter and His Times: The Reform Years.* New York: Free Press, 1982.

Posner, R. *Cardozo: A Study in Reputation.* Chicago: University of Chicago Press, 1990.

Pullen, C.H. *The Life and Times of Arthur Maloney: The Last of the Tribunes.* Ottawa: Dundurn, 1994.

Sturm, P. *Louis D. Brandeis: Justice for the People.* Cambridge, MA: Harvard University Press, 1984.

———. *Brandeis: Beyond Progressivism.* Lawrence: University of Kansas Press, 1993.

Swayze, C. *Hard Choices: A Life of Tom Berger.* Toronto: Douglas & McIntyre, 1987.

Thayer, J.B. *John Marshall.* New York: Da Capo, 1974.

Thomas, E. *The Man to See: Edward Bennett Williams — Ultimate Insider, Legendary Trial Lawyer.* New York: Simon & Schuster, 1991.

Thorne, S.E. *Sir Edward Coke, 1552-1952.* London: Quaritch, 1957.

Warden, L.C. *The Life of Blackstone.* Charlottesville, VA: Michie, 1938.

Weinberg, A. and L. Weinberg, *Clarence Darrow: A Sentimental Rebel.* New York: Antheneum, 1987.

White, G.E. *Justice Oliver Wendell Holmes: Law and the Inner Self.* New York: Oxford University Press, 1993.

Williams, D.R. *Duff: A Life in the Law.* Vancouver: University of British Columbia Press, 1984.

———. *Just Lawyers: Seven Portraits.* Toronto: University of Toronto Press, 1995.

Williams, J. *Thurgood Marshall: American Revolutionary.* New York: Times Books, 1998.

Index

P